Comparative Politics

Comparative Politics

Approaches and Issues

Howard J. Wiarda

With the Assistance of
Esther M. Skelley

ROWMAN & LITTLEFIELD PUBLISHERS, INC.
Lanham • Boulder • New York • Toronto • Plymouth, UK

ROWMAN & LITTLEFIELD PUBLISHERS, INC.

Published in the United States of America
by Rowman & Littlefield Publishers, Inc.
A wholly owned subsidary of The Rowman & Littlefield Publishing Group, Inc.
4501 Forbes Boulevard, Suite 200, Lanham, Maryland 20706
www.rowmanlittlefield.com

Estover Road, Plymouth PL6 7PY, United Kingdom

British Library Cataloguing in Publication Information Available

Library of Congress Cataloging-in-Publication Data

Wiarda, Howard J., 1939–
Comparative politics : approaches and issues / Howard J. Wiarda ; with the
assistance of Esther M. Skelley.
    p.   cm.
  Includes bibliographical references and index.
  ISBN-13: 978-0-7425-3035-5 (cloth : alk. paper)
  ISBN-10: 0-7425-3035-3 (cloth : alk. paper)
  ISBN-13: 978-0-7425-3036-2 (pbk. : alk. paper)
  ISBN-10: 0-7425-3036-1 (pbk. : alk. paper)
1. Comparative government. I. Skelley, Esther M. II. Title.
  JF51.W47 2007
  320.3—dc22

                                                        2006012679

Printed in the United States of America

♾™ The paper used in this publication meets the minimum requirements of
American National Standard for Information Sciences—Permanence of Paper for
Printed Library Materials, ANSI/NISO Z39.48-1992.

Contents

List of Tables and Figures

TABLES

FIGURES

Acknowledgments

The author wishes to express his gratitude to the following publishers and organizations for permission to include materials published earlier in preliminary form. All these materials have been thoroughly reworked, reorganized, rethought, updated, and rewritten for inclusion in the present book.

Westview Press, for materials from Howard J. Wiarda, *New Directions in Comparative Politics* (Boulder, 2002), used in chapter 2.

Harcourt Publishers, for materials from Howard J. Wiarda, *Introduction to Comparative Politics* (Fort Worth, 2000), used in chapters 3, 4, 10, and 11.

M. E. Sharpe, for materials from Howard J. Wiarda, *Corporatism and Comparative Politics* (New York, 1997), used in chapter 5.

American Enterprise Institute, for materials from Howard J. Wiarda, *Ethnocentrism and Foreign Policy: Can We Understand the Third World?* (Washington, D.C., 1985), used in chapter 6.

Harper Collins, for materials from Dankwart A. Rustow and Kenneth Paul Erickson (eds.), *Comparative Political Dynamics* (New York, 1991), used in chapter 7.

Harcourt Publishers, for materials from Howard J. Wiarda, *Comparative Democracy and Democratization* (Orlando, 1992), used in chapter 8.

Westview Press, for materials from Howard J. Wiarda, *Civil Society* (Boulder, 2003), used in chapter 9.

Third World Quarterly, for materials from Howard J. Wiarda, "Is Comparative Politics Dead," 19 (1998): 935-49, used in chapter 12.

Preface

C omparative politics is one of the most exciting and dynamic fields in political science. Its area of inquiry, its "living laboratory," is *all* of the world's political systems—all 244 of them.[1] Comparative politics seeks to study and understand these political systems analytically, systematically, and comparatively; it looks for patterns, regularities, and systemic changes within and among them. How do political systems change? What are the differences between developed and developing countries? How do political systems transition from authoritarianism to democracy? What are the trends in global politics that lead to greater freedom, democracy, and pluralism? How do different political systems handle such issues as health care, education, and social welfare? These are only some of the essential questions with which comparative politics wrestles.

I first began studying comparative politics at the University of Michigan and the University of Florida quite a few years ago; I then won a scholarship that for the first time took me abroad to Latin America. I was fascinated by Latin America—the Cuban revolution, the struggle for democracy in the area, and the effort to achieve development and modernization—and spent most of the 1960s living, working, doing research, and writing about the area. Then, during the 1970s I moved to Europe and wrote several books on European politics, meanwhile keeping up my interest in Latin America. In the 1980s and 1990s my research and writing interests became more general and diverse, and I spent large amounts of time in Asia, Russia, Eastern Europe, the Middle East, and sub-Saharan Africa. It has been a fun and exciting research life, but it also gave me the background to write comparatively about many areas of the globe.

This is a book not about all these individual countries and regions; there are already quite a few textbooks (including some of my own[2]) that do that. Rather, it is a book that provides a set of "handles" or suggestions for enabling us to better comprehend and understand these countries. The issue is: when you go to some other country, how do you go about understanding and coming to grips with it, what approach do you use, what conceptual framework best helps you comprehend that country? You do not just go there with your backpack, sit in the central park (or maybe a sidewalk café), and watch the world go by—fun and interesting though that also is. Instead, if you are a serious student, you go there equipped with an idea, a thesis, a larger issue that you want to explore and test out. Is the country or area democratizing, is it developing, what is holding it back, what is pushing it forward, what is the impact of globalization, what are the forces of both change and continuity? To think through and analyze these issues you need an approach, a conceptual framework for thinking about them, and, in scientific or analytical terms, a hypothesis.

That is what this book provides. It tells the history and explores the field of comparative politics by focusing on the main approaches or conceptual frameworks that have been used by scholars over the years. These include developmentalism (focused, as the name implies, on the developing nations); dependency theory; the study of political values and beliefs, or political culture; the role of the state and state-society or state-interest group relations; corporatism or how governments try to control interest group activity; indigenous and non-Western theories of change; the role of institutions; rational choice theory; political economy; civil society; and transitions to democracy. The author has been an active participant in the debates over these alternative approaches over the years and has written extensively about them. In this book he seeks to capture the essence of–and the controversy that swirls about—these several approaches.

This book is meant to be used as a textbook in courses and seminars on comparative politics. All the main approaches, the history of the field, and its alternative conceptual frameworks are here. Because it covers all these approaches briefly and analytically, students and faculty members alike have discovered this book is especially useful in preparing for exams, thinking through the main issues of comparative politics, and determining which of these approaches is most useful in their research.

Several of the chapters in this book have appeared before in preliminary form as papers at major conferences and articles in scholarly journals. For this volume they have been thoroughly reorganized, rethought, updated, and rewritten, and much new material and chapters added. That, after all, is how scholarly work and research proceeds: first by the setting forth of some preliminary ideas, then by the testing of them in academic conferences and through field work, and finally their reformulation in more refined and complete versions.

The author would like to thank his collaborators on this book, which is part of a four-volume series published by Rowman & Littlefield on Latin America, comparative politics, Southern and Eastern European democratization, and American Foreign Policy. Hillenbrand Fellow (and my research assistant) Esther M. Skelley has once again been so helpful and her advice so sound in preparing this book that she merits mention on the cover. Doris Holden has been helping me edit, refine, and put book manuscripts in final form since the mid-1970s; here she has worked her usual magic. And Dr. Iêda Siqueira Wiarda, herself a distinguished political scientist (imagine, two in one family), has been providing indispensable moral, intellectual, logistical, and familial support even longer than that. This book, and the series, could not have been completed without the invaluable assistance of these individuals—my team! However, the author alone is responsible for the book and its approach and interpretations.

Howard J. Wiarda
Bonita Hills
Athens, Georgia
Fall 2006

NOTES

1. There is, I discovered on one of my own research adventures abroad, an association of travelers called the International World Travelers' Club (IWTC), headquartered in Tunisia, that keeps track of these numbers and decides on controversial cases of "nationhood"—e.g., the Palestinian Authority, Kosovo, the Panama Canal Zone. Three of its members have visited all 244 of these "political entities" (not all of them are countries); others are striving for that goal. In my career I have lived, traveled, and done research in sixty-seven countries.

2. Howard J. Wiarda and Harvey F. Kline (eds.), *Latin American Politics and Development*, 6th ed. (Boulder, CO: Westview Press, 2006); and Howard J. Wiarda (ed.), *European Politics in the Age of Globalization* (Fort Worth: Harcourt Brace, 2000).

I

THE FIELD OF COMPARATIVE POLITICS

1

Introduction

Comparative politics is one of the most interesting and exciting fields in political science. Particularly nowadays, after the 9/11 attack on the World Trade Center and the Pentagon, with the war on terrorism, with armed conflict raging in Iraq and Afghanistan, differences and disputes between the United States and its allies, and U.S. forces both military and diplomatic committed in so many areas of the globe, international affairs are once again at the forefront of our thinking. Issues of foreign policy, international relations, and comparative politics are among the most important that we face today.

the year Comparative politics seeks to come to grips with and understand *all* of
1995 the world's political systems—as indicated in the preface, that presently
countries includes some 244 "political entities." Not all of these are countries; the list includes the Vatican, the Palestinian Authority, Puerto Rico, the Virgin Islands, and other political or administrative units that are not full-fledged, independent countries. Nevertheless, the list of fully independent countries, recognized by or members of the United Nations, is now over two hundred. Those *plus* the units that are not independent countries give us plenty of political systems to study and understand. It can literally be said that the domain or territory of comparative politics encompasses the entire globe. The whole world is our laboratory of study.

Comparative politics concerns itself with a great variety of issues. These include the comparative study of institutions (political parties or legislatures) in different political systems, interest groups and their relations to the state or government, political culture or political values in different countries, and public policies (health, education, social welfare) in different countries. Comparative politics also studies the processes by which countries become developed, modern, and democratic; how civil society (intermediary groups between the citizen and the state) emerges in different countries; and the effects of economic growth and social change on the developing nations. There are many other exciting topics, which comparative politics seeks to study; many of these, including transitions to democracy, social policy, and the impact of globalization's pressures, are among the most interesting, exciting, and important topics in both the policy realm and the social sciences.

COMPARATIVE POLITICS DEFINED

Comparative politics may be defined as the systematic, comparative study of the world's political systems. It seeks to explain both similarities and differences among political systems and to develop comparisons between them. In exploring these issues, comparative politics seeks to be as rigorous, analytic, and systematic as possible. It develops hypotheses (for example, why some countries are more democratic or developed than others), seeks to be rigorous in its use of evidence (using scientific public opinion surveys, for example, in place of purely personal impressions), and tries to fashion rigorous propositions that can be tested by other scholars in other countries or research settings.

A great variety of kinds of studies can be undertaken within comparative politics. These include single-country case studies, comparisons of two or more countries, or studies of some dimensions of the entire global universe of countries. Studies in comparative politics can include an in-depth examination of a single country or of a particular institution within that country, studies of the same institution (the political role of the military, for example) in two or more countries, or a cross-cultural study of trends (e.g., rising literacy and its effect on democratization) among all nations. One can study a particular institution within one or several nations, the same or parallel trends (the rise of neoliberalism, for example) across a variety of nations, or a theme (let us say, democratization or civil society) and whether it has universal validity or not. Numerous other studies can be conceived within the comparative politics rubric.

Comparative politics can study a single institution or trend among several or many countries at a given point in time, which we call the snapshot approach. That is, you "freeze" your camera at a certain point in time (usually the present), and you study how a given institution works, in one or more countries, at that particular instant. Or (and here the going gets trickier—and more intriguing) you study the same phenomenon in different countries but at different points in history. For instance, we know that in the West, economic development and industrialization gave rise to social change, which, in turn, sparked greater pluralism and democratization. The question is whether those same processes will give rise to democratization in Afghanistan, Iraq, and today's developing nations. In other words, can we use the experiences of the already-developed nations (industrialized, modern, democratic) to predict what the future of today's developing nations will look like? Do the developed nations today provide a mirror by which we can see what the developing nations will look like in the future? Or are the circumstances of today's developing nations so fundamentally different from those of the past that they cannot be expected to follow the model of the earlier developers?

The above discussion brings us to our last preliminary point, which is the use of "models" or hypotheses in comparative politics. Comparative politics uses many such models. Models are simplifications of reality, but they are useful in our thinking and in the organizing of our research. One such model posits that there is a strong correlation between economic development and democracy, that countries that are economically developed also *tend to be* democratic. That does not mean that all wealthy countries are democratic (Kuwait, Borneo, and Saudi Arabia are wealthy but nondemocratic) or that all poor countries are undemocratic (Costa Rica is poor but very democratic). But it is to say that there is a *correlation* between national wealth and democracy, even if it is not exactly one-to-one. This "model," therefore, of the relationship between wealth and democracy, while not always exact, points us in a useful research direction, suggests a pattern or a relationship that we may not have thought of before, and indicates a research hypothesis that can then be tested empirically in the field or by using comparative data for all the world's countries. Such models are, therefore, useful but they should not be worshiped or reified. For sometimes, as we shall see in the case of some early theories of Third World development, the models may need to be scrapped altogether as new facts come in that do not fit the theory.

THE END OF THE GREAT SYSTEMS DEBATE?

Since the French Revolution of 1789, three great *systems* or paradigms of organizing politics have vied with each other for control and dominance. These are (1) revolutionary socialism (eventually Marxist-Leninist and totalitarian), (2) reactionary conservatism or authoritarianism in various manifestations (including fascism as well as Third World despotism), and (3) liberal democracy. During most of the nineteenth and twentieth centuries these three major systems vied for control of much of the world's populations.

In the post-World War II period, this historic political debate as to the best system of rule was given a new formulation that reflected the division of the world's political systems into First, Second, and Third "Worlds." The First World was the modern, developed, liberal-democratic states, mostly of the West but including Japan as well. The Second World included the developed communist states led by the Soviet Union and Eastern Europe (actually, these countries turned out to be not nearly so developed as thought at the time). And the Third World consisted of the poor states, mostly underdeveloped and authoritarian, of Africa, Asia, Latin America, and the Middle East. This formulation and the three-part division of the world's political systems held sway for a long time, from the 1950s until well into the 1980s.

But then something quite remarkable, unexpected, and astonishing happened that undermined and may have destroyed this earlier classification. First, beginning in the mid-1970s in Portugal, Greece, and Spain, and then spreading to Latin America, East and Southeast Asia, and parts of Africa and the Middle East, a great wave of change swept aside many of the existing authoritarian regimes and led to a transition to democracy in many countries of the area. Second, beginning in 1989 and continuing through 1991, the Soviet Union imploded, leading to democratic transitions there and in many of its former Eastern Europe satellite countries. Essentially, the Second World of developed communist states disappeared, destroyed under the weight of both internal and external pressures, while in the Third World the opening toward democracy undermined any unity within that category.

These changes toward democratization in both the Second and Third Worlds destroyed the old categorizations and the division of the world into essentially three types of regimes or systems. Not only had democracy triumphed in many parts of the globe but now democracy appeared to be "the only game in town." All the others had been vanquished or were on their way to oblivion. Two trends were immediately present. The first was a kind of triumphalism that "our side," our model democracy, had triumphed, that the historical systems debate stretching back over two hundred years was settled, and that all other countries were also fated to become democratic. The second was a new emphasis in the comparative politics field on transitions to democracy, on the comparative processes and institutions involved, including the fascinating question of whether the transition from Marxism-Leninism in Russia and Eastern Europe could be studied using the same categories and approaches as those developed from the study of right-wing authoritarianism in Southern Europe and Latin America.[1]

Recent events, however, force us to rethink the issue of whether history really is "over," whether democracy has actually triumphed, and what the implications of these reinterpretations are for comparative politics. Consider the following: *Read this, carefully - which of these ff is not [illegible]*

1. Many of the so-called democratic countries are only formally democratic; real, liberal, pluralist democracy is still deficient in many countries.
2. Not all authoritarian countries have transitioned to democracy; there are still many authoritarian regimes in the world.
3. Not all Marxist-Leninist states have transitioned to democracy; Cuba, Vietnam, and North Korea are still totalitarian Marxist states, while China still uses a Marxist-Leninist system politically even while liberalizing its economy.
4. Many countries, in the Third World particularly, are mixes or hybrids of some democratic and some authoritarian features.
5. After a decade or two of experimentation, many countries are disillusioned with democracy, faulting it for failing to deliver needed social and economic reforms. In quite a number of these, sentiment is rising to return to "strong government."
6. It's become clear that many persons in such countries as Afghanistan and Iraq, among Islamic fundamentalists more generally, and in quite a number of non-Western countries, do not want democracy, see it as destructive of their values, and prefer their own institutions to the Western imported ones.

These comments make it obvious that "the great systems debate" is not quite over yet, at least in some countries. History has not "ended." Democracy has not yet fully triumphed, let alone become "the only game in town." There are still quite a few other options.

How, then, to strike a balance? We can say, first of all, that among *developed* countries, democracy really is the only game in town. Neither the Marxian communist option nor the reversion to authoritarianism is conceivable at this stage in *any* of the developed countries. Second, among developing countries, the overwhelming majority—certainly in Latin America, much of Asia, parts of Africa—now adhere to the principles of a democratic, open, pluralist society. Some of these countries may not always live up to democratic precepts, but that is clearly their goal and aspiration. Certainly the overwhelming trend in the last three decades has been toward greater liberalism and democracy.

That leaves still quite a number—but a dwindling minority—of "outlier" states: countries that do not conform to the general pattern and current trends. These include the Marxist-Leninist states of China, Cuba, North Korea, and Vietnam; but few countries nowadays want to imitate them, and while China and Vietnam remain Marxist-Leninist in their political controls, both have moved to open up their economies, which may eventually help produce more democratic political systems. Much of Africa also remains nondemocratic, but that is mainly due to underdevelopment, poverty, weak institutions, and weak civil society, and that condition can be expected to change as Africa, too, develops. That leaves chiefly the Islamic Middle East, or roughly three-quarters of the countries there, as the one area not only nondemocratic but in many cases often hostile to democracy. But even in the Middle East, democracy is growing in some countries; it may be that our view of that area as nondemocratic is skewed by the heavy media coverage of such non- or even antidemocratic states as Afghanistan, Iran, Iraq, and Saudi Arabia.

DISTINCT APPROACHES

The triumph of democracy and the presentation of it as "the only game in town" was undoubtedly overstated. There are too many nonconforming outlier states, too many reversals of direction, too many incomplete or limited democracies for us to be to sanguine about democracy's triumph. The trends and patterns are in the *direction* of democracy but the process is still incomplete and, for some countries, may never arrive.

It is safe to say, however, that in *most* countries the great systems debates of the past are largely over. Communism, fascism, totalitarianism, Marxism-Leninism, authoritarianism—almost no one wants to go back to the bad old days of these types of regimes. There are hangovers from the past and sometimes, in fits of disillusionment with democracy, some people express a desire to return to an often heavily romanticized vision of supposedly rosier earlier times; but, on balance, most people in most countries, deep down, prefer democracy.

If that is so, however, if the great systems debates of the past are largely over, then what is there left for comparative politics to do? Actually, quite a lot. For even within democracy, there are a variety of forms that democracy can take. In addition, many questions are involved in the *consolidation* of democracy—such "second-generation" reforms as the overhaul of the judiciary, building respect for the rule of law, strengthening civil society, and strengthening democratic institutions (parties, legislatures, and the like). Moreover, the transitions in such presently nondemocratic states as China, Cuba, and perhaps Iran will be fascinating to watch.

The main focus in this book, however, is on the major *approaches* employed in comparative politics to study these changes. How do we get a grip, a handle, on the change processes underway? How do we know what to study and where do we start? What conceptual framework should we use? How do we know what's relevant and what's not? In short, we are concerned here with assessing how we go about *doing* comparative politics, what questions to ask and what approaches to use, how to assess both changes and continuities, in a context now where the great systems issues—democracy, freedom, open markets, or a mixed public-private economy—have mostly already been decided. And in the process of assessing these distinct approaches, we will also be surveying the modern history of comparative politics and offering suggestions about the future.

The early stages of comparative politics in the 1930s, 1940s, and 1950s were dominated by what has come to be called the formal-legal or institutional approach. That is, students of comparative politics focused on the formal-legal *institutions* of government, such as the executive, legislative, judiciary, and bureaucracy. It concentrated on the rules of the political system, the powers of the various institutions, and how the constitution or formal structures worked. This was a useful approach; it is important to understand the institutions. But most scholars came to see this approach as too constraining: other factors besides formal institutions were important. Particularly as political science in the 1950s came to focus on the more informal and dynamic aspects of politics—public opinion, political behavior, interest group lobbying, decision making, political processes—comparative politics was similarly changed from within by these influences from the broader political science profession.

In the late 1950s, early 1960s, the new or developing nations (the Third World) burst upon the world scene, and that also forced a conceptual (and a geographic) change in how comparative politics approached its subject matter. Heretofore, comparative politics had largely focused on the developed, well-institutionalized (hence, the formal-legal or institutional approach) European states; now it came to concentrate on the emerging nations of Africa, Asia, Latin America, and the Middle East. Because in the countries of these areas the formal institutions of government did not always work very well, scholars instead concentrated on such informal aspects as political communications, patronage networks, how interests get mobilized and organized, government favoritism and cronyism, military intervention in politics, coups, and revolutions. The approach was also strongly reformist: not only would we *study* developing areas but we (the United States) would also *bring* development to the Third World through such agencies as the Peace Corps, the Alliance for Progress, and the Agency for International Development (AID).

The study of political culture emerged at about the same time as did the study of the developing areas, and the two went forward hand-in-hand. Political culture involves the comparative study of political beliefs and values, the influence of religion on politics, and the lasting impact of accumulated historical experiences on a country. To the extent possible, political culture studies need to be based on careful, comparative, public opinion surveys;

otherwise, they run the danger of employing unacceptable, discredited national stereotypes ("Germans are this," "Italians are that," "Muslims are such-and-such"). But if we can say with some certainty, based on our opinion surveys, that Latin Americans tend to be skeptical of whether democracy is working very well in their countries, or that the people of Afghanistan prefer strong government over representative rule, that should be useful information in assessing the prospects for democracy.

The study of political development flourished during the 1960s but then in the 1970s it was discredited as an approach and went into decline. Part of the reason for its decline was the general political climate of the time: Vietnam protests, the Watergate scandal that brought down President Richard Nixon, political assassinations (Robert Kennedy, Martin Luther King Jr.), various societal discontents. But the political development approach also had serious logical and methodological flaws: it was ethnocentric; it was based too heavily on the U.S. and European experiences that didn't apply in the Third World; it devalued the cultures and institutions of the developing countries; it assumed the end product of development would be a country that looked just like the United States; and it was too closely (and often destructively) tied to the U.S. Cold War goals of anticommunism. By the end of the 1970s the political development approach was in decline—although in later decades, as we shall see, it enjoyed something of a comeback.

Replacing political development was a number of new approaches, no longer a single one. The unity in the comparative politics field that had persisted through, first, the formal-legal-institutional approach, and then the political development approach, now evaporated. In its place came a variety of approaches—the analysis of which lies at the heart of the presentation in this book. Most scholars in the field thought this new diversity of approaches to be healthy for comparative politics, but some of those who had championed the earlier approaches were disturbed both by the criticisms of their approach and by the absence of unity in the field. Here we only briefly introduce these approaches: they are analyzed in greater detail later in the book.

Corporatism was one of the new alternative approaches that emerged in the late 1960s and 1970s. Corporatism, related to communitarianism, has a long history in political theory; in modern times it has come to mean the regulation or control of interest groups and their integration into the decision-making apparatus of the state. There can be religiously based corporatism and secular, bureaucratic corporatism, state corporatism (dictatorial, authoritarian—Franco's Spain) and societal corporatism (democratic, participatory—modern Sweden). What distinguished corporatism from the earlier approaches was (1) its willingness to look at countries in terms of *their own* (corporatist) arrangements rather than through the lenses of U.S.-preferred solutions; (2) its presentation as having either democratic *or* authoritarian versions and outcomes; and (3) the idea that corporatism represented a quite distinctive model and system of politics, fundamentally different from either liberal-pluralism or Marxist totalitarianism.

2. State-society relations was another related approach that emerged in the 1970s. Its focus was the complex legal, political, and institutional arrangements between the state or government *and* the component units that make up society: labor, business, farmers, bureaucracy, religious groups, armed forces, etc. Some countries have strong states and weak societies (Russia, China) while others have weak states and strong societies (the United States). In some countries the relations between the state and societal units are corporatist (state control, regulation, limits on group activities); in others, liberal (full freedom of association). One can see how this would be an interesting and useful way to classify countries and also, in its regulation of societal or interest groups, how it relates to corporatism.

3. A third alternative approach that emerged during this period was called dependency theory. In contrast to the developmentalist approach which saw rich country and Third World development going ahead in tandem, dependency theory saw First World wealth as coming at the expense of poor countries. The rich got rich on the backs of the poor; to remedy this exploitive situation, poor countries would need to band together, break relations with their exploiters in the First World, and develop their own statist or socialist economies. As will be surmised, dependency theory owed a lot to Marxism; although one can be a dependency theorist without being a Marxist (I am; after all, big wealthy countries do, regularly, intervene and muck around in the politics of smaller, poorer countries), most advocates of the dependency approach tended to be Marxist in their thinking. But dependency theory didn't work out very well: its Marxist approach was often off-putting; most poor countries quickly realized they still needed rich-country investment; and with the collapse of the Soviet Union and Eastern Europe in 1989–1991, socialism was discredited as an effective economic growth model.

Still a fourth alternative approach to appear during the 1980s was called "indigenous theories of change." It emerged out of rising disillusionment in the Third World with both developmentalism and Marxian dependency theory. Both of these other approaches were imports from the First World and neither worked very well in Third World settings; hence, the rising call on the part of Third World leaders to fashion *their own* developmental solutions to their problems based on homegrown or indigenous practices and institutions. We will call this the Frank Sinatra solution, who so famously sang "I did it *my* way." The idea of an indigenous (Islamic, Confucian, Buddhist, African, Latin American) model of change was undoubtedly

attractive; but in the long run, as we shall see, there were numerous problems with this formulation as well.

There are some interesting parallels and commonalities between these
four alternative approaches. First, they all find fault with the earlier institutionalist and developmentalist approaches. Second, they all are enormously sympathetic to the efforts of Third World peoples and nations to
find a way out of their underdevelopment. And third, in one way or another, they all seek to formulate a theory or approach that derives not
from imported Western models but is closer to actual Third World institutions and ways of doing things.

Our analysis now moves, although more briefly, to some of the other alternative approaches that have emerged in comparative politics in recent
years. The *political economy* approach provides a useful way of looking at the
interrelations between politics and economics; although it largely emerged
out of earlier Marxian and dependency analyses, one does not have to be a
Marxist (witness Adam Smith) to recognize the utility of this approach.

Rational choice is an approach that has swept some political science departments in recent years, although it has been less successful in the international relations or comparative politics fields. Rational choice seeks
to develop a model of political behavior similar to economics based on rational self-interest, and to use that as a means to explain electoral choice,
congressional voting behavior, interest group politics, and governmental
decision making.

Finally, the new institutionalism (students should consider whether it is
different from the previously discussed old institutionalism) returns the
field back to its earlier emphasis on institutions. Here the focus is on constitutional design—executive, parliament, local government, court system, legal structures, bureaucratic roles. One can see that in its emphasis
on bureaucratic controls, for example, the institutionalist approach could
overlap with the corporatism and state-society relations approaches;
some advocates of the new institutionalism, in fact, define it so broadly as
to even include such topics as political culture, interest group conflict, and
decision making, which to others may seem like a bit of a stretch.

HOT ISSUES

In recent years some scholars of comparative politics have moved away
from the earlier emphasis on approaches. They simply assume, as most of
us do, that the corporatist, state-society relations, political economy, and
other approaches noted above are so thoroughly integrated into the field,
so widely accepted, that we don't need to argue about them anymore. We
use them, or some combination of them, where they are useful; the choice

among approaches, most of us believe, should, therefore, be eclectic and pragmatic, and not based on great ideological or methodological hang-ups. Taking for granted the usefulness of these approaches and moving on from there, quite a number of scholars have now gone on to focus on *problems* and *issues*.

One of the most important of these is the issue of transitions to democracy. How do countries transition from authoritarianism or communism to democracy? Are there parallel processes or is each country unique? What institutions and political processes are involved in the transition? Which formula works better: corporatism, liberal democracy, or some combination of these? Is the model to be found in the Western experience or indigenously? Is democracy everywhere the same or can there be local, homegrown versions? Just posing the questions this way shows (1) how interesting this issue is and (2) how one can use the theories and approaches discussed previously to shed light on it.

A second major issue, related to the first, is civil society. Almost all scholars of comparative politics agree that, for democracy to succeed and last, it requires a web of intermediary associations (civil society) between the individual and the state, both to protect the individual from state intrusion on civil liberties and to serve as transmission belts between citizens and the government. But how can civil society be created in countries, such as Haiti or Afghanistan, that have never had civil society? Can it be imposed by outside powers or must it grow from indigenous roots? What if we don't like the particular kind of civil society (caste associations, tribalism, Islamic fundamentalism) that emerges and consider it inimical to democracy? These can be thorny issues, but once again one can readily see how the approaches offered up earlier (developmentalism, corporatism, state-society relations, political economy, rational choice, dependency theory, the new institutionalism) can each offer their own insights on the issue.

A third issue is the developing nations and what works (versus what doesn't) in achieving development. We now have about fifty years of experience with the developing nations; scholars of the issue and foreign assistance practitioners now know pretty well how to help countries achieve growth and development. There are still controversies, of course, over such issues as globalization and neoliberal economic reforms, but in most policy areas we generally agree as to what is helpful and what is not. The chapter on developing nations in this book spells this out; in addition, it shows how several of the approaches described above can be useful in understanding and advancing the processes involved.

Finally, in the section on issues we include a chapter that examines some of the new, hot, frontier issues seen from a comparative perspective. These include women in politics, drug policy, immigration, regionalism and decentralization (is "small" really beautiful?), gay rights, and environmental issues and pollution. It is an intriguing chapter, in part, because it covers so many issues in a short space, but also because it once again illustrates the main theme of the book: the utility of comparative politics models and approaches in enabling us to better understand both the diverse countries in the world *and* the hot issues that they face.

THE ORGANIZATION OF THE BOOK

The following chapter reviews and explains in more detail the definition, methodology, and background of comparative politics, and how and why it should be studied.

Part II of the book discusses, analyzes, and critiques the main *approaches* that comparative politics has employed over the years to study the nations of the world and their political systems. These approaches include, in successive chapters, developmentalism, political culture, corporatism, and indigenous theories of change. A catch-all chapter includes briefer discussions of dependency theory, bureaucratic-authoritarianism, political economy, state-society relations, rational choice theory, and the new institutionalism.

In Part III we turn our attention to the major *issues* and problems that have emerged in recent years. In successive chapters these include transitions to democracy, civil society, what works in development, and, again, a catch-all chapter that discusses women in politics, drug policy, immigration, decentralization, gay rights, and the environment.

In Part IV, the Conclusion, we return to the themes raised here in the Introduction. Is "the great systems debate" between Marxism-Leninism, authoritarianism, and democracy really over? Are democracy and neoliberalism really the "only games in town"? What other alternatives, if any, are there? How does comparative politics best go about exploring these issues? What approach, or approaches, are the most useful and appropriate to use in our studies? Are we likely to see a revised and reformulated development theory applied to the Third World? And finally, what are the unexplored research terrains, the new frontiers, to which comparative politics should turn its attention?

NOTE

1. See the other volumes in this series, *The Dilemmas of Democracy in Latin America: Crises and Opportunity* (Lanham, MD: Rowman & Littlefield, 2005) and *Development on the Periphery: A Comparative Analysis of Democratic Transitions in Southern and Eastern Europe* (Lanham, MD: Rowman & Littlefield, 2005).

2

New Directions in Comparative Politics

ᔆ

Comparative politics has long been considered one of the leading fields within political science—maybe *the* leading field. It covers a vast research terrain: the entire world. Comparative politics deals with *all* of the world's diverse and fascinating political systems along with critical, current, and overarching themes such as democratization, integration, and globalization.

Over the past forty years, comparative politics has produced some of the most intriguing, innovative, and stimulating theory and approaches in political science. These include developmentalism, political culture, corporatism, dependency theory, state-society relations, comparative political economy, indigenous theories of change, comparative public policy, and, recently, rational choice theory and the new institutionalism. In addition, within most political science departments, the comparative politics faculty is frequently the largest and often the most prestigious, partly because it has so much of the world to cover. Comparative politics scholars are usually well-traveled, have lived abroad for long periods of time often in exotic places, and have seen the world. It is a fun, exciting, and important field.

COMPARATIVE POLITICS DEFINED

Comparative politics involves the systematic study and comparison of the world's political systems. It is systematic in that it looks for patterns, regularities, and trends among all these political systems; it is comparative in seeking to explain similarities and differences, as well as developmental

15

changes among and between these systems. For example, we might explore how presidential systems work in different countries, the differences between presidential and parliamentary systems, or how and why countries adopt one constitutional form or another.

We can study two-party versus multiparty systems, unitary versus federal systems, and dictatorships versus democracy. This list just begins to scratch the surface of the many subject matters to which comparative politics turns its attention.

Note that all the subject matters indicated above are static, in the sense that they compare the same, similar, or contrasting institutions *at a given point in time*—usually the present. In this sense they are like a camera taking a snapshot, first of one political system or a particular institution in it, and then another, and comparing the two. But now suppose we add a dynamic element to the picture, a moving picture that takes its portraits at different points in time. Suppose we compare the United States or Western Europe, for example—highly developed and industrialized countries—with some of the less-developed countries of the world. Will these less-developed countries, as they also modernize, go through the same developmental steps and stages as the already developed countries, and eventually come to resemble them in their stability, democracy, and efficient economies? Do the already developed countries provide a backwards reflection of what the developing nations will look like in the future? By studying the advanced countries today, will we know what the emerging nations will look like tomorrow?[1]

There are also more complicated questions, around which great debates in comparative politics have swirled. Are the developing nations fated to be just pale, somewhat retarded imitations of the developed ones? Or do the emerging countries have cultures, dynamics, and political institutions of their own? Times and conditions have changed dramatically since the nineteenth century, when the United States and Western Europe began *their* modernization. So will developing nations' experiences be fundamentally different from today's already developed nations? One can readily see why these questions are bound to raise complex, nationalistic, and culturally sensitive issues in many parts of the globe.

As we proceed, keep in mind these two approaches in the comparative politics field:

1. The easier *snapshot approach* where we simply compare two identical or roughly similar institutions, policies, or political processes at the same point in time, in two or more countries.
2. The harder *developmentalist approach* where we try to foretell the future of one group of countries on the basis of the earlier developmental experience of another group of countries.

PAST AND PRESENT IN COMPARATIVE POLITICS

Comparative politics has had a long and distinguished history as a political science field.[2] Here we provide a brief overview of the field and of its major shifts of emphasis and direction as a way of putting current issues into better perspective.

Aristotle was the first comparativist twenty-five hundred years ago with his analysis of the various Greek city-states—not just their formal constitutional provisions but also their underlying social, cultural, and economic bases and how these changed over time. The Greek Plato and the Roman Cicero also used a comparative approach not only to classify political systems but to suggest the best form of political system. In the post-1500 modern era, Machiavelli, Jean Bodin, and Montesquieu (the architect of the American system of separation of powers), were all comparativists. Adam Smith and Karl Marx were preeminently economists but they also studied political economy, and Marx particularly drew upon comparative data derived from his research and living experiences in Germany, France, and England.

Some of the best early studies of the United States in the nineteenth century, those by Frenchman Alexis de Tocqueville[3] and Englishman Lord James Bryce,[4] were excellent precisely because their authors were able to make comparisons between the United States and other countries. Similarly, Woodrow Wilson, the only political scientist ever to be elected president of the United States, greatly enriched his studies of executive-legislative relations in the United States by his understanding of the main European political systems.[5] Recently, the United States has been compared with Canada[6] as well as portrayed as "the first new nation."[7] Examining this rich intellectual history, one would be inclined to say that political science as a discipline has always been most illuminating when it employed a comparative approach, that the foremost thinkers in the history of political thought have rather consistently been students of comparative politics, and that even the study of American politics has been greatly enriched when a comparative perspective is brought to bear.

By the 1920s and 1930s, comparative politics had developed as one of the major fields within political science. The other fields were usually American politics, constitutional law, political theory, international relations, and sometimes state and local government.

Through the 1950s, the main focus of comparative politics was on the countries of Western Europe—primarily Britain, France, Germany, and the former Soviet Union. Those were considered the most important countries; indeed, in many universities the introductory comparative politics course *required* that these four countries be taught. The politics of Scandinavia or Latin America were sometimes taught but only in a handful of universities. Travel to foreign continents was difficult, slow, and very expensive in those pre-jet days, and most scholars considered themselves lucky if they got to travel abroad more than once or twice in their lifetimes.

Comparative politics mainly studied the formal, legal, constitutional *institutions* of government; indeed, in those days it was called comparative government. As in the rest of political science prior to the mid-1950s, there was little attention to more dynamic, informal aspects of politics such as political parties, public opinion, interest groups, decision making, or public policy.

The comparative politics field was strongly influenced by refugees from Europe during the 1930s and 1940s who themselves had been trained in constitutional law. The foremost scholars in the field during this period—Carl Friedrich, Herman Finer, Karl Deutsch, Hannah Arendt, Karl Loewenstein, among others—were all of European origins and had been trained in legal studies; in Europe, political science was not yet a separate discipline. A particularly interesting case is that of Loewenstein who, as the last student of the great sociologist Max Weber, was in his native Germany considered "too sociological" by his German law colleagues; but when he came to the United States he was thought of as "too legalistic" by his American political science colleagues. The influence of these European scholars tended to reenforce both the legalistic and the European focus of comparative politics.

Beginning in the early1950s, a revolution occurred in the comparative politics field, as well as in political science generally, that gave rise to the modern comparative politics. First, a new generation of post–World War II scholars emerged who were trained in political science rather than law and who brought fresh perspectives to the field. Second, within political science generally the emphasis came to be more on the informal aspects of politics, the study of political behavior, and systems analysis, and these approaches also carried over into comparative politics. Third, the sudden emergence as independent states of a host of new, Third World nations, coupled with the shift in the Cold War focus away from Central Europe and toward the new or emerging nations, led to a much greater emphasis on the developing areas of the world and less on Europe.

A key turning point was the publication in 1955 of Roy Macridis's tub-thumping, flag-waving little book called, innocuously enough, *The Study of Comparative Government*.[8] Macridis had been one of the "young activists" of the post–World War II generation of comparativists who had been advocating change and new directions. He charged that in the past comparative politics had been parochial in focusing so much on Western Europe; merely descriptive rather than analytic; formalistic and legalistic rather than concentrating on dynamic processes; and consisting more of case studies of individual countries rather than being genuinely comparative. The Macridis critique was strongly worded, posed the issues in sharp either/or terms, and had an enormous impact on the field. His little monograph was probably read by every aspiring graduate student in the field over the next fifteen years. The view that comparative politics should be nonparochial, nonformalistic, nonlegalistic, analytic, and genuinely comparative became the prevailing position among scholars and their students. The Macridis book ushered in a revolution in comparative politics and provides the launching pad for our consideration of the distinct newer approaches in the field, beginning with development theory (see chapter 3).

WHY STUDY COMPARATIVE POLITICS?

There are a number of reasons for studying comparative politics. First, it's fun and interesting, and one learns a lot about other countries, regions, and the world.

Second, studying comparative politics will help a person overcome ethnocentrism, defined as the inability to understand other countries except through one's own rose-colored lenses. All peoples and countries are ethnocentric, but Americans seem to be particularly afflicted. Instead of studying and trying to understand other countries through *their* eyes, in their own cultural and social context, and in their own language(s), Americans tend to look at the rest of the world from the perspective that our ways and institutions are best and these other countries should therefore learn from the United States. Americans seldom perceive that they could also learn from other nations' experiences or that they should study American as well as other countries' institutions *comparatively*, neutrally, without bias, from the pragmatic point of view of what works best rather than from a perspective of superiority and condescension.

Third, we study comparative politics because that enables us to understand how nations change and the patterns that exist. What accounts for the fact that some nations have forged ahead while others remain poor and backward? What can we learn from the recent, very heartening transitions from authoritarianism to democracy in so many parts of the world? And how does one explain the unraveling of so many Marxist-Leninist regimes and their transactions to more open politics and economies? Comparative politics may not have all the answers to such questions, but it does offer some, and it has an approach and methodology that enable us to get at quite a few others.

A fourth reason for studying comparative politics is that it is intellectually stimulating. Consider these questions: Why do some countries modernize and others not? Why are some countries democratic and others not? Why are interest groups and political parties structured one way in some countries and other ways in others? Why do some countries and their political systems fail while others succeed? These are among the

most challenging questions that one can face in today's world. Comparative politics helps us get at the answers by showing the change process in
all its dimensions, and by wrestling with the problems posed by the complexity and multiple causes of these processes.

Fifth, comparative politics has a rigorous and effective methodology.
The comparative method, really a way of thinking comparatively about
the world and its individual political systems, is both a sophisticated tool
of analysis and one that is always open to new approaches. (We have
more to say about the comparative methodology in a later section.)

Finally, comparative politics is necessary for a proper understanding of
both international relations and foreign policy. Without knowing thoroughly, from the inside, empathetically (the opposite of ethnocentrically),
the other countries with whom we conduct our foreign relations, we cannot have an informed, successful foreign policy. Hence, there is an inti-
mate connection between international relations, foreign policy, and comparative politics; in my view, these are distinct fields of study, but in the
real world they are also inseparable, complementary, and mutually necessary for an understanding of today's world.

TYPES OF STUDIES

Comparative politics seeks to explain systematically differences between as
well as similarities among countries. In contrast to journalistic reporting on a
single country, comparative politics is particularly interested in exploring
patterns, processes, and regularities among political systems. It looks for
trends, for changes in patterns; and it tries to develop general propositions or
hypotheses that describe and explain these trends. It seeks to do such comparisons rigorously and systematically, without personal, partisan, or ideological axes to grind. It involves hard work, clear thinking, careful and thorough scholarship, and (hopefully) clear, consistent, and balanced writing.

The world is our laboratory, so the types of studies that can be encompassed in comparative politics are (as would be expected) varied. Different scholars will have different preferences in these regards, but that
should not cause concern that the field has no one single focus. Rather, it
includes several different kinds of studies—and legitimately so, in my
view. Among the types of studies that students of comparative politics actually do are the following:

1. *Studies of one country,* or a particular institution (political parties, mil-
   itaries, parliaments, interest groups), political process (decision making), or public policy (for instance, labor or welfare policy) in that
   country. Such single-country studies are probably the easiest for

young students in the field to do. But in focusing on only one country or institution, it will be necessary in an introductory statement or
paragraph to put that study into a larger comparative framework.
That means we should tell why the subject is important and where it
fits in a larger context. For instance, if we're interested in military intervention in the politics of a country, then we should explore the
general literature on interventions as well as studying the politics of
that particular country. We should also offer a set of comments, usually called a "model" or "conceptual framework," that explains the
broader implications of the study and its possible relevance to the
same or similar issues in other countries or to global trends. In other
words, even though our study may concentrate on a single country,
we are still interested in the "bigger picture" and in *comparison*. Such
broader concerns, the effort to analyze patterns and general behavior, are what distinguish comparative politics from newspaper reporting or a historical survey of a single country.

2. *Studies of two or more countries.* Such genuinely *comparative* studies are
   harder to carry out, and they are usually more expensive in terms of
   travel and research costs. It is often difficult for the beginning student to understand and master one foreign country; two or more are
   even harder. Hence, often the student of comparative politics does a
   case study of one country first in the form of a paper, thesis, or doctoral dissertation; later he or she may move on to study a second (or
   third, fourth, and so on) country—and to elaborate the comparisons
   between them. Such a step is very important intellectually because it
   is in knowing and writing about two or more countries that students
   can begin to make genuine *comparisons*.

3. *Regional or area studies.* These may include studies of Africa, Latin
   America, the Middle East, East Asia, Southeast Asia, South Asia, Europe, or other subregions (Southern Europe or North Africa, for example). Such studies are useful because they involve *groups* of countries that may have several things in common—for example, similar
   histories, cultures, languages, geographic locations, legal systems,
   religions, colonial backgrounds, and so on. Such regional or area
   studies are often particularly interesting because they are almost like
   a science laboratory. That is, if a group of countries has many common features—let us say a colonial background or Catholicism in
   Latin America—the investigator can hold such factors constant
   while examining or "testing" for certain other features (for instance,
   the level or degree of authoritarianism in the society), almost as if
   one were carrying out a chemistry experiment. The investigator can
   then make statements about the area as a whole or make comparisons between countries within a given area. The danger lies in

overgeneralizing, in making comments about the area as a whole without sufficient attention to the specific differences of individual countries even within a particular region.

Among some scholars, area studies are controversial. Students may become so enamored of their own area that they lose objectivity. Or they may become so engrossed in one particular culture that they forget the larger goal of *comparison*. In addition, many issues today—human rights, democracy, the environment, drugs—are global; they are not limited to one country or area. Even with these potential problems, however, area studies have a very important role in comparative politics: They enable a student to study and become immersed in one particular area, they facilitate comparison among often similar or at least *comparable* countries, and it is out of such area studies, as we see later in the book, that some of the most exciting new approaches in the field—dependency theory, corporatism, bureaucratic-statism—have emerged.

4. *Studies across regions.* Such studies are becoming more prevalent, but at more advanced levels they are often expensive and difficult to carry out. One must know, master, and travel to not just one region but two or more. Such studies might involve comparisons of the role of the military in Africa and the Middle East, or of the quite different paths to development of the East Asian countries and Latin America. (My own research, for example, has involved comparisons among Latin America, Southern and Eastern Europe, and East Asia.) Such studies can be very interesting, although one must recognize that it is very difficult for a single scholar to stay well informed on so many countries and areas.

5. *Global comparisons.* With the improved statistical data collected by the World Bank, the UN, and other agencies, it is now possible to do comparisons on a global basis. We can, for example, trace the relationship in *all* countries between economic development and the growth of democratization, or between the size of the middle class and democratization, or between greater affluence and the decline of authoritarianism and Marxism-Leninism. Such studies can best be done through the use of statistical correlations. But such correlations cannot be said to prove *causation;* that is, that economic growth causes democratization. There is a relationship between economic growth and democracy, but the first does not necessarily *cause* the second. In addition, students of such global comparisons often lack expertise in the specific areas or countries studied and thus may make egregious mistakes. For example, Nicaragua under the dictator Anastasio Somoza was sometimes listed as "overdemocratized" for its level of economic development, because one of the indices

used to measure democratization—the presence of opposition members in the congress—was consistently high in that country. The global comparativists didn't know, however, what only an area or country specialist would know: that in Somoza's emphatically nondemocratic regime the constitution *required* one-third of the legislature to come from opposition parties so that the dictator could portray a false picture of his regime as more democratic than it really was.

Other problems involved in global comparisons include the frequent unreliability of the statistical data used and the problems of developing meaningful comparisons between countries and regions that are so different in their cultures and histories—such as Africa and Latin America or Asia and Europe—so that it's like trying to add apples and oranges. I think of such global comparisons as provocative, suggestive, and interesting, but they should be treated with a good dose of healthy skepticism, especially if one tries to draw too strong a conclusion out of them.

6. *Thematic studies.* Comparative politics focuses on themes as well as countries and regions. For example, some scholars may be interested in a comparative perspective on the changing role of the state, the process of military professionalization, the structure of class relations, or in the process of political socialization (how we learn about politics, where our political ideas come from). Others may be interested in such themes as dependency theory (the dependence of some countries on others), the processes by which emerging countries achieve democracy and national development, or the newer systems of interest group representation called "corporatism" (all of these terms and themes are examined in greater detail later in the book), viewed from a comparative perspective. Such studies are often complex, difficult, and at a theoretical level, and are usually carried out by more experienced scholars in the field because they presume a great deal of knowledge about various areas and require the ability to see the "big picture" at a high conceptual level.

Several interesting lessons emerge from this survey of the types of research that students of comparative politics do. First is the variety of approaches and perspectives used. Most of us find such diversity in the field healthy and stimulating. The important thing at this stage is not so much the *type* of study that one chooses to follow but to begin to think *comparatively*, in terms of the patterns and comparisons that exist between countries and regions.

A second admonition is to look at what students of comparative politics actually *do* in their studies rather than getting bogged down in the stale, often disruptive and inconclusive debates over approaches and methods that mar the field. Rich country, area, global, and thematic studies are "out there" that students should peruse in order to get a feel for the field; some suggestions along these lines are contained in the "Suggested Readings" at the end of the book.

Third, one should recognize degrees of difficulty. For the beginning student a single-country study or a two-country comparison may be appropriate, or an area study, or perhaps a topical study that cuts across regions; but remember that even these require an introduction and conclusion that places the topic in a broader comparative perspective.

THE COMPARATIVE METHOD

Comparative politics provides a means by which we can learn about other societies, how they work and how they change. Through comparison, we can learn that what works in one society may not work in another, and why. Comparative politics also provides an antidote to ethnocentrism—a method by which to understand other societies on their own terms and in their own context.

The comparative method, we have indicated, is usually thought of as involving two distinct levels of comparison. One is the snapshot approach: it is the easiest to comprehend and operationalize since it involves a comparison, a snapshot, of two or more countries or specific institutions within them *at a certain, given point in time*—usually the present. The second approach, trickier and more complex, involves a comparison of the same aspect or issue in two or more countries but *at different points in historical time*. For example, if we are interested in the comparative development of democracy or of political parties, can we perhaps compare Europe and the United States in the nineteenth century when parties and democracy first emerged, with late-twentieth-century development of democracy and political parties in many developing countries? In other words, to what extent do the already developed or industrialized nations of today present a picture of what the developing nations will be like in the future? Do the developed nations at every stage of their development provide us with a picture, a mirror, of what all nations must go through eventually on their road to development? Comparison, in other words, can be across nations at a single point in time, or it can involve comparisons across time periods to test if the same processes (economic development and greater social change, for example, giving rise to greater demands for democracy) are operating at different historical periods.

The comparative method has often been compared, somewhat pretentiously, to the scientific method in physics or biology. Like the natural sciences, comparative politics has its "laboratory": the world's political system. And with this image of a laboratory in mind, it appears that we could carry out scientific measurements involving those systems. In comparative politics we can sometimes hold one or more variables constant—religion, culture, social structure, a particular political institution, etc.—while we look comparatively at policy outcomes. For example, if we're interested in studying comparative welfare policy, we can control for some variables while we test for others. In this case welfare policy outcomes are viewed as the *dependent* variable while religion, culture, socioeconomic factors, and so on are the *independent* variables.

One can see why this method is sometimes compared to the laboratory methodology of the hard sciences. In this case the globe is our comparative politics experiment station, and we have over two hundred nations (plus other kinds of units) to consider. We also know how to test for certain variables and to control for others. In comparative politics, as in the laboratory sciences, we use hypotheses, tests, and "proofs." One can understand why it would be tempting to equate comparative politics' methodology with that of the natural sciences.

Although the analogy with the hard sciences is attractive, it should not be taken literally. Comparative politics is *not*, in most respects, a hard science. The field and its concepts—political culture, political socialization, interest group activity, decision making, policy implementation—are often vague and imprecise, and are not amenable to empirical scientific experimentation. In addition, the exact meaning and measure of these concepts may vary from country to country. Furthermore, too many variables in human affairs may intervene in unlikely or unanticipated ways, so that it is very difficult to be quantitatively precise about our findings. Nor, in the social sciences, can one readily isolate these variables and thus replicate the test and get the same results as in a science laboratory. Because the concepts often carry diverse meanings to different researchers and the tests are difficult to replicate, one cannot speak of comparative politics as a precise, empirical science as one would physics or biology.

A mistake is often made by beginning students in comparative politics, however, that involves the confusion of "science" with the experimental method. Not all sciences need to use the experimental method of the physics or chemistry laboratory. Those are more precise, to be sure, but other methods may also be used. For example, if science is defined as an "orderly body of knowledge," then surely comparative politics qualifies. It *may* use the experimental method, but it may use other, more interpretive methods as well—such as library research, interviewing, or participant observation in the country studied—that carry their own specific rules of data collection, logical argumentation, and interpretation. Here we emphasize comparison as a mode of inquiry or way of knowledge. To achieve the desired results, the experimental method *may* be employed, but the traditional approaches are also valid methods of research.

For some students, the fact that comparative politics is not a strict science in the sense that the natural sciences are is a cause for despair and even the abandonment of the field. That feeling is shared by some scholars in comparative politics, who have embarked on a sometimes frustrating quest to quantify and mathematicize, to find universal rules for the entire field. But the conclusions of most scholars of comparative politics lie in between these two extremes: That is, although comparative politics is not always as quantifiable as, say, chemistry, that's not a reason for us to throw up our arms in despair and abandon the field. At the same time, while recognizing that comparative politics is not and probably never will be a strict or hard science, that does not absolve us from trying to be as precise, systematic, and careful in our research as possible.

Where, then, does that leave us—or the field of comparative politics? The following injunctions may be helpful:

1. Let us recognize realistically that, for most questions, comparative politics is not a science in the same sense that, say, physics or biology are. It has its "orderly body of knowledge" like other sciences, but it cannot often replicate the experimental method of laboratory science.

2. Nevertheless, we need to be as careful and as rigorous as possible in setting forth our hypotheses and research plans, in testing our hypotheses, and in carrying out and reporting on our research.

3. Some of the methods used by comparative politics, such as interviewing and library research, are often not as exact as we would like them to be; they are useful methods but by their very nature may be open to different interpretations.

4. Nevertheless, the goal must remain a study that is as systematic and precise as possible.

5. We must also recognize that some of the new approaches in the field, employing statistics, mathematical modeling, regression analysis, multivariate analysis, and computers, enable us to use sophisticated and quantifiable measures that were previously unheard of. Every student of comparative politics now must master these techniques. Furthermore, while the field is unlikely to achieve the precision of an exact science in answering the most important questions that we are interested in, its scientific measures are expanding, and in the future it is likely that such mathematical and computer-based measures will be used even more frequently.

6. At this stage comparative politics mainly produces tendency statements rather than scientific proofs. For example, we can say that

countries with high income levels *tend* to be more likely to have democratic political systems than do very poor countries; table 2.1 clearly illustrates that relationship. Note that this is not an absolute statement, nor is it a scientific law of behavior, because there are numerous variations and exceptions; there is, however, undoubtedly a relationship, and a rather close one, between economic development and democracy, a relationship that is best described by "tendency statements" rather than absolute laws. In most areas of comparative politics, such tendency statements are at present about as much as we can hope for—although more rigorous "proofs" of hypotheses should be sought.

7. Above all, we need to avoid bias and special pleading in the field. Some people use the "soft science" underpinnings of comparative politics as an excuse to advance their own biases or ideologies or to grind their own pet political axes. Most scholars in the field deplore that approach. There may be biases in the field or in some parts of it, but that should not lead to an equally biased view on the other side. The goal should be not the celebration of one bias or another but rather a comparative politics approach that is as unbiased, unprejudiced, fair, and balanced as possible.

MODELS AND PARADIGMS IN COMPARATIVE POLITICS

Frequently, the field of comparative politics employs various "models," "frameworks," or "paradigms" as a way of simplifying and thus explaining various political phenomena more easily. In fact, the tracing, history, and analysis of these several approaches in the field lie at the heart of the presentation in later chapters. Examples of such models include the developmentalist approach, corporatism, and dependency theory. Each of these approaches is defined and explained in subsequent chapters. A model of this sort is a simplification of reality, and should not be confused with the real thing.

For example, if we say that the developmentalist approach helps us explain the modernization processes of various Third World countries or that corporatism helps us understand the relations between interest groups and the state or government, then we are using developmentalism or corporatism as a model or paradigm that explains some aspects of the political process. A model is a shorthand way of referring to a larger and more complex phenomenon or process. Again, such models as corporatism, developmentalism, or dependency represent simplifications of reality, not reality itself—they are metaphors for or abstractions of reality, not the genuine product. But such models are very useful in political

Table 2.1. Basic Development Indicators

Human Development Index (HDI) Rank	Total population (millions) 2003	Urban population (% of total) 2003[a,b]	GDP (US$ billions) 2003	GDP per capita (US$) 2003	GDP per capita annual growth rate (%) 1990–2003
High Human Development					
1 Norway	4.6	78.6	220.9	48,412	2.9
2 Iceland	0.3	92.8	10.5	36,377	2.1
3 Australia	19.7	91.9	522.4	26,275	2.6
4 Luxembourg	0.5	91.8	26.5	59,143	3.6
5 Canada	31.6	80.4	856.5	27,079	2.3
6 Sweden	9	83.4	301.6	33,676	2
7 Switzerland	7.2	67.6	320.1	43,553	0.5
8 Ireland	4	59.9	153.7	38,487	6.7
9 Belgium	10.4	97.2	301.9	29,096	1.8
10 United States	292.6	80.1	10,948.50	37,648	2.1
11 Japan	127.7	65.5	4,300.90	33,713	1
12 Netherlands	16.1	65.8	511.5	31,532	2.1
13 Finland	5.2	61	161.9	31,058	2.5
14 Denmark	5.4	85.4	211.9	39,332	1.9
15 United Kingdom	59.3	89.1	1,794.90	30,253	2.5
16 France	60	76.3	1,757.60	29,410	1.6
17 Austria	8.1	65.8	253.1	31,289	1.8
18 Italy	58	67.4	1,468.30	25,471	1.5
19 New Zealand	3.9	85.9	79.6	19,847	2.1
20 Germany	82.6	88.1	2,403.20	29,115	1.3
21 Spain	42.1	76.5	838.7	20,404	2.4
22 Hong Kong, China (SAR)	6.9	100	156.7	22,987	2.1
23 Israel	6.5	91.6	110.2	16,481	1.6
24 Greece	11.1	60.9	172.2	15,608	2.1

#	Country								
25	Singapore	4.2	100	91.3		21,492			3.5
26	Slovenia	2	50.8	27.7		13,909			3.1
27	Portugal	10.4	54.6	147.9		14,161			2.2
28	Korea, Rep. of	47.5	80.3	605.3		12,634			4.6
29	Cyprus	0.8	69.2	11.4		14,786			3.2
30	Barbados	0.3	51.7	2.6		9,708			1.4
31	Czech Republic	10.2	74.3	89.7		8,794			1.5
32	Malta	0.4	91.6	4.9		12,157			3.3
33	Brunei Darussalam	0.4	76.1	:		:			:
34	Argentina	38	90.1	129.6		3,524			1.3
35	Hungary	10.2	65.2	82.7		8,169			2.6
36	Poland	38.6	61.9	209.6		5,487			4.2
37	Chile	16	87	72.4		4,591			4.1
38	Estonia	1.3	69.5	9.1		6,713			3.3
39	Lithuania	3.5	66.8	18.2		5,274			0.5
40	Qatar	0.7	92	:	d	:	d		:
41	United Arab Emirates	4	85.1	:	d	:	d	c	-2.1
42	Slovakia	5.4	57.5	32.5		6,033			2.4
43	Bahrain	0.7	90	:	d	:	d	c	1.5
44	Kuwait	2.5	96.2	41.7		17,421		c	-2.3
45	Croatia	4.5	59	28.8		6,479			2.1
46	Uruguay	3.4	92.5	11.2		3,308			0.9
47	Costa Rica	4.2	60.6	17.4		4,352			2.6
48	Latvia	2.3	66.3	11.1		4,771			2.2
49	Saint Kitts and Nevis	(.)	32.2	0.3		7,397			3.1
50	Bahamas	0.3	89.4	5.3		16,571		c	0.3
51	Seychelles	0.1	50	0.7		8,610			2.2
52	Cuba	11.2	75.7	:		:		c	3.5
53	Mexico	104.3	75.5	626.1		6,121			1.4

(continued)

Table 2.1. *(continued)*

Human Development Index (HDI) Rank		Total population (millions) 2003	Urban population (% of total) 2003[a,b]	GDP (US$ billions) 2003	GDP per capita (US$) 2003	GDP per capita annual growth rate (%) 1990–2003
54	Tonga	0.1	33.5	0.2	1,603	2
55	Bulgaria	7.8	69.8	19.9	2,539	0.6
56	Panama	3.1	57.2	12.9	4,319	2.4
57	Trinidad and Tobago	1.3	75.4	10.5	8,007	3.2
Medium Human Development						
58	Libyan Arab Jamahiriya	5.6	86.2	.. [d]	.. [d]	..
59	Macedonia, TFYR	2	59.6	4.7	2,277	-0.7
60	Antigua and Barbuda	0.1	37.8	0.8	9,629	1.6
61	Malaysia	24.4	63.8	103.7	4,187	3.4
62	Russian Federation	144.6	73.3	432.9	3,018	-1.5
63	Brazil	181.4	83	492.3	2,788	1.2
64	Romania	21.9	54.6	57	2,619	0.6
65	Mauritius	1.2	43.3	5.2	4,274	4
66	Grenada	0.1	40.7	0.4	4,199	2.4
67	Belarus	9.9	70.9	17.5	1,770	0.9
68	Bosnia and Herzegovina	3.9	44.4	7	1,684	11.9 [c]
69	Colombia	44.2	76.4	78.7	1,764	0.4
70	Dominica	0.1	72	0.3	3,639	1.2
71	Oman	2.5	77.6	.. [d]	.. [d]	0.9 [c]
72	Albania	3.1	43.8	6.1	1,933	5.1
73	Thailand	63.1	32	143	2,305	2.8
74	Samoa (Western)	0.2	22.3	0.3	1,505	2.4
75	Venezuela	25.8	87.6	85.4	3,326	-1.5
76	Saint Lucia	0.2	30.5	0.7	4,314	0.3

No.	Country						
77	Saudi Arabia	23.3	87.6	214.7	9,532		-0.6
78	Ukraine	47.5	67.3	49.5	1,024		-4.7
79	Peru	27.2	73.9	60.6	2,231		2.1
80	Kazakhstan	14.9	55.9	29.7	2,000		0.4
81	Lebanon	3.5	87.5	19	4,224		2.9
82	Ecuador	12.9	61.8	27.2	2,091		0.1
83	Armenia	3	64.5	2.8	918		2.8
84	Philippines	80.2	61	80.6	989		1.2
85	China	1,300.00	38.6		1,417.00	1,100	8.5
86	Suriname	0.4	76	1.2	2,635		0.9
87	Saint Vincent and the Grenadines	0.1 e	58.2	0.4	3,403		1.8
88	Paraguay	5.9	57.2	6	1,069		-0.6
89	Tunisia	9.9	63.7	25	2,530		3.1
90	Jordan	5.4	79.1	9.9	1,858		0.9
91	Belize	0.3	48.4	1	3,612		2.2
92	Fiji	0.8	51.7	2	2,438		1.8
93	Sri Lanka	20.4	21.1	18.2	948		3.3
94	Turkey	71.3	66.3	240.4	3,399		1.3
95	Dominican Republic	8.6	59.3	16.5	1,893		4
96	Maldives	0.3	28.8	0.7	2,441	c	4.7
97	Turkmenistan	4.7	45.4	6.2	1,275		-1.3
98	Jamaica	2.6	52.2	8.1	3,083		(.)
99	Iran, Islamic Rep. of	68.2	66.6	137.1	2,066		2.1
100	Georgia	4.6	52	4	778		-2.7
101	Azerbaijan	8.3	50.1	7.1	867		-2.6
102	Occupied Palestinian Territories	3.5	71.1	3.5	1,026	c	-6
103	Algeria	31.9	58.8	66.5	2,090		0.6

(continued)

Table 2.1. (continued)

Human Development Index (HDI) Rank	Total population (millions) 2003	Urban population (% of total) 2003[a,b]	GDP (US$ billions) 2003	GDP per capita (US$) 2003	GDP per capita annual growth rate (%) 1990–2003
104 El Salvador	6.6	59.4	14.9	2,277	2.1
105 Cape Verde	0.5	55.9	0.8	1,698	3.3
106 Syrian Arab Republic	18.1	50.2	21.5	1,237	1.4
107 Guyana	0.7	37.6	0.7	965	3.6
108 Viet Nam	82	25.8	39.2	482	5.9
109 Kyrgyzstan	5.1	34	1.9	378	-2.4
110 Indonesia	217.4	45.5	208.3	970	2
111 Uzbekistan	25.8	36.7	9.9	389	-0.5
112 Nicaragua	5.3	57.3	4.1	745	0.9
113 Bolivia	8.8	63.4	7.9	892	1.3
114 Mongolia	2.6	56.8	1.3	514	-2.5
115 Moldova, Rep. of	4.2	46.1	2	463	-5.7
116 Honduras	6.9	45.6	7	1,001	0.2
117 Guatemala	12	46.3	24.7	2,009	1.1
118 Vanuatu	0.2	22.9	0.3	1,348	-0.3
119 Egypt	71.3	42.2	82.4	1,220	2.5
120 South Africa	46.9	56.9	159.9	3,489	0.1
121 Equatorial Guinea	0.5	48	2.9	5,900	16.8
122 Tajikistan	6.4	24.8	1.6	246	-6.5
123 Gabon	1.3	83.7	6.1	4,505	-0.4
124 Morocco	30.6	57.4	43.7	1,452	1
125 Namibia	2	32.4	4.3	2,120	0.9
126 São Tomé and Principe	0.1	37.8	0.1	378	-0.2
127 India	1,070.80	28.3	600.6	564	4
128 Solomon Islands	0.5	16.5	0.3	553	-2.5

129	Myanmar	49.5	29.5	..	.	5.7	
130	Cambodia	13.5	18.6	4.2	315	4	c
131	Botswana	1.8	51.6	7.5	4,372	2.7	c
132	Comoros	0.8	35	0.3	538	-1.3	
133	Lao People's Dem. Rep.	5.7	20.7	2.1	375	3.7	
134	Bhutan	2.1	8.5	0.7	797	3.6	
135	Pakistan	151.8	34.1	82.3	555	1.1	
136	Nepal	26.1	15	5.9	237	2.2	
137	Papua New Guinea	5.7	13.2	3.2	578	0.2	
138	Ghana	21.2	45.4	7.6	369	1.8	
139	Bangladesh	136.6	24.3	51.9	376	3.1	
140	Timor-Leste	0.8	7.7	0.3	389	..	
141	Sudan	34.9	38.9	17.8	530	3.3	
142	Congo	3.8	53.5	3.6	949	-1.4	
143	Togo	5.8	35.2	1.8	362	0.4	
144	Uganda	26.9	12.3	6.3	249	3.9	
145	Zimbabwe	12.9	35	.. d	.. d	-0.8	c
	Low Human Development						
146	Madagascar	17.6	26.6	5.5	324	-0.9	
147	Swaziland	1	23.6	1.8	1,669	0.2	
148	Cameroon	15.7	51.4	12.5	776	0.2	
149	Lesotho	1.8	18	1.1	635	2.3	
150	Djibouti	0.8	83.6	0.6	886	-3.3	
151	Yemen	19.7	25.7	10.8	565	2.4	
152	Mauritania	2.9	61.7	1.1	384	1.6	
153	Haiti	8.3	37.5	2.9	346	-2.8	
154	Kenya	32.7	39.3	14.4	450	-0.6	
155	Gambia	1.4	26.2	0.4	278	-0.1	
156	Guinea	9	34.9	3.6	459	1.6	

(continued)

Table 2.1. *(continued)*

Human Development Index (HDI) Rank	Total population (millions) 2003	Urban population (% of total) 2003[a,b]	GDP (US$ billions) 2003	GDP per capita (US$) 2003	GDP per capita annual growth rate (%) 1990–2003
157 Senegal	11.1	49.6	6.5	634	1.3
158 Nigeria	125.9	46.6	58.4	428	(.)
159 Rwanda	8.8	18.5	1.6	195	0.7
160 Angola	15	35.7	13.2	975	0.4
161 Eritrea	4.1	20	0.8	171	1 [c]
162 Benin	7.9	44.6	3.5	517	2.2
163 Côte d'Ivoire	17.6	44.9	13.7	816	-0.4
164 Tanzania, U. Rep. of	36.9	35.4	10.3	287	1
165 Malawi	12.3	16.3	1.7	156	0.9
166 Zambia	11.3	35.9	4.3	417	-0.9
167 Congo, Dem. Rep. of the	54.2	31.8	5.7	107	-6.3
168 Mozambique	19.1	35.6	4.3	230	4.6
169 Burundi	7	10	0.6	83	-3.5
170 Ethiopia	73.8	15.7	6.7	97	2
171 Central African Republic	3.9	42.7	1.2	309	-0.4
172 Guinea-Bissau	1.5	34	0.2	160	-2.4
173 Chad	9.1	25	2.6	304	(.)
174 Mali	12.7	32.3	4.3	371	2.4
175 Burkina Faso	12.4	17.8	4.2	345	1.7
176 Sierra Leone	5.1	38.8	0.8	149	-5.3
177 Niger	13.1	22.2	2.7	232	-0.6

Without HDI Rank

Afghanistan	27.2	23.3	4.7	..	..
Andorra	0.1	91.7	..	..	..
Iraq	27.3	67.2	..	..	..
Kiribati	0.1	47.3	0.1	567	2.7
Korea, Dem. Rep.	22.3	61.1	..	..	..
Liberia	3.2	46.7	0.4	131	4.2
Liechtenstein	(.)	21.6	..	..	..
Marshall Islands	0.1	66.4	0.1	2,017	..
Micronesia, Fed. Sts.	0.1	29.4	0.2	1,952	-1.4
Monaco	(.)	100	..	..	..
Nauru	(.)	100	..	..	..
Palau	(.)	68.7	0.1	6,281	..
San Marino	(.)	88.7	d	..	..
Somalia	7.7	34.9	..	..	..
Tuvalu	(.)	55.1	..	..	..
Serbia and Montenegro	10.5	52	20.7	2,558	3.5 c

Source: United Nations Development Program, "Human Development Report, 2005."

Notes:

a. Data refer to medium-variant projections.
b. Because data are based on national definitions of what constitutes a city or metropolitan area, cross-country comparisons should be made with caution.
c. Data refer to a period shorter than that specified.
d. Data refer to 2002.
e. Population estimates include Taiwan, province of China.

analysis—indeed they are used all the time—enabling us to simplify for discussion purposes what are often very complex processes.

A model is a heuristic device—a kind of teaching aid—used to sort out, organize, and simplify more complex processes. An effective model simplifies reality by dividing it into clear and manageable components. But reality is always more complex than any single model or even several models can capture. A model is a very helpful tool in social science and comparative politics analysis, but it should not be confused with the even more complicated kaleidoscope that is reality itself. A model helps us understand and come to grips with events and processes that otherwise would be so disorganized, complex, and random that they would not make sense. At the same time, we should understand that the term *model* is a neutral one; when we use that word, we are not making a value judgment. A model is simply an intellectual device; in contrast to the term's popular usage it implies neither approval nor disapproval.

What then is the utility of our employing such models in our analysis of comparative political systems? To recap:

1. Models help us organize, highlight, and give coherence to otherwise diverse events, processes, and institutions.
2. Models help put many seemingly unrelated events in a larger context, enabling us to see the "big picture," to provide perspective.
3. Models enable us to think more clearly about complicated events.
4. Models are heuristic devices; they teach us things and enable us to see patterns.
5. Models help simplify complex events, enabling us to understand them more clearly.

Models should also be seen as pragmatic instruments. To the extent they are useful and helpful in terms of the purposes outlined above, we can use them to help order our thinking. But such models as used in comparative politics should not be worshiped or reified. They are not forever. They are not sacrosanct. New events or facts—the unraveling of the communist world, for example, or the emergence of democracy as a near-universal political system—often force us to alter our interpretations, obliging us to change or revise our models, or to scrap them altogether. Often students of comparative politics become so attached to their particular model—as happened with developmentalism in the 1960s—that they fail to recognize that it must be reformulated or that it has outlived its usefulness. Models are devices to be used as long as they are useful and help us shed light on events, but we should not hesitate to rethink or replace them when they have outlived their utility. The overall usefulness—and limits—of models should be recognized.

APPROACHING THE SUBJECT dn't study.

Studies of all the world's political systems using a global model and statistical correlations are useful in some respects in suggesting relationships
and patterns that otherwise we might not be aware of. However, such
studies ignore regional and cultural differences and, as noted, too frequently involve the inappropriate mixing of apples and oranges. In any
case, they are not for the beginning student. Beginning students should
probably begin by studying a single country, a pair of countries, or a
group of countries in a single region or with other comparable features.

How then should we proceed? I have found it useful in my own studies to use the following outline, which can also be thought of as a potential table of contents for a book or thesis. The outline also suggests numerous topics for a smaller, narrower term paper or thesis and shows
where they might fit in the broader scheme of things. Someone doing a
complete country study should probably have chapters on each of the
subject areas; someone writing a research paper would probably be advised to narrow the focus and try to cover only one aspect within this
larger outline.

I. *Introduction.* The introduction should try to interest, stimulate, or
"grab" the reader, state why the particular country or subject
matter is important, and why someone should spend time researching or reading about it. The introduction should also "introduce" the subject and the author's preliminary ideas or hypotheses about it, explore the previous literature on the subject,
and tell precisely what the author intends to do in the study. A
good introduction should also explain the methodology of the
study and present a plan so readers have a "road map" of where
they are going.

II. *Political History.* History is so important in so many countries,
where the shadow of the past still lingers, that it is useful to have a
chapter on the historical background. One need not necessarily do
original research for this information, but one ought to review all
the secondary literature in order to trace the historical pattern of
the country's formative development, to place the study in historical context, to bring the history right up to the present, and thus to
provide a setting for the author's own study. One can also, if one
wishes, do a comparative political history of two or more countries.

III. *Political Culture.* Political culture refers to the values, ideas,
norms, belief systems, and patterns of behavior of a particular
people or country. History obviously helps shape the political
culture, but other factors are also involved. An assessment of the

political culture can derive from the art, literature, religious beliefs, modes of expression, and ways of behaving of the society—particularly as these affect politics and give it a certain style. To be more accurate and quantitative, however, assessments of political culture should be based on public opinion surveys. In studying political culture, one should avoid national stereotyping, but careful research can show what political-cultural patterns exist and how they influence countries.

IV. *Socioeconomic Background*. This chapter or section should present information on the country's level of economic development and how it compares with other countries. What is the nature of its economy? What does it produce? What is its relationship to outside markets and economic forces? This chapter or section should also contain data on the country's level of social modernization, its class structure and social relations, and how these are changing. Is it an agricultural or an industrial country? Does it have two traditional social classes (elites and masses), or is it more pluralist? What are its ethnic, caste, tribal, and other divisions? In short, the writer needs to outline the social and economic basis of politics. And here, most often, political scientists will have to do their own research because economists and sociologists frequently do it badly, not at all, or in a form that political scientists cannot use.

V. *Interest Groups*. It is often a short step from socioeconomic data and class structure to interest groups. Many interest groups—business, farmers, middle-class associations, labor, peasants—are economic, but others—the armed forces, religious bodies, ethnic associations, student groups, professional associations—are not. In addition, many countries have outside actors—the U.S. embassy, multinational corporations, the International Monetary Fund, the Vatican, the German, Japanese, or Russian embassies—that are so powerful that they function like domestic interest groups. One can study any one of these interest groups in a particular country or group of countries, or one can try to gauge the overall structure of interest group power in a particular country. One should also try to determine if the interest group system is based on an authoritarian, democratic, corporatist, or totalitarian pattern.

VI. *Political Parties*. Almost all countries now have political parties, or, if not, they frequently have socioeconomic, class, clan, caste, or tribal groups that function like political parties. That is, they educate their people in a certain belief or interest system (called political socialization), and they bring people together as an effective political movement (called interest aggregation). One can study a particular political party, a group of similar parties (socialist, conservative, communist, Christian-democrat) in different political systems, various functions (leadership recruitment, electioneering) of the parties, or the entire political party spectrum, left to right, or structure (one-party, two-party, multiparty) of a particular country.

VII. *Political Communications.* This topic involves how ideas and interests are communicated to government officials. In a less-developed country, political communication may take place mainly via interpersonal communications, family networks, or gossip; in more-developed countries, the mass media (radios, newspapers, television, the Internet) tend to be more important. Political communication is thus related to levels of literacy, newspaper circulation, and per-capita radio or television ownership. It is also important to know who owns the media, what are its biases, and how the media both manipulates and is manipulated by political leaders. Another important issue is the new trend toward globalization of news and culture, what some have called the "world culture" of rock music, blue jeans, television ("Friends," "Seinfeld"), and Coca-Cola, along with demands for democracy and freedom.

VIII. *Institutions of Government.* We now move from what are called the "inputs" of politics, or what goes "into" the political system (history, political culture, socioeconomic data, interest groups, political parties, political communications), to the actual institutions and decision-making processes of government. This topic may either be subdivided into three separate chapters or sections, or combined in a more abbreviated form into a single unit. The first of these subdivisions looks at the institutions of government: the legal system, the constitutional structure, president/prime minister, congress/parliament, justice and the court system, local government, and so on. There are many topics to study in this category (comparative federalism, presidentialism versus parliamentarism, executive-legislative relations, decentralization, and so on), which, since it focuses on the institutions of government, is what many beginning students think of as the proper realm of political science or governmental research.

IX. *Bureaucracy and the State.* Because the state system and bureaucracy in the United States are comparatively small, most Americans do not spend much time thinking about these subject areas. In some other countries, however, the state plays a far larger role, either in directing the economy, in controlling interest groups (corporatism), or in providing a fuller range of social programs. Thus, in this second subdivision of government institutions, one would want to show how the state system and the bureaucracy are organized, who controls them, their role in social welfare and directing the economy, and so on. Or, in this new era, how does the state handle downsizing, privatization, and reform campaigns?

X. *Decision Making.* This is the third subdivision in our analysis of government institutions. It focuses on who makes decisions, how they are arrived at. What influences are felt? For example, I once had the president of a Latin American country tell me that when he made important decisions he checked first with his armed forces chiefs, then with his country's economic elites, and third with the American embassy—but not necessarily in that order! If he had time he might check with other groups, but such was rarely the case. That rank-ordering certainly tells us a lot about the structure of power and decision making in his country. Comparable information on decision making in other countries would likely reveal parallel or divergent, but perhaps equally striking, patterns.

XI. *Public Policy.* Moving from governmental structures and decision making to the actual decisions that come out of the political system, we arrive at the subject area of public policy. Comparative public policy is one of the fastest-growing subjects in the field. There are a great variety of public policies that can be studied comparatively: housing policy, economic policy, industrial policy, social policy, agrarian reform, education, population policy, environmental policy, and so on. One can also compare the foreign policies of different countries. In some country and comparative studies, domestic policy and foreign policy will be combined within a single chapter or section; in others the two subjects will be divided into two discussions.

XII. *Conclusion.* In this chapter or section we will want to sum up our findings, examine the patterns that emerge, look back at our original hypotheses to see if they can be confirmed or denied, and draw out the assessments of our research. What makes this country or political system unique? In what ways is it comparable to others? What lessons can be learned? Does the system work? Is it functional? How do its parts fit together? What are its weak or missing links? A good conclusion should not only sum things up in this fashion but might also indicate what gaps still exist, and thus point in the direction of another, future research project.

A number of things should be reemphasized about this chapter or paper outline and organizational scheme. First, and most obviously, it offers a practical guide both to the range of subject areas encompassed within the comparative politics field *and* a plan for organizing them in book or thesis form. Second, it is quite appropriate for students to focus on only one or a few aspects within this outline, not on the "big picture" as one would do in a complete, sophisticated comparative country study. Third, this outline can easily be expanded or contracted like an accordion; depending on the time frame, motives, or particular research focus, chapters or sections can be either combined or further subdivided.

In addition, as perceptive students will note, there is a logic, coherence, and sequence to the way these materials are presented. We proceed from the most general (history, political culture, socioeconomic background) to the more specific (interest groups, parties, political communications, government institutions, decision making, public policy). Finally, the outline follows a systems or process model of the polity (see figure 2.1); that is, it has "inputs" that go into the political system in the form of values, history, interests, and so on; it has a government or decision-making system that processes these demands; it has "outputs" in the form of government decisions and policies; and it has "feedback," by which those decisions and policies have an effect on values, interests, and behavior, as well as what again goes "into" the political system.

I hasten to add, however, that this systems plan is purely a heuristic device, a teaching aid, a picture that helps us envision the interrelated parts of the system, an outline that seems to make some logical sense but that can be modified to fit new facts and particular circumstances. For example, this schema, with its focus on interest groups and political parties, may be more appropriate for a liberal-pluralist polity than it would be for an authoritarian or totalitarian regime, where some modifications in the outline might have to be introduced. The organizational plan presented here should be used where it is useful and helpful, and modified where it is not.

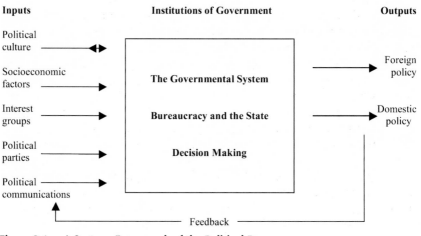

Figure 2.1. A Systems Framework of the Political Process

ASPECTS OF CHANGE

Change within the system presented in figure 2.1 can take a variety of forms and stem from a variety of sources. Change may take peaceful evolutionary or violent revolutionary directions, or it may stem from the use of limited structured violence to achieve limited goals. Change may come under authoritarian, totalitarian, or democratic auspices, and it may come gradually or rapidly. Change is ubiquitous, but it takes many forms, and the processes of change have themselves often been the subject of comparative study.

What are the causes of change? Over the past decades, students of comparative politics have gotten into some terrible arguments over this question. Is it historical, political-cultural, value-based, or ideological forces that drive change? Or is it socioeconomic forces, foreign investment, the class system, the ownership of the means of production and of distribution (mainly a Marxist interpretation) that initiate change? Or is it political-structural factors: the organization of the state system, the strength of political parties, the coordination of business and labor to achieve national development? Or could it be biological and genetic forces—what is now called sociobiology—that are involved?

My answer is that probably all of these factors are involved—and at the same time it is often a silly debate, like asking which came first, the chicken or the egg. No one knows the answer to that either—the question can never be answered—so it doesn't get us anywhere to even ask it.

Clearly, in studying the change process in comparative politics, cultural, socioeconomic, and political-structural factors are always involved. If one does not know or understand the role of religion and cultural factors in Asia or Latin America, for example, then that is an admission that one knows little about the area. Similarly, one must understand the power of the great motor forces of economic development and industrialization in giving rise to class changes (the rise of an entrepreneurial class, a middle class, and an organized working class), which, in turn, affect politics and political institutions at all levels. At the same time, political institutions are themselves often "independent variables," filtering the process of cultural and political change and shaping the form, direction, and speed of economic development.

Hence, if we ask, as in our chicken-egg dilemma, whether it is culture change that sets the conditions in which economic growth can begin, or is it economic change that changes the culture and the political system, the answer is *both*. That is, culture helps determine the form of the economy and, at the same time, is itself changed by economic growth. Meanwhile, political factors affect both culture and the economy and are, in turn, changed by them. Change is, therefore, not one-way or monocausal but multifaceted; the image we should draw on is that of a trellis in a rose garden with multiple routes to development and various crossing members that mutually influence one another.

Having said that, we should also recognize that the relative influence of these three main factors—cultural, socioeconomic, political-structural—and doubtless other factors (accidents, biology, chance, geography, and so on) as well, may vary over time and from country to country. Culture may be the most important factor at some points in history; at other times it will be socioeconomic factors; and at still others the main forces will be political and institutional. Moreover, in some countries and areas the cultural influences will be stronger, in others the economic forces will be strongest, and so on. It will be up to students of comparative politics to wrestle with these issues, to sort them out, and to try to draw conclusions from them. The issues are complex; those who simply assert the predominance of one factor over another or jump to hasty conclusions about them are probably making an ideological statement rather than engaging in serious scholarship. For *serious* students of comparative politics these issues, and our minds, must remain open; there is no simple or pat formula. Rather, it is one of the joys and enthusiasms of the field that we must remain open-minded, pragmatic, and always willing to explore new relationships.

NOTES

1. A good analysis of the philosophical bases of comparative politics is Mattei Dogan and Dominique Pelassy, *How to Compare Nations* (Chatham, NJ: Chatham House, 1984).

2. For a detailed survey, see Howard J. Wiarda, *An Introduction to Comparative Politics: Concepts and Processes*, 2nd ed. (Fort Worth: Harcourt Brace, 2000).

3. Alexis de Tocqueville, *Democracy in America* (New York: Knopf, 1960).

4. James Bryce, *Modern Democracies* (New York: Macmillan, 1924).

5. Woodrow Wilson, *The State* (Boston: Heath, 1918).

6. Seymour Martin Lipset, *Continental Divide: The Values and Institutions of the United States and Canada* (New York: Routledge, 1990).

7. Seymour Martin Lipset, *The First New Nation: The United States in Historical and Comparative Perspective* (New York: Norton, 1979).

8. Roy Macridis, *The Study of Comparative Government* (New York: Random House, 1955).

II

APPROACHES
TO THE FIELD

3

Political Development

We saw in the last chapter that the field of comparative politics has had a long and distinguished history. As it emerged as a separate field in political science in American universities between World Wars I and II, comparative politics was dominated by a formal-legal approach that emphasized constitutions, laws, and the formal procedures of government. That approach continued into the 1950s when it faced a challenge by a younger group of scholars who sought to emphasize the informal processes of politics: public opinion, interest groups, decision making, and the like.

By the late 1950s there were already several "schools" within the field of comparative politics. Some scholars, whose background often included legal training, continued to do research—often very interesting and valuable research—on what was now considered rather old-fashioned topics by younger scholars: constitutional and governmental institutions. Most of these senior scholars concentrated on European affairs and continued to do the noncomparative, case study projects that Macridis and others had strongly criticized. Other scholars, though not so numerous as those in the first group, were area specialists whose concentrations included "newer" areas such as China, Japan, the Soviet Union, or Latin America. But there was also a third and younger group beginning to form that was intrigued by the politics of the newly independent and gradually emerging nations in Asia, Africa, and the Middle East. Over the course of the next decade, the 1960s, not only did this group become the most numerous, but its theory and approach—called "political development" and focused on the politics of the developing nations—became dominant in the field.

ORIGINS OF THE DEVELOPMENTALIST APPROACH

At least seven major influences help explain the new focus in comparative politics on the politics of the developing nations.

The first, already discussed in the previous chapter, was the new emphasis in political science on political behavior and the more informal aspects of politics: political socialization, interest group activity, and decision making. This focus came at the expense of attention to the more legal-formal aspects of government. But in the developing nations, it was reasoned, the formal rules and constitutions did not work very well anyway. Moreover, with the strong influence in the developing nations of tribal associations, caste associations, and family, clan, and patronage networks, it was appropriate to focus on these informal aspects of politics. In short, the field of political science was already moving toward a focus on informal actors, and in the developing areas, given the weaknesses of laws and constitutions, that focus seemed particularly appropriate.

A second reason for the new interest in the developing nations was the sudden entrance in the late 1950s and early 1960s of a host of new nations onto the world's stage. Several Middle Eastern countries had become independent with the breakup of the Ottoman (Turkish) empire in World War I; after World War II, India, Pakistan, and several others became independent; the People's Republic of China emerged from the fallout of the Chinese Revolution; Indonesia became independent from Dutch colonial rule in the early 1950s; and Indochina became independent from France. By the late 1950s and on into the early 1960s, a large number of newly independent African and Caribbean, and more Asian and Middle Eastern, nations had emerged onto the scene. The independence of all these new nations more than doubled the number of political entities available for comparative politics to study; it enormously expanded our universe of countries and provided whole new laboratories for the study of political change.[1]

Some distinctions need to be introduced at this point. Most of the Latin American countries had become independent from Spain and Portugal as early as the 1820s, so it was hardly appropriate to lump them together with the new nations. In addition, Latin America was at that time considerably more developed economically and institutionally than was most of Asia and Africa, occupying intermediary or middle-level positions in most of our indices, so it was not useful either to consider all these nations together with the poorer, less-institutionalized developing nations. Because Latin America didn't fit very well in the "new nation" category, it was either left out of or treated peripherally in most of the books dealing with development produced during this period. The same was often true for such nations as Iran and Egypt: These were old cultures and civilizations dating back thousands of years, with proud and sometimes glorious histories. They often resented being included with the other "new nations" that lacked their long histories; and they were sometimes especially resentful of the United States and its scholarship for using the "developing nations" designation. After all, U.S. history spanned only two to three hundred years as compared with their thousands, so who were the Americans or U.S. professors to treat them disparagingly and lump them with nations that lacked similar backgrounds or histories?

A third reason for the focus on the developing nations had to do with the former colonial powers themselves. As Belgium, France, Great Britain, the Netherlands, and eventually (the mid-1970s) Portugal withdrew from their colonial possessions, they often sought to keep in place both a political system and a framework for change that would protect their long-term interests. Developmentalism seemed to serve that purpose since it provided for cooperation with rather than hatred toward the former colonial masters and since it seemed a reasonable, centrist, nonradical formula for growth. Already we see that developmentalism had political purposes as well as strictly academic ones.

A fourth reason for comparative politics' focus on the "new" or "developing" nations was the growing influence of new academic hybrids in the social sciences that seemed particularly appropriate for studying the developing nations: the emerging fields of cultural anthropology, political anthropology, political sociology, and political economy. In the developing nations, less institutionalized, less specialized, and generally less egalitarian and democratic than the nations of the West, it was almost impossible to separate social position based on family, clan, or patronage headship from political power, or to separate economic wealth from political influence. Hence, the fields of political anthropology, political sociology, and political economy, then coming into their own in any case and *combining* the insights of anthropology, sociology, economics, and politics, offered particularly useful categories and ideas for the study of the developing nations.

A fifth important reason was U.S. government policy. With the Chinese (Communist) Revolution in the late 1940s, North Korea's invasion of South Korea in 1950, and the attraction of socialism as an ideology and Marxism-Leninism as a formula for seizing and holding power in many developing nations, the United States became worried. It feared that unless the West offered an attractive alternative, much of the developing world would be tempted to socialist solutions and would provide the Soviet Union with important allies and access to immense natural resources in the Cold War. Hence, as early as 1952, the U.S. government began meeting with economists and students of comparative politics to try to devise a foreign policy strategy for dealing with the new or developing nations, and to fashion a model or ideology of development that would serve as an alternative to Marxism. This effort received added impetus after the Bandung (Indonesia) conference of 1956, which gave rise to the nonaligned movement (what we would today call the *South* of poor, developing nations), and which was strongly sympathetic to socialism and strongly critical of the United States. Hence, the U.S. government (often using

CIA money) began during this time to fund various centers for the study of international affairs that focused on the developing nations, asked scholars to provide an alternative, noncommunist model of development, and, with Castro's revolution in Cuba in 1959, provided fellowship programs for a whole generation of young graduate students to study the developing nations.[2]

Once again, some further explanation and distinctions are necessary. There is nothing wrong with the U.S. government getting involved in these issues of the future of the developing nations. It is in our interest to know as much as we can about these nations and the development processes involved. However, it was probably not appropriate to covertly use CIA money for these purposes, and, as we see later on, the U.S. government's involvement probably skewed the research results in various ways. Moreover, it must be emphasized that the scholars of development who worked on these matters were not of one mind on the issues. Some were idealistically committed to the developing nations and wanted only to help them out, while others were cynically intent on using the focus on development as a way of manipulating the emerging nations for purely Cold War and ideological purposes. But the vast majority of scholars who got involved in these programs wanted to serve both purposes at once and saw no contradiction or incompatibility between them. That is, they wanted both to assist the developing nations in advancing their economies and building democratic institutions, *and* at the same time to assist U.S. foreign policy by putting forward a noncommunist model of development. They believed their idealistic goal of advancing development would also assist U.S. foreign policy goals, which they identified with the same purpose.

Note that this position stands in marked contrast to, and is less simplistic than, the inaccurate charges of some radical critics, who argue that the United States and the scholars of development wanted to keep the new nations poor and "in chains."[3] In fact, nothing could be farther from the truth: Both the U.S. government and the scholars it supported wanted the developing nations to advance and develop, and saw such development as the best way to guard against Marxian advances. Thus they put forward a positive model of development, an alternative to Marxism to be sure, but one based on the notion that the developing nations and U.S. policy interests would *both* be best served by a strategy that advanced development rather than holding it back.

A sixth reason for the new interest in the developing areas was the sheer excitement of it. Here were fifty to sixty new nations that no one had ever studied before. There were neither theories nor models to work with, nor much factual knowledge about them. Here was a chance to do truly pioneering work in unexplored research terrains. To a scholar, this is heady, exciting stuff. This was a chance to advance and test new concepts, to acquire new knowledge of countries few people had studied or written about before—a chance to be an innovator. Few scholars could resist those attractions.

The final factor that stimulated research on the developing nations was modern jet travel. In the late 1950s to early 1960s, when all these new nations were emerging, commercial jet travel was becoming widespread for the first time. A few years earlier, for example, it would have taken three or four days to travel by propeller plane from the United States to Jakarta, Indonesia. Now all these research sites in Africa, Latin America, the Middle East, and Asia were only one day away or less. Plus, there was new research money for scholars to undertake the travel. Whereas before a scholar of comparative politics had been able to spend a year or even a few months in a new country maybe once or twice in a lifetime, now, with jet travel and adequate research funds, he or she could go abroad for extended periods virtually every year—often several times per year. Thus, not only could the researcher keep current on a favorite research country, but it also became possible to study several countries and areas at the same time. The revolution in modern travel enormously facilitated our ability to do comparative politics.

THE EARLY DEVELOPMENT LITERATURE

The Economists

The earliest literature on development was written by economists. The main contributors were Karl Polanyi, who wrote a classic book around the time of World War II on European industrialization,[3] Everett von Hagen and Bruce Morris, who wrote in the 1950s on economic development,[4] and Robert Heilbroner and W. W. Rostow, who similarly wrote on global economic development but were also concerned with the emerging nations.[5]

All of these books used Europe or the United States as their models of how economic development occurs. That was quite natural given that there were abundant data about Europe and the United States, scholars knew and understood their historical patterns of development, and these were considered the most developed regions at that time. It was simply assumed (and the terms used reinforced those assumptions) that the "less-developed countries" (they were no longer called "backward" or "primitive") would follow the same general path as the already developed ones. Europe and the United States would provide the examples, and the emerging nations, it was assumed, would follow the same trajectory and thus be able to "catch up." The model employed, of course, was one of liberal capitalism or perhaps a mixed form of capitalism combined with some elements of socialism and central planning. But the question of whether the new, emerging nations would, inevitably, follow the European or U.S. model—or whether that model was even appropriate given these countries' vast cultural and other differences in relation to the West—should have remained an open one.

Another problem, common to economists, was their inattention to political factors and the assumption—a large one, as it turned out—that social and political development would *inevitably* follow from economic growth. The economists who formulated the first plans for development in the emerging nations thought, again using the European and U.S. models, that the motor forces of economic growth and industrialization would inevitably give rise to a new entrepreneurial class, a moderate middle class, and organized labor and farmer groups that would in turn produce stable, responsive, pluralist, democratic governments. In much of the Third World, however, this "inevitable" progression toward pluralism, moderation, and democracy did not occur. Rather, economic and social change gave rise to radicalism on the one hand or authoritarianism on the other, at least as much as to democracy. Moreover, a good case can be made that the causation should be exactly reversed from what it was in the early development literature: that first a decent *political system* needed to be put in place, one that was really interested in and committed to economic development and pluralism (instead of simply using government power to attain personal wealth). In the short run at least, there was very little that was inevitable in the developing nations about economic growth automatically producing pluralism and a democracy that looked "just like ours."

The Sociologists

The next group to weigh in on development themes was the sociologists. Here one thinks primarily of Talcott Parsons,[6] Daniel Lerner,[7] Seymour M. Lipset,[8] and (although he was a political scientist) Karl Deutsch.[9] Parsons was a "grand theorist" at Harvard who never spent any time in the developing world but who nevertheless advanced a set of categories for comparing "modern" and "traditional" societies that he presented as having universal validity. He called these categories "pattern variables." Parsons suggested that traditional societies are based on ascription (birth, family name, clan, or tribe) whereas modern societies are based on merit, that traditional societies are particularistic or parochial (closed, narrow, confined, limited) in their viewpoints whereas modern societies are based on universal values, and that traditional societies are "functionally diffuse" (military, political, and economic functions may get all mixed up) whereas more developed societies are functionally specific and differentiated. (See figure 3.1.)

These are probably useful contrasts in some ways. In reality, however, most societies are complex mixtures of ascription and merit, of particularism and universalism, and of diffuseness and specificity. Nor in the Parsons scheme is there any indication of how societies move from one form to another (the assumption is, once again, inevitably, through economic development), or of why these three traits should be singled out and not others. In addition, the distinction between traditional and modern is too absolute, and often produced expectations about modernity that the developing countries could not possibly live up to. Nor, as with the economists, is there

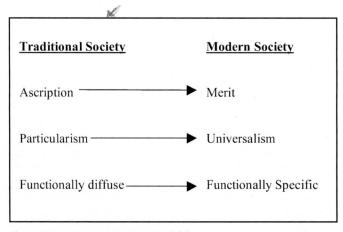

Figure 3.1. Parson's Pattern Variables

any mention by the sociologists of political factors; the processes involved are assumed to be inevitable. Parsons's goal was to present these "pattern variables" as "ideal types," but the result was some misplaced polarities in the study of the developing nations.

Lerner studied the effects of increased means of communications on modernization and development in the Middle East. His was a more detailed study than Parsons's grand theory, more down-to-earth and with real facts and countries involved. But Lerner's study rested on many of the same assumptions as did those of other sociologists writing during this period. He assumed that the process from traditional to modern was one-way, that the modernization brought on by new communications media produced inevitable political results (egalitarianism, democracy, and so on), and that these processes were universal. But the 1979 Islamic revolution of the Ayatollah Khomeini in Iran, and his use of tapes ("modern communications") to get his hateful, fundamentalist message across, should be sufficient to give us pause as to just how one-way, inevitable, and universal these changes produced by modern communications were.

In two seminal articles (see notes 9 and 10) published just as the interest in development was getting into high gear in the late 1950s and early 1960s, Karl Deutsch and Seymour M. Lipset focused respectively on "social mobilization" and the "social requisites of democracy." The two articles, though derived from distinct research, were remarkably parallel in their arguments. Both asserted that certain social requirements (high literacy, economic development, mobilization of peasants and workers, modern communications, education, consensus on the rules of the game, and so on) must be met before a society could become developed and democratic. Deutsch and Lipset were careful to argue that higher education levels do not cause democracy (in Franco's Spain, for example, new education campaigns were launched, but they taught authoritarianism rather than democracy), but they did argue that there is a close correlation between the two. However, their followers and disciples were not quite so careful as Deutsch and Lipset were, and in some circles the belief grew that social mobilization, education, and the like *would* cause democracy to flower.

For a long time (and even now) these ideas of the causative relationship between economic and social change *and* democratization represented the ideological foundation of the U.S. foreign aid program directed at the developing countries. That program had largely been designed in the early 1960s by the economist W. W. Rostow, so we should not be entirely surprised to find these same assumptions prevalent. Rostow had presented an analysis of the several "stages" of economic growth. The stimulus in proceeding from one of Rostow's "aeronautical" stages (first preconditions for take-off, then take-off, next drive to maturity, eventually the age of high mass consumption) to the next was economic growth. Economic growth, according to Parsons, Lerner, Deutsch, and Lipset, would inevitably produce social modernization and differentiation that would lead to democracy. All the United States needed to do, the argument ran, was to provide economic aid, aid to education, new communications media, aid to new social groups, and so on; democracy would presumably inevitably follow. And in terms of U.S. foreign policy and Cold War considerations, such development would carry the country past the stage where it would be susceptible to Marxist-Leninist takeovers (Rostow's book had called communism a "disease" of the transitional stages; once the country got beyond that stage, communism was no longer viewed as a threat). So, not only would U.S. aid produce development (ethically and morally good), but it would also serve our foreign policy purposes. As we will see, there are some enormous holes in this argument.

The Political Scientists

The high point of this early period of the study of development was the publication in 1960 of *The Politics of the Developing Areas*, edited by Gabriel A. Almond and James S. Coleman.[10] In his introduction to the volume, which also included contributions by other experts with country or regional expertise, Almond set forth a framework for studying development that was to have enormous influence on the field. The main ingredients were the following: First, Almond accepted the emphasis on process, informal actors, and genuine comparison set forth by Macridis and other younger scholars in the 1950s. Second, Almond adapted for comparative politics the systems framework (input → governmental decision making → output) that David Easton had suggested a few years earlier. Third, Almond took Parsons's pattern variables (ascription → merit; particularism → universalism; functionally diffuse → functionally specific) and applied them to the political differences between developing and developed nations. And fourth, because, Almond reasoned, the same functions had to be performed in all political systems regardless of the institutions in place, he set forth a *functionalist model* of political activity that presumably would be universally valid—even though Almond later admitted that at that time he had never visited a developing country.

On the input side, Almond had four functions:

1. *Political socialization*—how people learn about or are inculcated with political values and ideas.
2. *Interest articulation*—how interests are articulated and set forth, which sounds like interest group activity.
3. *Interest aggregation*—how interests are brought together and presented in the political system, which sounds like political party activity.
4. *Political communications*—how interests and influences are conveyed to political decision makers.

On the output side there were three functions:

1. *Rule making*—who makes the rules or laws.
2. *Rule execution*—carrying out and administering the rules or laws.
3. *Rule adjudication*—deciding conflicts over rules within the system.

A close look at these output functions reveals that they bear a striking resemblance (although called by different names) to the American system of tripartite separation of powers into legislative, executive, and judicial branches. However, Almond continued to insist that his categories had universal validity, that all these functions *had* to be performed by all the world's political systems.

Even at the beginning there was some skepticism of the Almond approach. Most Europeanists did not find his categories very helpful for their research on advanced societies. Similarly, senior Asia and Latin America specialists often felt the Almond design was an effort to stuff their countries into a set of categories that didn't really apply. Almond himself, meanwhile, had assumed the chairmanship of the important new Committee on Comparative Politics (CCP) established in the 1950s by the grant-making *cum* policy agency Social Science Research Council (SSRC); but even within this group not everyone accepted Almond's framework or the pattern variables of Parsons on which it was built. (The CCP/SSRC is discussed in more detail in the next section.) Nor did those with more experience in the field than Almond feel that his categories fit all their countries very well.

Nevertheless, the Almond design and *The Politics of the Developing Areas* had an enormous influence in the early to mid-1960s, particularly on younger scholars and graduate students. The reasons for this were several. First, the Almond design provided a means to understand, and an outline presumably applicable to, *all* the world's disparate political systems. Second, it told those who were just starting in the field what to look for: interest aggregation, rule adjudication, and so on. Third, what made it attractive was that Almond's approach was not only "scientifically" valid (or so many thought at the time) but also morally good. That is, not only could it be used to study development systematically, but it also suggested what might be missing in a country's development, which comparative politics or U.S. foreign aid could presumably correct (Almond later admitted that his writings in the John F. Kennedy era of the early 1960s were infused with the do-gooder, "Peace Corps mood" of the times). That was the fourth reason for developmentalism's popularity: Not only was it scientifically sound and morally right, it also, in this optimistic, romantic pre–Vietnam War period, was amenable to correcting by U.S. foreign aid. Who could resist an approach that had such an impressive combination of virtues?

So, armed with the Almond categories, a whole generation of young scholars went off to Asia, Africa, Latin America, and the Middle East to study "development." What they found, however, often bore little resemblance to what the Almond framework had suggested. We pick up the thread of why that was so and its implications later in the chapter when we review criticisms of the developmentalist approach, but first we must discuss the proliferation of developmentalist writings.

THE PROLIFERATION OF DEVELOPMENT STUDIES

During the1960s studies of development proliferated, and the developmentalist approach became the dominant one in the field of comparative politics. The Committee on Comparative Politics of the Social Science Research Council (CCP/SSRC) led the way under Almond's leadership, producing seven influential volumes in the 1960s and early 1970s, all published by the prestigious Princeton University Press. These included volumes on political parties and political development, communications and political development, bureaucracy and political development, political culture and political development, education and political development, political modernization in Japan and Turkey, crises and sequences in political development, and the European historical experience with development.[11]

But that was just the beginning. In addition to its own work, the CCP/SSRC also commissioned a large number of studies by others. It brought over two hundred scholars in as contributors to its various books and deliberations. Almond, the group's chairman, also began publishing a series of textbooks in comparative politics that built on his framework and became best sellers in the field. In addition to their work as members of the CCP/SSRC, such leading scholars as Lucian Pye, Myron Weiner, Joseph LaPalombara, Robert Ward, Sidney Verba, Leonard Binder, and James Coleman were also putting out a large number of studies on their own dealing with development themes.

The developmentalist approach soon spread far beyond the original CCP/SSRC group. The CCP/SSRC had served as a catalyst, but now a large number of other scholars were also publishing books dealing with modernization and other aspects of development. Entire bodies of literature soon sprang up around such popular themes as education and development, the armed forces and development, trade unions and development, religion and development, peasants or agrarian reform and development, and so on. A bibliography published in the mid-1960s contained over two thousand entries dealing with development themes; shortly thereafter, an entire book-length bibliographic volume was published focused exclusively on the topic of development.[12]

Development now shifted from being just one academic approach to being *the* approach underlying U.S. assistance programs for developing nations. Here Rostow had been the key person as one of the architects of the U.S. foreign aid program in the early 1960s, as head of policy planning under Kennedy at the Department of State, and later as national security adviser to President Lyndon Johnson. Once again the familiar developmentalist/policy assumptions were applied: If only we can provide enough economic assistance, the argument ran, then we can create middle-class, democratic societies that will be socially just and that can also resist the appeals of communism. To that end, a host of development-related programs—the Peace Corps, the Alliance for Progress, CIA aid to peasants and trade unions, aid to favored political parties, aid to education, aid in the development of mass communications, agrarian reform, community development, military assistance (the list goes on and on)—were put in place to help developing countries make the transition to modernity. It bears reemphasizing that such programs were designed to serve both the goal of assisting developing nations and U.S. foreign policy goals, which were seen as complementary; no possible contradiction between the two was seen at that time.

Few of us disagree with the policy goals in the developing nations of supporting peasant and worker organization, encouraging community development, building roads and highways, or helping with agrarian reform. The question was whether the model set forth in Rostow's and others' writings, based so heavily on the European and U.S. experiences, was really relevant in the particular circumstances of today's developing nations. For example, the model of citizen participation advanced always came out looking like a New England town meeting; the agrarian reform model bore a striking resemblance to conditions in rural Wisconsin. There was nothing inherently wrong with these programs per se, but they should have better taken into account local cultures and customs. Translated into U.S. aid policy, a manifest program of political development often left a great deal to be desired.

In addition to providing foreign aid to a great number of Third World countries, the U.S. government established a number of programs in American universities to advance the study of development. First, the CIA and then more

some subject areas *that were ignored*

overt sources provided the funding for a number of centers for the study of development. The U.S. government also provided stipends to some major foundations and research institutes for them to provide funding for other development projects. Various faculty members also received grants from the government to study the different aspects of development. For graduate students there was the National Defense Foreign Language (NDFL) program to help channel young people into programs that combined language training with Third World area specialization. Such blandishments provided enormous encouragement for the study of development.

Significantly, with all this encouragement of and money available for the study of development, some subject areas were completely ignored. For example, no one seriously studied business or entrepreneurship and development—possibly because in those days the assumption was that a centrally planned or perhaps "mixed" economy was the best way to achieve development, and few academics thought seriously about the contribution of business to development. Another glaring omission was the lack of studies of oligarchies or ruling classes and development—again, presumably, because this element was seen as inevitably fading away as development and social justice were advanced and because the democratically inclined persons who studied development were uncomfortable with oligarchies and ruling classes. But in the short run at least, these groups did not disappear and there was often precious little democratic advance; a strong case can be made that if we are going to study development, we had better be well informed about those elite groups with the capacity either to control, co-opt, or frustrate it. A third omission was the lack of study of any alternatives to democracy and Marxism-Leninism as routes to development—undoubtedly a result of the Cold War preoccupations of the time. There was no attention to such "third ways" or "halfway houses" as corporatism, bureaucratic-authoritarianism, or combined civil-military *juntas* in the process of development—all themes that came to the fore later and that are discussed in the following chapter.

Another omission was the absence of a clear definition of what precisely "political development" meant. In the less divisive, more consensual atmosphere of the early to mid-1960s, people simply assumed they knew what it meant and that others of good will would arrive at the same understanding. In fact, however, the term had diverse meanings. Some, chiefly the political sociologists, thought political development meant the greater differentiation and specialization of functions—rather like Parsons's or Almond's categorization of functions. Others, mainly political scientists, thought political development meant the growth of institutions: interest groups, political parties, bureaucracies, and the like. Still others equated political development with democratization, which made the process and institutions involved look just like the United States. Within the U.S. government, which had foreign policy interests in advancing political development, the term implied stability and anticommunism as well as democratization. Political scientist Lucian Pye once counted over twelve distinct uses of the term.

Most of those who wrote about political development in these early days were not very precise about the term's meaning. Most scholars probably incorporated all of the meanings just noted—specialization and differentiation, institutionalization, democracy, stability—without being very exact about it. Such vagueness was not so bad as long as there was a good general understanding of what was meant. However, the very looseness of the concept provided an opportunity for the critics to attack it. Moreover, unlike economic development (which can be measured quite simply and precisely in terms of Gross National Product or GNP per capita) or social modernization (which can also be measured precisely as levels of literacy, degree of urbanization, and so on), political development had no exact measures. How would we know when a country was politically developed or not? Or when it began the transitional phase? The dilemma was that there was no way of knowing. If we look back at table 2.1, we see that economic and social development can be measured according to various indices but there is not a single gauge for political development. These definitional and measurement problems would continue to plague the concept of political development.

Despite these omissions and the faults already hinted at, the developmentalist approach became *the* dominant approach in comparative politics in the 1960s. Thousands of articles and hundreds of books were written on development during that era, and hundreds of graduate students fanning out to all areas of the globe wrote doctoral dissertations during this decade on developmentalist themes. But what they found in their studies often had little to do with what Almond's famous analysis said they should find. Then came the protests against the Vietnam War, a war that seemed to demonstrate that the U.S.-favored development path was destructive and didn't work very well. By the late 1960s criticisms of the developmentalist approach were mounting.

CRITICISMS OF THE DEVELOPMENTALIST APPROACH

The young faculty and graduate students who went out to the emerging nations in the 1960s armed with the developmentalist categories and came back to write their books, articles, and doctoral dissertations often became the foremost critics of that approach. Recall that Almond's had been an abstract, deductive design based on no actual field experience in the developing nations. Many young scholars found that Parsons's pattern variables and Almond's functional categories had very little to do with their countries. The Almond design looked nice and logical on paper, but it had little to do with the realities these younger scholars observed in practice. The reality was usually not "interest aggregation" or "rule adjudication" but more likely caste, tribe, and clan

politics and conflict, vast patronage networks, favoritism and special privi-
leges, elite rule, military repression, a nasty scramble for power and money
rather than happy pluralism, and so on. Instead of concluding that the political systems they were studying were "dysfunctional" according to the Almond paradigm, more and more of these young scholars came to the conclusion that the paradigm itself was faulty. These criticisms came increasingly to
the surface in the 1960s and led eventually to a considerable rethinking of the
entire developmentalist approach.[13]

A second major influence was the war in Vietnam in the mid-1960s. In
South Vietnam the United States had tried all the programs that the developmentalist school suggested: agrarian reform, aid to democratic trade unions
and peasant associations, creation of political parties, reform and professionalization of the armed forces, assistance through the transition so the country
would not be susceptible to Communist revolution, and so on. But nothing
the United States tried seemed to work successfully or well. Furthermore—
and this was the main criticism—the United States, through its bombing campaign and by heavily Americanizing the war, seemed to be destroying the
country of Vietnam in the process. Given that so many of those (for example,
Rostow) who were the architects of development theory were also among
"the best and the brightest"[14] involved in the fashioning of U.S. policy in Vietnam, the souring Vietnam experience seemed to discredit the developmentalist approach. Out of Vietnam came the strong sense that the United States
and developmentalism not only didn't have the answers, but had provided
the *wrong* and destructive answers.

A third blow to developmentalism came with the publication in 1968 of
Samuel P. Huntington's influential *Political Order in Changing Societies*.[15]
Earlier development literature had argued that economic growth, social
modernization, and political development went hand-in-hand and were
mutually reinforcing. But Huntington showed convincingly that rapid economic growth and social mobilization, rather than leading to stability and
democracy, could be so upsetting of traditional ways that they produced
chaos and breakdown. Social modernization leads people to have increased
expectations for a better life often before their political institutions are capable of providing it, and the result is disappointment and frustration on a
national scale leading to societal unraveling or even revolution. Huntington
suggested that instead of focusing on social change, scholars and government officials should concentrate on building strong institutions capable of
handling change, such as armies, bureaucracies, and political parties.

A fourth criticism of development, growing mainly out of the experience
of many young scholars studying development abroad in the 1960s, was
that it was biased and ethnocentric. The development categories, the stages
of growth, and the processes involved all derived from the Western (European, U.S.) experiences with development, not from the developing areas
themselves. The experience of many young scholars in non-Western devel-

oping nations often led them to conclude that the Western tradition was of doubtful applicability in Third World areas whose culture and history were quite different.[16]

Fifth, it was argued that the international context for development in the late twentieth century was also different from that prevailing in the early nineteenth century when most of Europe began its upward ascent. Then, nations could largely develop autonomously and in isolation. In today's world, however, developing nations are much more involved in global markets, affected by world oil price changes, shaped by multinational corporations, and caught up in complex relations of dependency and interdependency. They cannot develop on their own but are inevitably involved in big-power relations and market forces over which they have no control.

+Sixth, the timing, sequences, and stages of development that the West experienced cannot be repeated in today's developing nations. The West had a long time to develop and could do so gradually, but the people in today's developing nations are aroused, impatient, and unwilling to wait the several generations that it took for the West to develop. The sequences are also off: Whereas in the West industrialization drew people out of the countryside and into urban jobs, in the Third World urbanization is preceding industrialization and leading to high unemployment and immense social problems. As regards stages, the West went from feudalism to capitalism, and, in some countries, to various forms of social democracy, But in the developing nations these stages have been jumbled together with the result that feudalism, capitalism, and sometimes socialism often coexist side-by-side in confused, overlapping forms.

Seventh, the developmentalist approach misrepresented the role of traditional institutions, such as the family, religion, the tribe, the caste, or the clan. Most of the development literature suggested that traditional institutions would either fade away or be destroyed as development proceeded. But many of these institutions are sources of pride and are quite functional in the developing nations. They often provide the "glue" that helps hold these countries together as they go through the wrenching process of transition. Moreover, in many developing nations, we have learned that rather than being swept aside as development proceeds, traditional institutions such as tribes and caste associations may be themselves capable of a great deal of modernization, often converting themselves into interest groups or political parties, and thus serving as bridges between tradition and modernity.

Eighth, within the developing nations there is a strong sense that the early development literature emanating from the West not only was biased but also raised false expectations for these societies to achieve. The developmentalist literature portrayed the process of development in happy, peaceful, almost antiseptic phrases when in fact the process is often bloody and wrenching. By underestimating the difficulties involved and by forcing on the developing nations Western institutions and practices that had no root in their cultures, the developmentalist approach often led to conflict, bloodshed, and military takeovers.

A ninth criticism focused on the logic and methodology of the developmentalist approach. Few scholars accepted fully the pattern variables that were part of Almond's analysis, or his functionalist approach. There were additional problems in comparing or "adding up" apples (Africa), oranges (Asia), and pears (Latin America). These areas were so different culturally and in other ways that it was difficult to compare them using the same criteria, and many scholars were not convinced of the feasibility of using a single set of indices to compare all the world's nations.

Tenth, radical critics charged that the development approach was all part of a Cold War strategy to keep the Third World under U.S. domination. That charge is probably too simplistic. The United States undoubtedly became more interested in the Third World because of Cold War concerns. The U.S. government provided fellowships and helped fund some research centers devoted to Third World affairs, and most scholars of development saw no incompatibility between their work and U.S. policy goals in the Third World. But the way to achieve those policy goals was to *promote* Third World development, since that would produce the moderation and stability the United States wanted, so it is hard to make a convincing case of a concerted effort by the U.S. government and development scholarship to retard modernization.

An eleventh criticism of the developmentalist approach was that, inadvertently, it sometimes wreaked havoc in the developing nations. By consigning "traditional institutions" to the ashcan of history, for example, developmentalism sometimes undermined the institutions that gave coherence and stability to these nations and that might have enabled them better to bridge the transition to modernity. Or, by its policy of aiding the armed forces in many developing nations, the U.S. government may have assisted the one institution that did not need strengthening, and therefore helped encourage oppression and military takeovers.

One final criticism of the developmentalist approach involves the selection of scholars to be included within prestigious publications, especially those issued by the CCP/SSRC. This criticism has to do with academic politics. Although the CCP/SSRC did make an effort to include some new persons, that was perceived as woefully inadequate by the rest of the field. Year after year as the CCP/SSRC volumes came out and as its conferences were held, the same scholars whose ideas seemed to be more and more shopworn were involved. Insufficient effort was expended to bringing in new, younger people who had new ideas. Eventually, these omissions bred resentments; quite a number of those not included in the CCP/SSRC's studies became among the strongest critics of the developmentalist approach.

These criticisms of the literature and approach of political development were powerful and devastating. Moreover, they were cumulative. By the end of the 1960s the criticisms were so widespread and so many case studies had been written in which the developmentalist approach had been found wanting that the basic theory and its assumptions were under attack. As we see in the next chapter, new approaches came to the fore and developmentalism was eclipsed.

As in the 1950s, a generational factor was also involved. In that earlier decade, the traditionalist approach adhered to by an older generation of scholars had been strongly criticized by the "young Turks" who wanted to go in new directions. But by the late 1960s to early 1970s the former young Turks were seen as older, part of "the establishment," and out of touch. A new generation of scholars that came of age during the civil rights and protest movements of the 1960s emerged. They had new ideas, a different agenda, and a variety of newer approaches that sometimes borrowed from but also often rejected developmentalism. This group and their new approaches would come to dominate the comparative politics field in the 1970s.

A REASSESSMENT OF THE DEVELOPMENTALIST APPROACH

Developmentalism was the dominant comparative politics paradigm of the 1960s. Its dominance within the field corresponded to a number of trends within the broader society: the rise of the developing nations, the sense of hope and optimism that accompanied the Kennedy era, and the emergence of a new generation of scholars committed to new ideas and a new approach. But by the end of the 1960s, with the assassinations of John F. Kennedy and Martin Luther King, Jr., the Vietnam War, and both new pessimism about and widespread questioning of earlier assumptions, the developmentalist approach also came under strong attack. Eventually, in the 1970s, it was superseded by other approaches.

The developmentalist approach, while open to various criticisms, nevertheless contributed significantly to our understanding of Third World nations. In its systems approach, its focus on change and decolonization, its emphasis on dynamic factors and genuine comparisons, developmentalism added significantly to our knowledge of Third World change. While many of the criticisms later leveled against it seem valid, one should not lose sight of the many contributions it made. Too often in comparative politics courses and seminars the developmentalist approach is reviewed and dismissed in a single session. But there are in fact rich insights, valuable information, and intriguing concepts in the developmentalist approach from which we can still learn. A first step would be to disaggregate or differentiate among and between the different developmentalist contributions, separating out those that deserve the criticism they have received (Rostow, Lipset, some of Almond's earlier writings) from those that present more nuanced and sophisticated interpretations (Apter, Huntington, LaPalombara, Macridis, Pye, Rustow, Weiner).[17]

Two themes dominate our thinking at the end of this chapter. One is that, in the history of comparative politics that we have been tracing, the developmentalist approach is to be supplanted in the 1970s by a number of other approaches, which are addressed in later chapters. The second is that, in the 1980s and 1990s, as democracy was reestablished in many of the developing areas and prosperity increased, the developmentalist correlations between literacy and democratization, social change and democratization, and economic development and democratization began to look better and better. Could it be that the Rostow/Lipset/Almond developmentalist school and approach, while wrong in the short run and containing many errors, might yet turn out to be correct in the longer run? And if that is so, could a reformulated, nonethnocentric, and less problematic developmentalist approach be resurrected and provide us with valuable insights concerning the development process? That is a subject to which we return later in the book.

NOTES

1. Karl Deutsch and William Foltz (eds.), *Nation Building* (New York: Aldine, 1963).

2. Max F. Millikan and W. W. Rostow, *A Proposal: Key to an Effective Foreign Policy* (New York: Harper, 1957); also Irene I. Gendzier, *Managing Political Change: Social Scientists and the Third World* (Boulder, CO: Westview, 1985).

3. Karl Polanyi, *The Great Transformation: The Political and Economic Origins of Our Time* (Boston: Rinehart, 1944).

4. Everett von Hagen, *On the Theory of Social Change: How Economic Growth Begins* (Homewood, IL: Dorsey, 1962); and Bruce Morris, *Economic Growth and Development* (New York: Pitman, 1967).

5. Robert Heilbroner, *The Great Ascent* (New York: Harper & Row, 1963); and W. W. Rostow, *The Stages of Economic Growth: A Non-Communist Manifesto* (Cambridge, UK: Cambridge University Press, 1960).

6. Talcott Parsons, *The Social System* (Glencoe, IL: Free Press, 1951); and Talcott Parsons and Edward Shils (eds.), *Toward a General Theory of Action* (Cambridge, MA: Harvard University Press, 1951).

7. Daniel Lerner, *The Passing of Traditional Society* (New York: Free Press, 1958).

8. Seymour M. Lipset, "Some Social Requisites of Democracy: Economic Development and Political Legitimacy," *American Political Science Review* 53 (March 1959), 69–105.

9. Karl Deutsch, "Social Mobilization and Political Development," *American Political Science Review* 55 (Sept. 1961), 493–514.

10. Gabriel A. Almond and James S. Coleman (eds.), *The Politics of the Developing Areas* (Princeton, NJ: Princeton University Press, 1960).

11. Social Science Research Council series, "Studies in Political Development": Almond and Coleman, *Politics of Developing Areas*; Lucian W. Pye (ed.), *Communications and Political Development* (Princeton, NJ: Princeton University Press, 1963);

Joseph LaPalombara (ed.), *Bureaucracy and Political Development* (Princeton, NJ: Princeton University Press, 1963); Robert E. Ward and Dankwart A. Rustow (eds.), *Political Modernization in Japan and Turkey* (Princeton, NJ: Princeton University Press, 1964); James S. Coleman (ed.), *Education and Political Development* (Princeton, NJ: Princeton University Press, 1965); Lucian W. Pye and Sidney Verba (eds.), *Political Culture and Political Development* (Princeton, NJ: Princeton University Press, 1965); Joseph LaPalombara and Myron Weiner (eds.), *Political Parties and Political Development* (Princeton, NJ: Princeton University Press, 1966); Leonard Binder, James S. Coleman, Joseph LaPalombara, Lucian W. Pye, Sidney Verba, and Myron Weiner (eds.), *Crisis and Sequences in Political Development* (Princeton, NJ: Princeton University Press, 1971); and Charles Tilly (ed.), *The Formation of the National States in Western Europe* (Princeton, NJ: Princeton University Press, 1975).

12. John Brode, *The Process of Modernization: An Annotated Bibliography of the Sociocultural Aspects of Development* (Cambridge, MA: Harvard University Press, 1969); and Saul M. Katz and Frank McGowan, *A Select List of U.S. Readings on Development* (Washington, DC: Agency for International Development, 1963).

13. The critical literature includes: Sidney Verba, "Some Dilemmas in Comparative Research," *World Politics* 20 (Oct. 1967), 111–27; Mark Kesselman, "Order or Movement: The Literature of Political Development as Ideology," *World Politics* 26 (Oct. 1973), 139–53; Philip H. Melanson and Lauriston R. King, "Theory in Comparative Politics: A Critical Appraisal," *Comparative Political Studies* 4 (July 1971), 205–31; Geoffrey K. Roberts, "Comparative Politics Today," *Government and Opposition* 7 (Winter 1972), 38–55; Sally A. Merrill, "On the Logic of Comparative Analysis," *Comparative Political Studies* 3 (Jan. 1971), 489–500; Robert T. Holt and John E. Turner, "Crises and Sequences in Collective Theory Development," *American Political Science Review* 69 (Sept. 1975), 979–95; R. S. Milne, "The Overdeveloped Study of Political Development," *Canadian Journal of Political Science* 5 (Dec. 1972), 560–68; Philip Coulter, "Political Development and Political Theory: Methodological and Technological Problems in the Comparative Study of Political Development," *Polity* 5 (Winter 1972), 233–42; and Ignacy Sachs, "The Logic of Development," *International Social Science Journal* 24, no. 1 (1972), 37–43.

14. After the title of David Halberstam's book, *The Best and the Brightest.*

15. Samuel P. Huntington, *Political Order in Changing Societies: The Governing of Restless Nations* (New Haven, CT: Yale University Press, 1968).

16. A. H. Somjee, *Parallels and Actuals of Political Development* (London: Macmillan, 1986); and Howard J. Wiarda, *Ethnocentrism and Foreign Policy: Can We Understand the Third World?* (Washington, DC: American Enterprise Institute for Public Policy Research, 1985).

17. See, for example, David E. Apter, *The Politics of Modernization* (Chicago: University of Chicago Press, 1965); Myron Weiner and Samuel P. Huntington (eds.), *Understanding Political Development* (Boston: Little, Brown, 1987); *Comparative Politics* I (Oct. 1968), articles by Rustow, Macridis, and LaPalombara; Lucian W. Pye, *Aspects of Political Development* (Boston: Little, Brown, 1966); Dankwart A. Rustow, *A World of Nations: Problems of Political Modernization* (Washington, DC: Brookings Institution, 1967); and Roy Macridis, *Modern Political Regimes* (Boston: Little, Brown, 1986).

4

Political Culture and
Comparative Politics

Political culture may be defined as the basic values, beliefs, ideas, attitudes, and orientations that citizens of different countries have about their political systems.[1] Political culture refers to core values, not ephemeral ones: whether people accept the basic premises of their political system (democracy, separation of powers, civil liberties, etc.), not whether or not one approves or disapproves on a daily basis of how well the president is doing his job. Clearly, political culture can vary greatly from country to country, with some countries having a democratic, participatory, and more-or-less egalitarian political culture; others being more elitist, top-down, and authoritarian; others believing in Marxism and/or statism; and still others being traditional and parochial with little interest or involvement in politics. It is the similarities as well as differences in beliefs and attitudes between countries and regions that stimulate comparisons and thus make political culture a subject of major interest to comparative politics.

The study of political culture gives rise to some very large issues in political science and in the social sciences generally; those include the questions of what drives politics or what produces political change. Is it values, ideas, and beliefs (political culture) or is it class structure and ownership of the means of production and distribution (Marxism)? Is it institutions—political, social, or economic—that shape and determine values and beliefs, or is it the values and beliefs, or ideas, that shape or determine what our institutions look like? Or is it biology and genetic makeup that, according to the growing field of sociobiology, trump all these other explanations? Or, as most social scientists tend to believe, is it some complicated, constantly changing combination of all of these explanations? Obviously, when we study political culture, we are making a statement that we think values, beliefs, and ideas are important—not necessarily that they are the only or most important factor in explaining differences between political systems (although some students of comparative politics believe that) but that political culture provides one important explanatory factor among several, including class and social structure, institutions, level of economic development, and—who knows—perhaps biology as well, although few political scientists know much about that.

The study of political culture arose at about the same time—the 1960s—as the study of political development, and in fact the two are closely interrelated. Recall the discussion in chapter 3 on development: while Rostow and the economists focused on economic growth and Lipset and the sociologists wrote about the social prerequisites of democracy, political scientists were mainly writing about political values or political culture. For example, the shifts that Talcott Parsons and then Gabriel Almond emphasized in their "pattern variables," from ascription to merit, from particularism to universalism, and from functionally diffuse societies to functionally specific, all involved values and value changes. In other words, the political development approach believed that, in order to achieve modernization, it was necessary not just to change the economy and social institutions but to change values as well—maybe even primarily to change values. Indeed, most of those pioneering scholars on political development in the influential Social Sciences Research Council/Committee on Comparative Politics (SSRC/CCP) were also pioneers in the study of political culture and believed that ideas and values were among the most important driving forces in history. The emphasis on values and ideas also served to distinguish the political culture approach from the Marxian model of class conflict; and since the Cold War was also being hotly waged at that time, doubtless that was a factor as well. In any case, for a long time the study of political culture and the study of political development were closely intertwined.

HISTORY OF POLITICAL CULTURE APPROACHES

When we say that political culture focuses on the ideas, values, and beliefs of a society, we are saying that the history, religion, and general sociocultural background and orientation of a country are important for understanding it. For example, it is probably no accident that modern capitalism and democracy arose in the Judeo-Christian West and that countries founded on Confucian, Buddhist, and Islamic principles took longer and have had a harder time becoming free-market democracies. Or, did the fact that Latin American politics had its roots in feudal and medieval Catholicism retard its historical development as compared with the relatively progressive Protestantism, Calvinism, pluralism, and freedom of religion of the British colonies in North America? Here we have some classic political-culture issues, involving the interrelations between religion and politics or religion (values) and economic development. We can also gain insight into the political culture by studying a country's music, literature, advertising, and television.

One of the first to study comparative political culture in a serious and systematic way was the great German sociologist Max Weber. In the late nineteenth century Weber embarked on a massive project to study the relations between religion and economic development.[2] He wanted to know why the countries of Europe, especially Northwest Europe (England, Holland, Germany), had so far outdistanced the countries of Asia and the Middle East in terms of economic growth. He was also interested in why the Protestant countries of the north of Europe had done better than the Latin or Mediterranean countries of the south. So he comparatively studied the values embedded in Buddhism, Catholicism, Confucianism, Islam, and Protestantism to get at the roots of these differences. His conclusion was not the simplistic one that people who have never read Weber often spout, that Protestants are good guys and that all these others are bad. Instead, his research revealed that in Protestantism, especially in its Calvinist variant in the Netherlands and other countries, the God-ordered emphasis on hard work, honesty, seriousness, and the thrifty use of money and time (both of these latter lent to us by God) was particularly conducive to business and capital accumulation. Other societies based on different religions lacked these qualities. Here, then, are a set of values—religious values—that provide a powerful explanation for why some countries forged ahead and others lagged behind.

More recently David S. Landes has embarked on a similar quest in his important book, *The Wealth and Poverty of Nations: Why Some Are So Rich and Some So Poor?*[3] Like Weber, Landes is interested in explaining why some countries have done so well and others remain undeveloped. And like Weber he is a careful researcher, emphasizing such geographic factors as climate, resources, and rainfall and such economic ones as trade and manufacturing. But the main factor, Landes argues, in explaining early industrialization in Western Europe and the relative lack of success of other areas, as well as the differences between Northwest Europe (Holland, England) and Southern Europe (Spain, Portugal, Greece) is cultural.

In Professor Landes's view, the industrial revolution occurred first in Northwest Europe for three reasons, all of them cultural: (1) autonomous intellectual inquiry was allowed to flourish regardless of any religious orthodoxies, (2) Europe was the leader in scientific experimentation which combined empirical observation and measurement, and (3) independent research was routine and respected and rewarded there as nowhere else. Landes ultimately comes to the same basic conclusion as did Weber: that it is ideas, values, and culture that are both the driving forces in change and that explain differences between countries, and not so much—at least initially—economic or institutional causes. In other words, in answer to the chicken-egg question posed earlier, both Weber and Landes argue that it is cultural factors that mainly explain political and economic outcomes, and not, as Marx argued, economic factors that undergird the cultural "superstructure."

Political-culture studies achieved widespread acceptance and popularity between World Wars I and II through the emerging field of cultural anthropology. Some of the most prominent cultural anthropologists—Franz Boas, Margaret Mead, and Ruth Benedict—became household names during this period, and their books about exotic places with often exotic cultural beliefs and practices became best sellers.[4] Cultural anthropology sought to study distinct cultures on their own terms, in their own languages, and within their own setting, without imposing on them the scholars' own (usually North American) lenses or making ethnocentric value judgments. The political uses and implications of cultural anthropology were exemplified during World War II when Benedict was commissioned to write a book about Japanese culture that could be utilized by the American government in the war effort.[5] A few years later Nathan Leites and his colleagues at the RAND Corporation, an Air Force think tank, completed a similar political-culture-based study of the Soviet Communist elite that was used in the Cold War.[6]

World War II proved to be a turning point in political-culture studies, however. By this time, in the press and in popular books, serious studies of cultural anthropology and political culture were being supplanted by what were called "national character studies" that often involved dangerous stereotyping. We are all familiar with the stereotypes involved: all Germans are authoritarian, all Frenchmen are great lovers, all Italians eat pizza, all Latins practice machismo, Arabs are all terrorists, etc. And within this genre, there were actually some good books written: Luigi Barzini's *The Italians*[7] and Salvador de Madariaga's *Englishmen, Frenchmen, Spaniards*.[8] But in less careful hands or among those with a political agenda, such national character studies can become the basis for ethnic slurs, prejudice, racism, hate crimes, and—in the eugenics movement of the pre–World War II period—selective human breeding.

Stereotyping people by religion, ethnicity, or national origins can be both dangerous and destructive, as, for example, when applied to Jews and

Gypsies by the Nazis during World War II. Or in the enmity between Greeks and Turks, Serbs and Croats, Jews and Arabs, French and Germans, Japanese and Chinese, Hutus and Tutsis, and a large number of other ethnic, religious, and nationality groups. Such stereotypes are not only inaccurate (it is false to say that all Englishmen or Dutchmen are this or that) but they frequently result in discrimination, pogroms, genocide, and mass slaughter being carried out by one people or nationality against another people or nationality. World War II and the Nazi experience as well as the various genocides that have followed brought these issues to a head.

In the aftermath of the war such national, ethnic, or racial stereotyping was denounced and discredited. Journalists (like Barzini) often continued to produce books involving nationality traits on individual countries and most scholars in comparative politics remained convinced that individual country or culture-area differences in values, history, religion, and ideas were important. After all, when one travels to France, Germany, Italy, or Spain, or to Asia, Africa, Latin America, or the Middle East, one knows immediately from the sights, sounds, smells, and colors that one is in one particular country or region, and not in another. So culture studies remained important, even though it was hard to do them systematically and without prejudice, with the result that for a time after World War II studies of political culture were often discredited and went into eclipse.

THE CIVIC CULTURE

A major breakthrough in the study of comparative political culture came with the publication in 1963 of Gabriel A. Almond and Sidney Verba's book entitled *The Civic Culture: Political Attitudes and Democracy in Five Nations*.[9] The book was a pioneering work for a number of reasons: first, it contained a sophisticated discussion of political culture; second, it involved a genuinely comparative study of five nations (Great Britain, United States, West Germany, Italy, and Mexico); and third, rather than being based on impressionistic interpretation as in the old national character studies, it was grounded on hard data generated from detailed public opinion surveys carried out by the investigators in each of the five countries. This last was particularly important because it enabled researchers to move away from dangerous national stereotyping and toward a more empirical or scientific examination of patterns of behavior.

The term *culture* can be obviously used in a variety of ways and with a variety of meanings. It encompasses music, literature, and art as well as how people conduct themselves and what they believe, think, and do. Almond and Verba indicate that they are particularly interested in the psychological orientation of peoples toward their political system, in the values and attitudes of citizens as they affect politics. By political culture, thus, they mean the cognitions, feelings, and orientations of people toward politics. The political culture of a nation is the "particular distribution of patterns of orientation toward political objects among the members of the nation."

Almond and Verba go on to distinguish three types of political cultures. Parochial political cultures are generally found in poor, illiterate, under-developed societies where people may focus on their own narrow (parochial) family, village, or tribe but have little sense of, or participation in, the larger, national political system. A subject political culture is one in which people are becoming aware of the larger political system but are not themselves participants in it; they are subjects of the state, which is usually top down and authoritarian, but they have few rights to involve themselves in its decision making. The third type is called participatory or "civic." By this, Almond and Verba mean a democratic political system where citizens can vote, have rights that are protected, and participate fully in the political process. It is clear that Almond and Verba (and most of the rest of us) prefer the third or civic type; moreover, there is a pro-gression of types here that reflects our earlier discussion of development. That is, parochial political cultures are most often associated with the less-developed nations; subject political cultures, with transitional regimes; and civic political cultures, with the developed, democratic countries.

The Civic Culture took over five years to research and write; it included interviews with over five thousand persons in the five nations repre-sented. These were in-depth interviews that called for responses on a great variety of issues relating to politics and the political system. The re-sults were not entirely surprising: that Great Britain and the United States were the most participatory, civic, and democratic of the five countries studied; that Germany and Italy occupied intermediary levels on these scales; and that Mexico was the least democratic with large numbers of peoples falling into the parochial and subject categories.

While the results were not surprising to people who know these coun-tries, what was impressive was the systematic and precise quantitative measures that the authors could give to the comparative study of political culture. Henceforth, it would not be acceptable to base political-culture explanations of different countries on the researcher's impressions alone; instead, survey results were needed to give such studies a more scientific base and to measure patterns of beliefs, not just stereotypes. For example, a country like Mexico might be partly parochial, partly subject, and partly civic; and by carrying out surveys like this we could tell the relative bal-ance among these diverse orientations within Mexico. We could also com-pare Mexico with the patterns in other nations. As a practical matter, most scholars sought to combine such survey results with other measures of political culture, such as historical studies, to arrive at a full and complete picture of political culture.

In the years following publication of the Almond and Verba book, studies of political culture blossomed. There were studies of political culture in Africa, Asia, Latin America, and the Middle East;[10] studies of Confucian, Hindu, Islamic, and Roman Catholic political cultures;[11] of the relations between political culture and religion;[12] of how political culture values were transmitted through the family or the school system;[13] of the relations between literature and political culture;[14] or between types of legal systems and political culture.[15] Other scholars studied how political culture changed or even underwent revolutionary transformation,[16] while still others studied the clash and conflict between two or more political cultures within a single political system, possibly leading to bloodshed or even civil war.[17] Meanwhile, the theoretical underpinnings of political culture studies and their relations to broader development themes also became more sophisticated.[18]

Recall, however, that in our model of the political system presented in chapter 2, political culture was only one part, one aspect, of a larger system and process. In the section on "Approaching the Subject," political culture and political history constituted only two of the twelve subject matters listed. That means, in the author's view, that while political culture is one important part of a full-length study of the political system, it is not the only part nor is it necessarily or always the most important part. Other factors or "variables," we have insisted, such as class and social structure, interest groups and political parties, government institutions and decision making, and public policy outputs, may be just as or, depending on the circumstances, more important.

The author's views on the issue probably come close to representing a consensus or majority view among students of comparative politics, but they are not the only views on the subject. I see political culture as an important factor but not the only factor in explaining comparatively the differences among nations. Political culture is thus a necessary subject of inquiry but not a sufficient one, in the sense that the researcher also has to consider other explanatory factors. But this position stands in contrast to the views of some scholars who want to elevate political culture into the sole, all-encompassing, and only explanation of national political differences. And of other scholars who want to eliminate political culture explanations altogether, presumably in favor of a class-based or some other single-cause explanation. To most of us in comparative politics, both of these alternative positions seem too rigid, too absolute, too driven by ideological considerations, and probably with too many axes to grind. Instead, most of us favor a middle position where political culture is seen as important but not all important, where a sophisticated political-culture explanation is viewed as a complement to other explanations and is used in conjunction with them.

CRITICISMS OF THE POLITICAL CULTURE APPROACH

During the 1960s and on into the 1970s, the study of political culture flourished. Ideas, values, beliefs, and overall political culture were all thought to be important and worthwhile subjects of inquiry—either by themselves or in conjunction with other factors. Political culture was thought to be particularly useful in studying as well as assisting the developing areas: many scholars believed that unless and until these countries got their political cultures reoriented toward honesty, fairness, egalitarianness, and serving the public good rather than the private self-enrichment of their ruling elites, no amount of economic aid or investment would do them much good.

Political culture's rise and decline ran parallel to that of the political development approach, with which it was closely related. Both of these approaches emerged as major breakthroughs in comparative politics. But then came Vietnam, assassinations of leading political figures, protest movements, Nixon, and Watergate. Both political development and political culture were strongly attacked. New and more radical approaches came to the fore. The political development approach went into a tailspin from which it never fully recovered—although much of U.S. government foreign aid is still based on this approach as is the emphasis on transitions to democracy (see chapter 8). Political culture also suffered and for quite a number of years no new or significant breakthrough occurred in that field. Most scholars continued to use political culture as one important explanatory factor among several, but political culture lost its place as an exciting new concept. First, we deal with criticisms that have been leveled against political culture; next, we treat the quite remarkable renaissance that political culture studies have recently experienced.

The main criticisms leveled against the political culture approach include the following:[19]

1. Political culture is used as a "residual category." That is, whenever we can't find any other explanation for a country's behavior, we blame it on "political culture." If a regime is corrupt or patronage dominated, or a country is unstable or authoritarian, the temptation may be strong to say, "Oh, it's just the political culture." But that is a form of circular reasoning that really explains nothing; obviously, more information and more explanation are necessary. In other words, political culture cannot be used simply as a "dumping

ground," an explanation to fall back on when we don't know what else to say. More details and greater precision are needed to make the link between the corruption, patronage, or instability that may be readily visible, and the aspects of political culture that explain those features. This criticism is directed at careless users of the political culture concept; careful, clear, and specific use of the concept can overcome the problem.

2. The concept of political culture is too vague. It seems to include everything: literature, art, music, values, political ideas, religion, history, behavior, whatever. In this sense, political culture becomes a kind of grab bag, and, when one throws everything into an explanation, one is left with really nothing. Once again there are elements of truth in this criticism. Political culture does cover a lot of territory. And one must be careful and discriminating in its use. But remember, political culture asks us only to consider the specifically political aspects of art or literature. Moreover, by the careful weighing of facts and evidence, it is possible to draw out of all these background factors the specific traits that help us explain modern-day politics. But great care, circumspection, and discrimination must be used.

3. In its focus on culture, the political-culture approach was accused of ignoring structure. By "structure" in this case was meant the class system and the ownership of the means of production and distribution. This was, in other words, the Marxist critique. Now, it is true that in their enthusiasm to study political culture, some scholars, naturally enough, overemphasized cultural factors; a handful ignored structural factors altogether. Most of us in the field, however, believe that both structure and culture are important, although we may still differ as to precisely how much weight to assign to each of these important explanations; the real challenge is to weave together both cultural and structural as well as other explanatory variables. If some scholars want, however, to focus their attention on the study of political culture because they find it interesting or important or both, that should not bother us too much—as long as we recognize that political culture is not the only answer as to why nations behave as they do and that other factors also need to be taken into account.

4. Another criticism of political culture was that it ignored international influences. Indeed, the focus in the early political culture literature was almost exclusively on domestic values and influences shaping political culture. But remember that all this early political culture literature was written before the onset of globalization; it was also written before most of the developing nations had very many radios or TVs, and before VCRs, satellites, and cable television. So we should not expect too much. On the other hand, even in these

early days, MIT political scientist Lucian Pye was writing about the "world political culture" (rock music. Coca-Cola, blue jeans, American TV, and—along with these others—freedom and democracy).[20] And, of course, by now, with the incredible spread of mass communications, including in the Third World, we would want to emphasize these factors even more. This criticism, therefore, seems valid but has since been corrected.

5. Political culture was also criticized as being ethnocentric. The values and ideas that were set forth as "most developed" or "most modern" always seemed to bear an uncanny resemblance to the United States or Great Britain and their democratic, participatory political cultures. This was particularly true of *The Civic Culture* volume where the most valued traits—the "civic" culture—corresponded exactly to the United States and Great Britain while other countries lagged behind. The "ethnocentrism" charge leveled against political culture was exactly parallel to the same charge raised in regard to political development.

   In response, it should be said that, as committed democrats (small d), most of us don't mind terribly if a democratic, egalitarian, participatory political culture and system come out as the model system for others—authoritarian regimes, totalitarian regimes, subject or parochial regimes—to live up to. At the same time, there is a lot of truth to the ethnocentrism charge. The ideal "civic" political culture does look exactly like the United States; moreover, it is in the longer view an idealized, even romantic, almost unrecognizable picture of the United States. In addition, the authors of *The Civic Culture* portray only one path to development when, in fact, there are multiple routes as well as many different kinds of democracies. So this criticism of *The Civic Culture* as being ethnocentric also seems valid— even though such criticism of one particular volume does not detract from the overall value of the political-culture approach, nor should it obscure that it was precisely students of political culture who themselves analyzed the several different forms and processes that development may take.

6. Finally, *The Civic Culture* was criticized for its methodology. Five thousand persons were interviewed for this book, which sounds like a large sample; but remember that five countries were involved, resulting in an average of one thousand persons interviewed in each. That is probably not a large enough sample for the size and complexity of the five countries studied. In addition, the samples overrepresented urban persons, particularly in the Mexico case, thus leaving rural persons and peasants woefully underrepresented. These methodological problems obviously need correcting; on the

other hand, it should also be recognized that in many quarters this study was praised for its pioneering and innovative methodology. For this was the first major comparative politics survey of political culture attitudes in five countries using such a sophisticated methodology, a cross-country research design, and a particularly detailed theoretical treatment of political culture itself.

THE RENAISSANCE OF POLITICAL CULTURE

During the 1970s and a part of the 1980s, political culture studies were often discredited in some quarters. In part, this reflected the criticisms listed above. But, in part, it reflected the times: Vietnam, Nixon, Watergate, protests, oil crises, recession, Jimmy Carter's "malaise." Many persons, particularly in the academic community, had become disillusioned with or lost faith in America and America's future; and, if we could not get our own house in order, who were we to foist off our versions and models of political development or political culture to the rest of the world? If during the 1970s much of the country was in a funk, why should we expect comparative politics and its main approaches to be immune from these influences?

A third factor accounting for the decline of political culture studies was the rise during this period of new and alternative approaches (treated in detail in subsequent chapters). These included dependency theory, corporatism, political economy, and a revived Marxism. All these approaches reflected, in part, the protest movements of those times; all focused on "structural" (class, economic) approaches to development and overall comparative politics; and in none of them was there much room for political culture. At the same time, we also need to recognize that, during this same period, there were some new and pathbreaking studies of political culture in Africa, Asia, Latin America, the Middle East, and Europe which, however, required a change in the times and academic atmosphere to be given due recognition.

The renaissance in political culture studies began in the 1980s with the publication by Almond and Verba of a new edition of their pioneering work entitled *The Civic Culture Revisited*.[21] In this new edition, Almond and Verba tried to answer the theoretical and methodological criticisms of their book raised over the nearly twenty years since its initial publication. They even invited some of the most vociferous critics to contribute chapters to the new edition! And they solicited chapters from experts on each of the five countries covered in their original volume dealing with the political culture of those countries, providing more refined analysis, and updating the materials presented. The result was more than a new edition; it was almost a completely new volume—although it had less of a splashy pathbreaking impact than did the original.

The revised or "revisited" volume of Almond and Verba was followed by a variety of new political culture studies by some of the leading figures in American political science. In 1981 Professor Samuel P. Huntington of Harvard University published a superb study entitled *American Politics: The Promise of Disharmony*[22] in which he moved away from his earlier emphasis on political institutions and, in looking at the American political system from a comparative perspective, toward a focus on political cultural factors. That was shortly followed by his work on transitions from authoritarianism to democracy in which Huntington clearly saw changes in political culture as the crucial factors in the transition.[23] Huntington, as well as another former American Political Science Association president Aaron Wildavsky and leading comparativist Harry Eckstein, published major articles on political culture in a short time span.[24]

At about the same time, MIT professor Lucian Pye, one of the early pioneers in the political culture approach, published a major work on Chinese political culture.[25] Pye argued that much of traditional Chinese political culture, founded on the Confucian belief system, had persisted into the modern era and continued to bind and limit China's Marxist-Leninist leadership from changing the system as rapidly as they wished. Pye focused particularly on the psychological constraints on Chinese political behavior. As a serious scholar, Pye made clear at the outset that in emphasizing cultural considerations he had no intention of disparaging other approaches to the study of politics. Nevertheless, he insisted on the importance of political culture as one key factor among several—and perhaps the most important one.

A variety of studies, both interpretive and quantitative, were published during this period on Latin American political culture. The interpretive studies suggested that, even though Latin America was mainly "Western" in its political beliefs and institutions, as a product of feudal, medieval Spain and Portugal, Latin America was governed by very different norms than is North American democracy. Latin America represented a fragment of the West from sixteenth-century Iberia—two-class, elitist, authoritarian, hierarchical—and, therefore, its political institutions and practices were quite different from U.S.-style liberalism, pluralism, and democracy.[26] Empirical studies refined this analysis, provided empirical tests of its validity and pointed out variations, both within and between countries.

In Asia the debate waxed strong over the emphasis on what were termed "Asian values."[27] Particularly as the Asian nations became more prosperous, successful, and economically powerful, Asian leaders and intellectuals began to reassert and champion their own values (largely

Confucian in origin) and to tell American and other critics of their political systems that they had no right to tell Asians how to govern themselves or to give them unwanted lectures on human rights. In some cases, the assertion of Asian values was a smokescreen for justifying authoritarian practices; but it also represented a widespread Asian resentment of Western criticism, of the United States and others telling Asian nations what to do, as well as an assertion by Asia of the importance of its own traditions and ways of doing things. Here we have political culture debates carried to the level of high national and international policy.

Much the same thing occurred in the Middle East and Africa. The Islamic-fundamentalist revolution in Iran in 1979, and the impact of some of the same cultural-nationalistic ideas subsequently in other countries, emphasized and sought to propagate an Islamic political culture and model of development. Edward Said's *Orientalism*[28] and numerous other studies similarly asserted Islamic cultural and political values as well as criticizing the West—including Western models of development—for attempting to impose its values and model on the area. Similarly, in Africa, rejecting that their political culture was "traditional" or "parochial," as much U.S. social science and political-culture literature had asserted, many African leaders and intellectuals sought to fashion an African model of development and to emphasize indigenous institutions rather than ill-fitting imported ones.[29]

Perhaps the most impressive of the new political-culture projects done during this period was the comparative study carried out by Professor Ronald Inglehart.[30] Like the original *Civic Culture* volume, Inglehart's study combined a sophisticated theoretical discussion of political culture with particularly rich public opinion survey data. Inglehart found that the peoples of different countries and areas not only have quite durable political-cultural attributes but that these often have major economic and political consequences as well. Importantly, he found that political culture was a crucial link in explaining the relations between economic development and democracy and that, if one asks why some economically developed or developing countries have democracy and others do not, the answer is to be found in their differing political cultures. Perhaps most important for our discussion here was Inglehart's conclusion that, when empirically tested against other explanatory variables, the political-culture explanation was a powerful tool of understanding.

The end of the Cold War in the early 1990s served as a further impetus to political-culture studies. For one thing, the decline of strategic factors in international politics enabled students of comparative politics to concentrate more on cultural differences. For another, the end of the Cold War brought ethnic, cultural, and nationality issues long bottled up by the superpowers to the forefront. Third, the collapse of Marxism-Leninism in

Russia and Eastern Europe, the failure of Marxist regimes in Cambodia, Cuba, and North Korea, and the abandonment of Marxian economics in China and Vietnam combined to lead to a general discrediting of Marxist or "structuralist" explanations and, hence, to a new emphasis on cultural factors.

One of the most important of the post–Cold War books was Samuel P. Huntington's *The Clash of Civilizations*.[31] Huntington argued that, with the Cold War over, future international conflict would involve not so much clashes between superpowers but clashes between civilizations, or cultures. He identified the major civilizations as Western, Confucian, Japanese, Islamic, Hindu, Slavic-Orthodox, Latin American, and African. He said that the cultural differences between these civilizations are far greater than the political, ideological, or economic differences. Writing at a time of particular conflict between the United States and Japan and the United States and fundamentalist Islam, Huntington saw the cultural differences as being paramount; as evidence he offered the clash between Slavic-Orthodox Serbs and the Muslims in the former Yugoslavia, ethnic and religious conflicts in many areas of the globe, as well as separatist movements in many Western nations. The Huntington thesis was controversial and probably overstated (can one really imagine a war between the United States and, say, Japan over cultural issues?), but it certainly stirred debate and served to reemphasize the growing importance of cultural explanations.

A second pathbreaking study that similarly emphasized cultural factors in explaining development differences was by Robert Putnam, another Harvard political scientist.[32] Putnam's country of interest is Italy, but his study, like other major works in comparative politics, is far more than a single-country case study. Putnam is interested in the larger question of what makes democracy work or not work, and he uses Italy's various regional governments to test his hypothesis. He concludes that democracy works best in those regions with high levels of "civic community," by which he means patterns of social cooperation based on tolerance, trust, and widespread norms of active citizen participation. All of these are essentially cultural attributes. What makes Putnam's study so valuable is not only his findings but the fact he also fairly and in a balanced way assesses other explanations (structural, institutional, class-based) before arriving at an assessment stressing cultural factors.

A third major work emphasizing cultural themes is that of Francis Fukuyama. Two of Fukuyama's books are of particular interest to us. The first, provocatively entitled *The End of History*,[33] argued that, with Marxism-Leninism vanquished and authoritarianism in decline in Asia, Latin America, and other areas, democracy was the only viable and legitimate form of government. With the triumph of democracy, the great systems debate in comparative politics between Marxist-Leninist, authoritarian, and democratic regimes was over. By his title—and it is often misinterpreted mainly by people who have not read the book—Fukuyama did not mean literally that history was over, only that the struggle between grand political ideas had largely ended and that democracy was the system of government that virtually all peoples everywhere desired. In a subsequent volume entitled *Trust*[34] Fukuyama elaborated on these themes and emphasized much like Putnam that mutual trust and civic responsibility were the keys to good government.

A SUMMING UP

In the right hands, and with a balanced point of view, political culture can be a powerful explanatory tool. All of us know that political culture is important in explaining differences and similarities between countries; the question is how to use this tool of analysis in the most analytic, balanced, and nonprejudicial way.[35]

We, therefore, conclude this chapter with a number of cautionary admonitions:

- Use political culture, but with caution.
- Keep in mind that political culture is dynamic; it is not fixed but changing, usually in conjunction with larger social, economic, and political changes.
- A country may have more than one political culture, and these may be in conflict.
- Political culture is often manipulated by different political elites for their own advantage; another reason to be cautious.
- Political culture provides a useful but still partial explanation; avoid elevating it into a single, monocausal, all-encompassing explanation; remain open to other explanatory factors.

NOTES

1. A particularly useful introductory comparative politics volume that employs a political-cultural approach while also integrating political culture into the larger political system is Gabriel A. Almond and G. Bingham Powell, *Comparative Politics: A Developmental Approach* (Boston: Little Brown, numerous editions).

2. Weber, *The Protestant Ethic and the Spirit of Capitalism* (New York: Scribner's, 1958).

3. (New York: Norton, 1998).

4. Franz Boas, *Anthropology and Modern Life* (New York: Dover, 1986); Margaret Mead, *Coming of Age in Samoa* (New York: Morrow, 1961); Ruth Benedict, *Patterns of Culture* (New York: Mentor Books, 1957).

5. Benedict, *The Chrysanthemum and the Sword: Patterns of Japanese Culture* (London: Routledge and Kegan Paul, 1967).

6. Nathan Leites, *The Operational Code of the Politburo* (Santa Monica: RAND, 1951).

7. Luigi Barzini, *The Italians* (New York: Athenium, 1964).

8. Salvador de Mariaga, *Englishmen, Frenchmen, Spaniards* (New York: Hill and Wang, 1969).

9. (Princeton: Princeton University Press, 1963).

10. George Ayittey, *Indigenous African Institutions* (New York: Transnational Publishers, 1991); Sang-bok Han (ed.), *Asian Peoples and Their Culture: Continuity and Change* (Seoul: Seoul National University Press, 1986); Anwar Syed, *Pakistan: Islam, Politics and National Solidarity* (Lahore: Vanguard, 1983); Lloyd I. Randolph and Suzanne Rudolph, *The Modernity of Tradition* (Chicago: University of Chicago Press, 1967); and Howard J.Wiarda (ed.), *Non-Western Theories of Development* (Fort Worth: Harcourt Brace, 1998).

11. Peter Moody, *Tradition and Modernization in China and Japan* (Belmont, CA: Wadsworth, 1995); Glen Dealy, *The Public Man: An Interpretation of Latin American and Other Catholic Countries* (Amherst: University of Massachusetts Press, 1977); A. H. Somjee, *Development Theory: Critiques and Explorations* (London: Macmillan, 1991); and Ahmet Davutoglu, *Alternative Paradigms: The Impact of Islamic and Western Weltanschauungs on Political Theory* (Lanham, MD: University Press of America, 1994).

12. Donald E. Smith, *Religion and Political Development* (Boston: Little Brown, 1970).

13. Richard K. Dawson, Kenneth Prewitt, and Karen Dawson, *Political Socialization* (Boston: Little Brown, 1977); and Ola Westin, *On Political Socialization and Education* (Uppsala, Sweden: Uppsala University Press, 1981).

14. Doris Somner, *Foundational Fictions* (Berkeley: University of California Press, 1991).

15. John Henry Merryman, *The Civil Law Tradition* (Stanford: Stanford University Press, 1969).

16. Richard Fagen, *The Transformation of Political Culture in Cuba* (Stanford: Stanford University Press, 1969).

17. Marc Belanger, *Rethinking Political Culture: Counterinsurgency, Democracy, and Political Identity in Guatemala* (Amherst: University of Massachusetts Ph.D. Thesis, Department of Political Science, 1993).

18. Lucian Pye and Sidney Verba, *Political Culture and Political Development* (Princeton: Princeton University Press, 1966).

19. For the criticisms, see Carol Pateman, "Political Culture, Political Studies, and Political Change," *British Journal of Political Science*, 1 (1973); and Robert C. Tucker, "Culture, Political Culture, and Communist Society," *Political Science Quarterly* (Jan. 1973), 173–90.

20. *Aspects of Political Development* (Boston: Little Brown, 1965).

21. (Boston: Little Brown, 1980).

22. (Cambridge, MA: Harvard University Press, 1981).

23. *The Third Wave: Democratization in the Late Twentieth Century* (Norman: University of Oklahoma Press, 1991).

24. Wildavsky, "Choosing Preferences by Constructing Institutions: A Cultural Theory of Preference Formation," *American Political Science Review*, 81 (March 1987); and Harry Eckstein, "A Culturalist Theory of Political Change," *American Political Science Review*, 82 (September 1988), 789–804.

25. *The Mandarin and the Cadre: China's Political Cultures* (Ann Arbor: University of Michigan Press, 1988).

26. Howard J. Wiarda (ed.), *Politics and Social Change in Latin America*, 4th ed. (Westport, CT: Greenwood, 2003).

27. For example, Raul S. Manglapus, *Will of the People: Original Democracy in Non-Western Societies* (Westport, CT: Greenwood Press, 1987).

28. (New York: Vintage, 1978).

29. Ali Mazrui, *The African: A Triple Heritage* (London: BBC Publications, 1986).

30. "The Renaissance of Political Culture," *American Political Science Review*, 82 (December 1988), 1203–30; also by Inglehart, *Culture Shift in Advanced Industrial Societies* (Princeton: Princeton University Press, 1990).

31. (New York: Simon & Schuster, 1996).

32. *Making Democracy Work: Civic Traditions in Modern Italy* (Princeton: Princeton University Press, 1993).

33. *The End of History and the Last Man* (New York: Maxwell Macmillan International, 1992).

34. *Trust: The Social Virtues and the Creation of Prosperity* (New York: Free Press, 1995).

35. A good, recent collection is Larry Diamond (ed.), *Political Culture and Democracy in Developing Countries* (Boulder: Lynne Rienner, 1994).

5

Corporatism and Comparative Politics

INTRODUCTION

From time to time, entire disciplines and fields of study are challenged—turned topsy-turvy, forced to rethink and reexamine all their earlier assumptions and ways of approaching their subject matter—by the impact of a single concept or a new approach. We call such approaches *conceptual models* or *paradigms*; when a fundamental change occurs in how we understand or conceptualize a particular subject matter or approach to the discipline, we call that a *paradigm shift*.[1] In this chapter, the disciplines and fields of study we are talking about where this shift has occurred are political science, political sociology, and political economy, particularly the subfields within these disciplines of comparative politics (Latin America, Western Europe), comparative development, and comparative public policy studies. The concept or paradigm that has forced this rethinking, this reconceptualization, this paradigm shift, is corporatism.

Since the late 1960s, corporatism, or the corporative approach, has emerged as one of the leading approaches in these fields. Corporatism has taken its place alongside liberal-pluralism and Marxism (both explained in chapter 1) as one of the three main approaches in these several fields. For this reason, we call corporatism "the other great 'ism'" because it now stands next to these other two as the third great paradigm—though far less known than the other two—in the social sciences. The emergence of this new approach has sparked great controversy as well as a vast outpouring of case studies and new theoretical writing designed to test and explain the corporatist paradigm.

Make no mistake about it, corporatism is a controversial subject, and a lot of misunderstanding surrounds it. Many identify corporatism with fascism from an earlier era; others confuse it with the modern business corporation; still others try to dismiss corporatism or wish it away, preferring to hang on to the earlier approaches even though they may no longer represent accurate or complete pictures of social and political reality. But the corporatism phenomenon cannot be so easily dismissed, and certainly the societies and political institutions organized on a corporatist basis or exhibiting corporatist characteristics are not about to disappear simply because some writers wish they would. Corporatism is here to stay!

It is important to acknowledge up front, especially to an American audience, the political sensitivity associated with drawing attention to corporatism and elevating it to the status of a viable political alternative. The topic is sensitive because the individualistic and liberal-pluralist ethos and ideology are so strongly ingrained in the American political consciousness. Americans are often reluctant to admit the power of certain groups in our society to control the economic and political system. But powerful interest groups tied into a strong state are precisely what corporatism is all about. Moreover, that seems to be the direction—despite recent talk about privatization, downsizing, and the like—in which we and other modern as well as developing nations are heading. This chapter helps get the corporatism phenomenon out of the closet and onto the table for examination and discussion.

At the same time, there remains great confusion about corporatism: Is it an ideology like Marxism or liberalism? Is it a form of social and political organization found in various countries? Is it a new and important social science approach? Or is it, somehow, all of these? This discussion seeks to sort through the controversies and confusion surrounding corporatism in order to arrive at some careful, balanced conclusions about this new (but also very old) concept.

Let us here define corporatism provisionally as a system of social and political organization in which major societal groups or interests (labor, business, farmers, military, ethnic, clan or patronage groups, religious bodies) are integrated into the governmental system, often on a monopolistic basis or under state guidance, tutelage, and control, to achieve coordinated national development. Even using this preliminary definition, we can see that a country or regime based on corporatism is going to be quite different from one based on liberal-pluralism (where interest groups are free and independent from the state) and from Marxism as well, because corporatism likes to claim that it is based on group and class harmony rather than on the Marxist concept of class conflict.

But corporatism can also take many different forms: quasi-medieval, as in some parts of Latin America; ethnic- or clan-communal, as in many areas of Africa or the Middle East; Confucian-communal, as in Asia; or the modern, participatory, social-welfare forms, as in Western Europe. Corporatism may take statist or authoritarian forms, or it may take more liberal and democratic forms; it can be present in one form in developing nations and another form in developed ones. Corporatism is thus present in many types of societies and regimes, and it may well be growing (*creeping corporatism*) in the United States. But if corporatism exists in so many forms and in so many different societies, what is its usefulness as an explanatory device for the social sciences? This chapter provides answers to these questions by examining the complex, multifaceted dimensions of corporatism worldwide and its impact on and gradual acceptance in the fields of comparative politics, Latin American studies, European studies, political sociology, and the developing nations.

LIBERALISM, MARXISM, AND CORPORATISM: THE THREE GREAT "ISMS" OF THE MODERN WORLD

During the past fifty years—ever since World War II—there have been two great, rival, alternative approaches in the field of comparative politics and in development studies and the social sciences more generally. These two approaches, or paradigms, are: (1) liberal-pluralism and (2) Marxism. Liberal-pluralism was largely found in the Western, democratic nations (the United States and Western Europe), and in the approaches scholars in these countries used to study comparative politics; while Marxism, otherwise known as *scientific socialism*, although not entirely absent in the Western tradition, remained a distinctly minority strain there and was concentrated more in the Soviet Union, the Eastern bloc countries, and a number of developing nations—for example, China, Cuba, Vietnam, and North Korea. It is obvious even from these opening comments that not only did liberal-pluralism and Marxism serve as the two major competing approaches in the social sciences for many decades, but also that these two *intellectual paradigms* were products of, bound up with, and a part of the Cold War, superpower rivalry of the last half-century.

To these two major, more familiar approaches has now been added a third major approach: corporatism. The recent resurgence of corporatist approaches to studying comparative politics; the politics of developing nations; public policy making in advanced industrial societies; and a variety of issues relating to social change, labor relations, social welfare policies, and other topics had their origins in the 1960s and 1970s when a number of pioneering scholars suggested that neither the liberal-pluralist nor the Marxian approaches were fully adequate to treat the new phenomena they were observing in their studies. These new phenomena included the incorporation of interest groups into the decision-making machinery of the modern state; social pacts to guarantee labor peace, involving unions, management, and government regulators; industrial policies undertaken by various governments that involved obligatory participation by business and labor; and public policy in the areas of social security, welfare reform, education, and social and economic change more generally in which the state, or government, specified which groups had to be brought in and consulted both in the making of the policy and its implementation. In none of these issues and policy areas did the traditional liberal-pluralist approach, or the Marxian one, prove adequate or provide the intellectual framework to fully comprehend the processes involved. Either these approaches were silent on the topics or they furnished inadequate categories for coming to grips with and understanding them. It is in this context that the corporatist approach arose, because it did seem to offer the intellectual framework that was either lacking or incomplete in the other main approaches.

Here, then, is the contribution and the attraction that the corporatist approach provided: it offered us a handle, a method, an approach for understanding some new social, economic, and political phenomena (the role of the state, the formal incorporation of interest groups into government decision making, new areas of public policy making, and so on) that the other approaches failed to provide. The corporatist approach was and is primarily an honest attempt by scholars to understand some new phenomena in modern societies (for example, the increasing rationalization and bureaucratization of society, the changing structure of labor and industrial relations, the involvement of interest groups in actual policy making and implementation), to respond to new socioeconomic and political phenomena that the liberal-pluralist and Marxist models were not especially helpful in providing. In this sense, the corporatist approach should be seen as going beyond the earlier approaches and providing students of comparative politics (as well as policy makers) with a set of conceptual tools for understanding modern politics.

But at the same time, the corporatist approach should be seen, in my view, not as entirely supplanting these other earlier approaches but as complementing them in various ways and helping to provide answers to questions for which the other paradigms proved inadequate. Meanwhile (and this is the fun and often controversial part), the study of corporatism and even the term itself became caught up in many of the ideological, political, and intellectual battles that surrounded and came to characterize the liberal-pluralism and Marxism approaches, often confusing or complicating the issues and causing great controversy.

Liberal-pluralism, Marxism, and corporatism have for a long time offered competing perspectives on society, governance, and state-society relations. But they have also, at different times in history, presented competing ideological visions as well. Here we try only to explain the basic structural or institutional differences among liberal-pluralism, Marxism, and corporatism. In all three concepts the focus is on the relations between society as represented by interest groups and the state or government, and hence on the dynamics of what are called state-society relations.

In liberal-pluralism, which is often considered to be the dominant reality as well as the main political ideology and approach to studying politics in the United States and Western Europe, interest groups are free, unfettered, and completely independent from the state. Interest groups can organize on any issue; in the modern liberal state there are few if any restrictions on interest-group activities. As a result, there are thousands of interest groups in the United States, at the local, state, and national levels, all competing in the political arena. Such free and vigorous interest-group activity and the overlapping webs of associations to which most Americans belong (churches and synagogues, unions and business associations, PTAs and grassroots associations, lodges and clubs) have long been considered among the glories of American democracy. Moreover, it is out of the competing interest-group struggle, a long and rich literature in the liberal-pluralist tradition approach suggests, that good and effective public policy emerges. For the plethora of competing groups serves not only to advance a great variety of policy positions but also forces everyone to compromise, to accommodate and reach a democratic solution. And in this intense competition among interest groups, according to liberal-pluralist theory, the state (executive, legislative, judicial branches) plays a relatively minor role. It umpires and referees the group struggle but does not try to control it; the state, in this theory, serves as a transmission belt and filter for interest-group activities, but it does not dominate the process or seek to impose its own purposes on it. In liberal-pluralism the interest groups and their activities are the main focus of the political system.

Under Marxism and especially in its Leninist form, the opposite characteristics apply: the state is powerful ("the *dictatorship* of the proletariat," as Marx put it), while interest groups are subordinated. Of course, we all understand that there are also democratic and parliamentary versions of socialism or social democracy (such as in Scandinavia and other Western European countries) in which interest groups are also free, but here we are talking about the totalitarian version of Marxism as it was long practiced in the Soviet Union, Eastern Europe, and other Marxist-Leninist states. The word "totalitarian" itself implies total control: no groups or associations are allowed to exist freely or apart from the state. Under totalitarian Marxism (fascism, too, as practiced in Nazi Germany) the state may create its own, *official* interest groups, but such groups have no independence or autonomy apart from the totalitarian behemoth. Quite unlike liberal-pluralism, under totalitarianism it is the state that makes all the important decisions, while the "interest groups" serve as window dressing to the regime in power, at times also helping to implement the state's policies. It is one of the hallmarks of such totalitarianism that there is no grassroots participation from below in decision making (through public opinion, elections, interest groups, or in any other way), only top-down authority (from the state or all-powerful government).

Corporatism occupies an intermediary position between liberal-pluralism and Marxian-totalitarianism or fascism. Corporatism's advocates like to say that they represent "the third way," an alternative route to modernization that avoids the disadvantages of the other two. On the one hand, corporatism advocates a strong, guiding, directing state but not one that is totalitarian. On the other, corporatism is usually characterized by state-structured and regulated interest groups, but not by total control as in Marxism-Leninism nor the completely unfettered interest-group struggle (which corporatists argue produces chaos and often paralysis) of liberal-pluralism. At the same time, corporatism advocates class and interest-group harmony over conflict and seeks to accomplish this by incorporating interest groups representing all sectors of society into the decision-making structure of the state. So under corporatism we have (1) a strong but not totalitarian state, (2) structured (neither totally controlled nor fully free) interest groups that are usually limited in number and functions, and (3) interest groups that are part of the state—as distinct from completely independent, as found under liberal-pluralism. Whenever we see government control, structuring, or licensing of interest groups, we are likely to see corporatism.

Hence, in picturing the differences between liberal-pluralism, Marxian or fascist totalitarianism, and corporatism, we need to think of a spectrum rather than either-or choices (see figure 5.1). At one end of the spectrum (liberal-pluralism) we have a weak state and, usually, strong interest groups. At the other, Marxist-Leninist or fascist, end of the spectrum we have a totalitarian state and weak, totally controlled interest groups. In

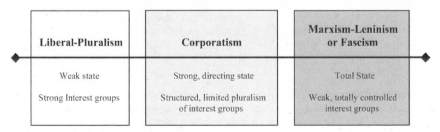

Figure 5.1. A Spectrum of Regimes

between, where corporatism lies, we have a strong (but not total) state and structured interest groups (partly free, partly controlled) that are limited in number. Different regimes may be strung out at various points on this spectrum, including some that may involve varying degrees or combinations of these features.

A considerable variation in types of regimes may be found within the corporatism category. Some corporatist systems (such as those in Scandinavia) allow relatively free interest groups, permit widespread public participation, and have a limited state; this is usually referred to as "societal corporatism," "open corporatism," "democratic corporatism," or "corporatism of free associability." This version of corporatism is often based on a constitution or contract or series of contracts negotiated between the state and its component corporate units (business, labor, agriculture, religious groups, military, etc.) that spell out the rights and responsibilities of all parties—giving corporatism a legal, constitutional, and democratic character. Other corporatist systems (such as Franco's Spain or Salazar's Portugal) had a strong state and strict controls over interest-group activity; these regimes can verge on dictatorship, authoritarianism, even fascism. We must remember, therefore, that there are "hard" as well as "soft" versions of corporatism, secular as well as religiously based corporatism, open as well as closed systems of corporatism, participatory versus exclusionary corporatism, and democratic versus authoritarian versions of corporatism.

While considerable variation exists among corporatist regimes, the distinguishing characteristics seem to be (1) a strong, directing state—stronger than most Americans with our freewheeling pluralism and freedom would be willing to allow, (2) restrictions on interest-group freedom and activity, and (3) incorporation of interest groups into and as part of the state system, responsible both for representing their members' interests in and to the state *and* for helping the state to administer and carry out public policies. In other words, under corporatism, interest groups often become part of the state, incorporated into it; they are agencies that are no longer just private but that have taken on *public* responsibilities. We need to keep these criteria in mind as we consider the growth of corporatism in the United States.

Furthermore, some corporatist systems have mixes of, for example, corporately represented bodies whose members are chosen by functions (military, religion, agriculture, commerce, industry, etc.) and democratically elected chambers whose members are chosen on the basis of one person, one vote. So, just as corporatism in its "open" or "societal" varieties can verge toward liberal-pluralism on one end of our spectrum of regimes and toward dictatorship and totalitarianism (Mussolini's Italy) on the other, there can also be liberal-pluralism systems that begin verging toward corporatism (the United States at present) as well as Marxian-socialist regimes (the People's Republic of China, for example) that may have various corporatist features. The discovery, or rediscovery, of corporatism shows that, if nothing else, we need to open our minds to a wide range of regime possibilities and variations that go considerably beyond earlier methods of classifying regimes (dictatorship versus democracy, for example, or liberalism versus fascism).

Overall, what bears emphasis is:

1. Corporatism's emergence as a social science and regime-type alternative to liberal-pluralism and totalitarian Marxism-Leninism or fascism.
2. The distinctions in terms of interest groups' freedom versus control and the role of the state in these three types.
3. The considerable variety of regimes that can fall under the corporatist category.

THE CORPORATISM PHENOMENON: HOW WIDESPREAD?

Corporatism may be said to be present when the following conditions apply:

1. Society is organized, in whole or in part, not on an individualistic basis (as in the case, historically, of the United States), but in terms of the functional, societal, or "corporate" units (family, clan, region, ethnic group, military organization, religious body, labor or business unit, interest groups, etc.) that make up the nation.
2. The state seeks to structure, limit, organize, or license these groups as a way of controlling them (limited pluralism).
3. The state tries to incorporate these groups into the state system, converting them into what are often called "private-sector governments"; while the groups themselves seek both to take advantage in terms of programs and benefits for their members from such incorporation, and at the same time preserve some autonomy or independence from the state, usually contractually defined (as in a constitution or basic law).

The countries and regions where these conditions apply, we are now discovering, are far more widespread than anyone had earlier imagined. Moreover, there is little evidence—again, contrary to earlier theorizing—that these countries and regions characterized in whole or in part as corporatist are moving inevitably or universally toward individualism and liberal-pluralism on the U.S. model. Corporatism is not only widespread but also ubiquitous and present not only in a great variety of regimes but also expanding even in countries like the United States or Western Europe, previously thought to be strongly in the liberal-pluralist mode.

A partial listing of these regimes will serve not only to show how widespread corporatism is and its considerable varieties but also to give a clearer picture of what is meant by and encompassed in the term "corporatism":

- In the communalist, organic, Confucian, group-oriented, nonindividualist, clan, family, tribal, and local community-oriented societies of East and Southeast Asia, one can find the germs of corporatist society—the forerunners of the modern corporatism of Japan and other countries.*
- Latin America is primarily Western in its culture, religion, politics, and society; but it is also a colonial offshoot of sixteenth-century Spanish and Portuguese Europe and organized historically on a group, communal, clan, family, and organic basis.
- Africa is also organized in part on a clan, ethnic, or tribal basis ("precorporatism"), which many scholars are now seeing as more important than the often artificial national boundaries imposed by the colonial powers.
- In the cultural and social traditions of India and South Asia, there are similar organic, communal, group-oriented social organizations—such as the caste associations—that can also be seen as providing a "natural corporatist" or "precorporatist" basis to society.
- Similarly, Islamic society contains roots that are strongly clan, tribe, and community-oriented—not all that different from the other corporate or community-based societies listed here.
- Western Europe practices an advanced or social-welfare form of corporatism, where major societal interests are often formally represented inside the state and help carry out social and economic programs on a sectorial (often called "neo-corporatist") basis.
- The United States has long been considered a predominantly liberal and individualistic country, but this is now changing as the United States, too, moves toward a more sectorally and functionally based society.

---

*The author's earliest writings on corporatism were concentrated on Latin America and Southern Europe. But—and this is one of the pleasures of writing in a public forum—as a result of these writings, the author received numerous communications from Asia and other areas saying, "Oh, your model applies in my country [India, Thailand, South Africa, South Korea, Saudi Arabia, Egypt, Tanzania, Japan, the Philippines] as well."

- Russia, the Commonwealth of Independent States, and Eastern Europe (the former Soviet Union and its empire) evidence considerable corporatist influence from their past histories; even under communism there was a sectoral (workers, peasants, military, intelligentsia) organization of society. Now in the wake of the Cold War and the breakup of communism, some of these historic communalist traits are being resurrected or reorganized; but in many of the former communist states there is still great confusion as to which form of society (liberal-pluralist, corporatist, authoritarian, revived communism, various mixed forms) will prevail.

This brief survey illustrates two major theses: (1) how widespread corporatism is in different regions and countries of the world and (2) the different forms that corporatism may take, ranging from "natural" or "historical-cultural" corporatism in its tribal, ethnic, regional, or social group-oriented forms, to the modern welfare-state forms of postindustrial European and North American society.

THE CORPORATISM PHENOMENON: WHY SO CONTROVERSIAL?

Not only has corporatism had a profound effect on the social sciences, offering a third and alternative social science model to liberal-pluralism and Marxism, but also it is widespread, characteristic of a wide variety of regimes and movements in both the Third World of developing nations and the First World of modern industrial states. For a long time (about forty years) corporatism was largely neglected by social scientists and students of comparative politics who saw it as a throwback to the 1930s and World War II. But in recent years corporatism has reemerged—although not without great controversy. As we go through the following list of reasons as to why corporatism is so controversial, we will see that this concept, like many concepts in the social sciences, is loaded with political, ideological, and emotional baggage. But this is even more so in the case of corporatism.

In this section we merely introduce the reasons for the controversy surrounding corporatism.

1. In the popular mind, corporatism is, or was, often associated with fascism and, therefore, carries highly emotional connotations. That is because in the 1920s and 1930s such fascists and semifascists as Mussolini in Italy, Hitler in Germany, Franco in Spain, and Salazar in Portugal used, in part, a corporatist system of organizing their

economies and political systems. But, in fact, corporatism can take many forms, left and center as well as right, Christian as well as secular, socialist as well as fascist.**

2. A second, related reason for the controversy is that corporatism is often assumed by historians to be a product of the period between World Wars I and II, a thing of the past now superseded. But, in fact, not only is corporatism now reemerging in various regimes and forms, but we are also discovering that many supposedly liberal and pluralist regimes have been practicing a disguised form of corporatism for many years.

3. In the past, corporatism was often denounced by its opponents as a "smokescreen" for authoritarianism or as a "confidence trick" played on workers. In some regimes and in some circumstances, corporatism may have been or done those things. But corporatism has also had many other and often more positive usages: as a way of organizing diverse and fragmented societies; as a means of filling a void in a nation's associational or organizational life; as a way of centralizing and concentrating political power; as a system of organizing and implementing social programs; as a way of integrating both business and working-class elements into political society or, alternatively, of controlling and regulating their participation; and as an alternative model of society that seeks to preserve unity, class harmony, and a sense of community as modern mass society begins to emerge.

4. A connection has been discovered between corporatism and capitalism and between corporatism and big bureaucratic states. Indeed some analysts have gone so far as to argue that some form of corporatism is virtually inevitable in all large, advanced, industrial societies where there are strong currents of national economic planning and modern social-welfare programs, and hence the need to rationalize and organize societal interest groups to provide input into and to help implement these programs. Could it be, in other words, that all big, advanced, bureaucratic societies evolve toward a system of corporatist organization?

5. Corporatism is often accused of being a right-wing, conservative, and elite-directed way of dealing with the great pressures brought on by industrialization and modernization, and indeed corporatism has often provided a basis for conservative and/or authoritarian

---

**The association of corporatism with fascism was brought vividly home to the author when he lectured on corporatism in the Netherlands. An elderly member of the audience came up afterward and told the author that he had fought against corporatism, the German occupation, and fascism during World War II while trying to liberate his country from the Germans and, therefore, that it was difficult for him to accept either the resurgence of corporatism or that it could be used as a neutral, social science term.

politics. But we know now that corporatism can also take liberal, pluralist, populist, social-democratic, socialist, and even communist directions; after all, Joseph Stalin, the communist dictator of the USSR, once accused his one-time partner and later foe Leon Trotsky of being a corporatist.

6. In the study of corporatism, some intense personal, scholarly, national, and regional rivalries and jealousies are involved. Corporatism began as a European phenomenon, then was revived in the area of Latin American studies, from whence it spread back to Europe once again. But the Europeanists seldom acknowledge the Latin Americanists' contributions to the literature; Latin Americanists are seldom aware of what the Europeanists are researching; and meanwhile other areas (Africa, Asia) have come up with their own versions of corporatism that are seldom known to the other two.

7. Corporatism, in some of its manifestations, has not been very acceptable to reformers. For corporatism is not just a set of political, economic, and social institutions; in some societies the corporate, organic, group-oriented way of thinking and acting is so deeply embedded in the society that it has become part of the political culture. If corporatism is so entrenched, then it will likely require two or three generations to change, not just some revision in the legislation. And that kind of cultural continuity as well as the long time span are often unacceptable to those who wish a more rapid reform.

8. Recently, corporatism has begun to be popular again as an ideology, in ways that have not been the case since the 1930s. Because of the lingering connotations of fascism, it is seldom explicitly called corporatism; instead, the terms used are communalism, solidarism, cooperatism, or even ethnic pride. All of these terms refer to the renewed longing for a sense of community, togetherness, and belonging that seem to have been eroded under the pressures of modern, impersonal, bureaucratic, mass society. But it was precisely the attempts to maintain or recapture the communalist community ties and values that helped give rise to corporatism in the first place.

9. Finally, and most importantly for the purposes of this book, corporatism is controversial because it serves as an alternative social science/comparative politics approach to the other great "isms" of the modern world: Marxism and liberal-pluralism. Particularly in its more religious and Christian-democratic manifestations, corporatism has long been strongly opposed to Marxism and Marxism-Leninism; and now with the collapse of the Soviet Union and the disintegration and discrediting of Marxist-Leninist regimes virtually everywhere, the Marxist approach is in strong disrepute. But corporatism often also stands in contrast to the dominant liberal-pluralist

approach of American and European social sciences and presents an alternative approach and model. This has sometimes earned corporatism the antipathy of those who are committed to liberal-pluralism; more than that, the corporatist approach has challenged the currently dominant liberal-pluralist orientation of American foreign policy to refashion governments abroad—especially in the Third World, where many of them are founded on corporatist principles—in the American liberal-individualist mold as wrong-headed, ethnocentric, and destructive of local institutions and ways of doing things. So the debate over corporatism not only has important comparative politics and social science implications but also is crucial in thinking about American foreign policy as well.

Over the past three decades, these issues and themes have stimulated an enormous amount of interest in the corporatism phenomenon. Moreover, these are important and very controversial themes. They get at the heart of many of the key issues of national and cross-national social and political development and public policy, and they importantly affect the way we perceive, grapple with, and seek to understand not just foreign societies (where corporatism has long and often been strong) but also that of the United States (where corporatism is growing). At the same time, corporatism and its attendant implications touch some raw political and ideological nerves. The corporatism issue has received so much attention precisely because it relates to and impacts the most important issues of our day.

THE FOUR FORMS OF CORPORATISM

Corporatism tends to emerge in societies that emphasize group or community interests over individual interests. The strong individualism of the United States, for example, helps explain why, until recently, corporatism seldom found a receptive breeding ground in America. Earlier, we had provided some preliminary guideposts to help us identify where and when corporatism was present: (1) a strong but not a totalitarian state; (2) interest groups that are usually limited in number; and (3) interest groups that are part of the state, usually existing in some form of contractually defined relation to the state, rather than complete independence from it as in liberal-pluralism. Whenever we see government control, structuring, or licensing of interest groups, we said, we are likely to find corporatism present.

Corporatism exists in a number of forms, cultures, and time periods, which makes it difficult to offer a single definition that covers all its forms. For now, let us keep in mind our "guideposts" rather than try to formulate a final definition, because in many respects corporatism represents a mood, a way of thinking (functionalist, statist, communalist), an approach that defies hard-and-fast rules. Here we try to explain what corporatism is, to try to understand it.

In this chapter we identify four forms of corporatism. These four forms have existed in different time periods, but there is often a progression or evolution from one form to the next. Moreover, as would naturally occur during an evolution, there can be various mixed forms, thus accounting for the considerable diversity of corporatisms that we find. In addition, because there is a progression from one form to the next, we posit that there are dynamic factors—explainable using the corporatist model—that help account for the changes. The four forms of corporatism are: (1) historical or "natural" corporatism; (2) ideological corporatism; (3) manifest corporatism; and (4) modern neo-corporatism. In addition, we also offer at the end of this discussion some preliminary considerations concerning a general model of corporatism.

1. Historical or "Natural" Corporatism

Historical or "natural" corporatism can be found in a great variety of premodern societies, especially those founded on traditions that emphasize solidarity, group identity, and community. Such societies tend to value group solidarity over individualism, which is what makes it hard for many U.S. foreign assistance programs—based naturally on the American tradition of individual initiative—to operate successfully in these societies, a theme to which we shall return later. By historical or natural corporatism we have in mind the ethnic, clan, and tribal basis of much of African politics; the emphasis on group and community that ties together many of the Confucian-based societies of East Asia; the similarly group-, clan-, and caste-based societies of South Asia; and the solidarist conceptions that tie together ruler and ruled into mutually supportive roles in those societies based in part on the Koran. Even in the West, by which we mean Western Europe (before the onslaught of the Renaissance, the Enlightenment, and the Industrial Revolution), there were many natural-corporatist institutions: the extended family, the neighborhood, the community, the parish, regional and ethnic loyalties (now often being reasserted), military orders, guilds, the Roman Catholic Church and its orders, and the aristocracy or nobility. These are all *historic* corporatist institutions; they tend to have been there almost from time immemorial, to have grown *naturally* in the society.

Historical or natural corporatism is often the glue, the cement, that holds together societies in their early premodern stages. It emphasizes the seemingly natural, timeless, and basic institutions of society. It often predates the formation of the modern nation-state. It is frequently a part of the historical political culture of the society; hence, the emphasis in the analyses of some writers on the connections between culture and corporatism. Rulers of the emerging or new states may try to use these historic and natural corporatist institutions as a basis for their own power, as a way of holding society together during the early, difficult stages of modernization and nationhood, or as a way to emphasize local or nativist values and institutions to keep out intruding foreign ones. At the same time, the historic corporate groups may try to keep the ruler or the emerging nation-state at arm's length as a way of retaining their own identity. Usually in the first stages of modernization a tug-of-war goes on between the central state trying to establish, consolidate, or augment its power versus the corporate groups that want to keep autonomy and a contractually defined independence from the central state. Where the central state completely snuffs out these autonomous corporate units, tyranny, absolute despotism, and dictatorship usually result; but where the corporate bodies continue to exist in some mutually satisfactory and legally defined relationship to the central state, that is usually called "constitutionalism," even "democracy," in the emerging nations. But note how different that is from American-style constitutionalism.

Very often these historic, "natural," and precorporatist groups continue to exist after the formation of the nation-state and in some, often uneasy, relations with it. Witness the continuing importance of ethnic institutions in Africa, caste associations in India, tribal rights in states based on the Koran, and the Roman Catholic Church and the armed forces (heirs to the tradition of autonomous military orders) in Latin America. In Asia, too, it is clear that group, community, and solidarist features persist into the modern age, standing in marked contrast to American-style individualism, often making it difficult for Westerners to understand these countries where Confucianism still holds considerable sway. The central government must then negotiate with these groups or snuff them out, which is becoming less acceptable; the result is a type of corporatism that often looks considerably different from the Western or European type.

2. Ideological Corporatism

The emphasis on the individual and on individual rights accelerated in the West during the eighteenth-century Enlightenment; in the course of the French Revolution beginning in 1789, and subsequently throughout most of the rest of Europe, group rights (of the Roman Catholic Church, the guilds, and other groups) were extinguished. Thereafter, at least in the West, the atomistic individual ruled supreme, while the older system of historic or natural corporatism was snuffed out.

But many, especially Catholics and conservatives, rejected what they saw as an excessive emphasis on the individual and longed for the solidarity, organized society, and group rights of the *ancien régime*. At first their message was entirely reactionary, an attempt to turn the clock back to a bygone *status quo ante*. However, beginning in the mid-nineteenth century, a number of writers, intellectuals, and religious figures began to formulate a more positive response to the alienation and anomie of the modern, industrial age. They called their new ideology *corporatism*, and throughout the remainder of the nineteenth century and the early decades of the twentieth their philosophy and recommendations gained many adherents. Corporatism became the "other great ism," alongside liberalism and Marxism, of the twentieth century.

Under corporatism, society was to be organized not on an individualistic or liberal basis but in terms of society's component groups: the family, the parish, the neighborhood, organized labor, fishermen, peasants, business, industry, religion, armed forces, university students, professional associations. These groups would help decide economic and social policy; they, along with the state, would regulate their own members. Rather than on an individual, one-person, one-vote basis, representation in government bodies under corporatism would be on a group basis: seven seats for the military, eight for business, and so on. A number of "corporations," representing both labor and management, would be created to help regulate wages, prices, and production in specific industries. In this way, group interests and solidarity would become stronger than the individual ones as represented in liberalism; similarly, the class-conflict model of Marxism would be replaced by the presumedly class harmony model of corporatism.

The corporatist ideology proved to be very attractive early in the twentieth century in societies where liberalism and individualism seemed to be producing near-anarchism (Spain, Portugal), where class conflict was feared to be getting out-of-hand or producing conditions for a Bolshevik-like revolution (Germany, Italy), and/or where the state or government needed to get a handle on the national economy in the face of depression or completely unbridled capitalism and its accompanying social ills (virtually all countries). In fact, throughout Europe as well as Latin America, corporatism was extremely popular as an ideology during the 1920s, 1930s, and early 1940s (before the end of World War II). Hundreds and even thousands of books, articles, and news stories were written about it. Corporatism was becoming so popular that a Romanian political philosopher wrote a book in French that became a best seller throughout Europe in which he proclaimed that the twentieth century would be the century of corporatism just as the nineteenth had been the century of liberalism.[2]

It should be noted that there were several different forms of corporatism at this time. Some were authoritarian; some, more democratic. Some were religiously based, grounded, for example, on the Catholic encyclicals *Quadregessimo Anno* and *Rerum Novarum*, while others were secular in orientation. Some provided only for group representation, while others combined this with geographic or individualistic representation. The unifying feature in all these regimes, however, was the emphasis on group rights and representation over that of individualism. In the heyday of corporatism between World Wars I and II, Austria, Belgium, France, Germany, Greece, Holland, Hungary, Italy, Norway, Poland, Romania, Portugal, Spain, Sweden, and Switzerland all were attracted to or experimented with various forms of corporatism.

It was only in the West (Europe and, by extension, Latin America) that historical or natural forms of corporatism turned eventually into a full-fledged ideology of corporatism. Other areas—Africa, Asia, areas under Islamic sway—often continued to practice their historic forms of corporatism, group solidarity, and communitarianism but without developing ideological corporatism. One suspects the reason for this lack of a corporatist ideology is that these non-Western societies were never inundated—until recently—by the West's emphasis (exaggerated, some would say) on individualism. So these societies continued to practice their historic and natural forms of corporatism on into the modern era. Only when they, too, began to be impacted by the onslaught of Western-style individualism and capitalism in the late-twentieth century did these areas also begin to fashion a corporatist philosophy both to manage the processes of modernization and to help preserve their traditional, group-oriented ways.

3. Manifest Corporatism

Corporatism sounded nice on paper, in theory, perhaps even as an ideology (solidarity, community, class harmony), but in actual practice corporatism did not work out very well—at least in the short term and in terms of the kinds of corporatist regimes that actually came to power. Fascist Italy, Nazi Germany, Vichy France, Franco's Spain, Salazar's Portugal, Metaxas's Greece, Dolfuss's Austria, Vargas's Brazil, Perón's Argentina—none of these was an exactly happy, friendly, admirable regime. All of these began to turn—or turned rather quickly, once in power—to authoritarian or totalitarian forms of rule. Their human rights records were often atrocious at best. Rather than presiding over a system of class harmony, these corporatist regimes frequently used dictatorial means to suppress *all* interest groups—especially organized labor. So it is not surprising that, with the defeat of Germany and Italy in World War II, the ideology and system of government associated with them should be thoroughly discredited—even though in some countries (Argentina, Brazil, Portugal, Spain) authoritarianism and corporatism continued to linger on although now de-emphasizing their discredited and manifestly corporatist aspects.

The corporatist regimes of the interwar period faced numerous similar problems, which help account for the failure of these forms of manifest corporatism. First, the storm clouds of war were already hovering over Europe in the 1930s, making the kind of social engineering envisioned by the corporatist writers and intellectuals difficult at best. Second, the global depression of the 1930s meant that there were inadequate financial resources available for the corporatist restructuring. Third, all these regimes came quickly to realize that they needed big business to keep their governments afloat economically, which meant the business sector of the economy was often able to escape thoroughgoing corporatization. Fourth and related, the control and licensing mechanisms of the corporate state came down heaviest on organized labor, which—in an era ripe with the possibility of Bolshevik revolution—was seen as the greatest threat to the regime in power and a source of potential revolutionary upheaval. Hence, the corporatist idea of class harmony became instead one in which the trade unions were suppressed, often viciously so.

Because of the general discrediting, corporatism went into eclipse after World War II. For the next thirty years the term "corporatism" was seldom mentioned. Even in those regimes that continued as corporatist hangovers from the earlier epoch—Franco's Spain and Salazar's Portugal—corporatism was either forgotten or redefined as a system to deliver social welfare. Interestingly, however, in a number of developing nations (Argentina, Brazil, Chile, Egypt, Indonesia, Peru, South Korea, Taiwan, Tazania, and others) that in the 1960s and 1970s began to experience development problems and crises parallel to those experienced by the European nations in the 1920s and 1930s—rising labor unrest and thus the need for social harmony, a level of pluralism that was producing chaos, the drive to better manage and control rational economies requiring closer tightening and coordination—a corporatist system of social organization looked very attractive. But because of the earlier discrediting of corporatism, these newly emerging countries usually preferred to avoid that label and call it something else: "new democracy," "communitarianism," "guided democracy," "tutelary democracy," or something similar. However, if one scratched below the labels, it was often a form of corporatism that one found in these developing nations, aimed at maintaining order in the face of change and at keeping control on increasingly pluralist societies. Corporatism thus continued to be practiced, but it was done in new areas of the world outside of Western Europe and under new guises.

4. Modern Neo-Corporatism

Modern neo-corporatism is very much different from the kind of authoritarian, top-down, and statist corporatism that was characteristic of Europe in the interwar period and of many developing nations in the 1960s and 1970s. Neo-corporatism, which is often called "societal" or "open" corporatism, is characteristically present not in developing nations but in already modern, industrial, social-welfare-oriented countries. Neo-corporatism incorporates societal or interest groups directly into the decision-making machinery of the modern state on such issues as industrial policy, social welfare, pensions, and economic planning. Usually the groups involved in such incorporation are economic: unions, employers, and farmer groups—though, depending on the policy issue, cultural, social, and professional groups may also be involved. Neo-corporatism implies formalized consultation between the state and its major societal interests, with the main difference from U.S.-style pluralism being the incorporation of these groups usually under state auspices *directly* into the decision-making process and their (usually) formal representation and vote (which often implies veto power) on the vast regulatory and planning apparatus of the modern state. Neo-corporatism thus stands in contrast to the historically laissez-faire quality and independence from the state of most U.S. interest groups. And, instead of the often authoritarian corporatism of the past, neo-corporatism is clearly compatible with parliamentary democracy, with a form of pluralism, and with modern social welfarism.

Neo-corporatism is mainly present in the advanced European countries where business, labor, and the state have often reached a tripartite agreement, or what is often called a "social pact." Usually such social pacts, carried out under government tutelage and direction, involve labor's giving up its right to strike in return for employers granting wage increases and expanded benefits. Cooperation, consultation, negotiations, and compromise are the usual routes to such agreements, not coercion—which help explain why this is called "modern," "neo-," or "societal" corporatism as contrasted with the authoritarian corporatism of the past. Such pacts are mutually beneficial: labor gets more money and benefits; business gets stability and continuous productivity; and the government "buys" social peace.

Neo-corporatism is also present in welfare programs when workers, the unemployed, mothers, older persons, and other groups are brought into a formal consultative role in the administration of social welfare. This entails not just an occasional expressing of views, as in American interest-group pluralism, but a system in which the groups affected become themselves a part of the state agencies responsible for carrying out their programs. Neo-corporatism may also be present when central planning or negotiations over industrial policy is at issue and the state needs to have all the formal interests "on board" for its programs. Or, when wage restraints are necessary and the state wants to assure that both employers and organized labor will accept the new conditions. Neo-corporatism may thus be present in the modern era over a variety of issues—and also in a variety of forms: strong corporatism, as we see in more detail later on, in Austria, Sweden, and Switzerland; weaker corporatism in France, Germany, and Great Britain. But all of them have this in common (which distinguishes corporatism from liberal-pluralism): the formal incorporation of interest groups *into* the actual decision-making apparatus of the modern state, rather than their remaining freewheeling, independent interest groups, as under liberal-pluralism.

CORPORATISM AS SOCIAL SCIENCE MODEL

Corporatist institutions and practices, we have seen, have now become pervasive in a variety of regimes: developing and developed nations, and authoritarian systems as well as democratic ones. Corporatism and the corporatist approach have become so pervasive, in fact, that they have recently emerged as a distinct model or paradigm in the social sciences. Note that we are here shifting directions in our description and definitions of corporatism. We are no longer describing a specific regime in a specific region or time frame; instead, we are talking about an approach, an intellectual framework, a way of examining and analyzing corporatist political phenomena across countries and time periods. We are not here trying to present an exact mirror of any single country's corporatist ideology or movement; rather, our goal is to provide a general picture, a model, that tells us what to look for if we are interested in studying corporatism.

The attempt here is not to present a formal or mathematical model of corporatism, as is often done in the natural sciences, but to offer a social science model that is necessarily less precise, more informal. Ours is what is called a *verstahen* approach, a way of looking at things, a set of suggestions as to what to look for, an *approach* and a *framework* rather than a quantifiable formula. We seek not some final or absolute model but instead a set of informal guidelines to help direct our thinking, studying, and analysis.

Corporatism is both a description of an existing regime *and* a model, in the same way that both liberal-pluralism and Marxism are, at the same time, both descriptions of existing regimes and models of more general phenomena. When we call a regime liberal-pluralist, it conjures up in our minds such things as elections, checks, and balances, competitive interest groups, democracy, and civil liberties. These ingredients are part of the liberal-pluralism *model*. Similarly, when we speak of Marxism or Marxism/Leninism, some of the elements in that model include the labor theory of value, class struggle, the dialectical theory of history, and dictatorship of the proletariat. In this manner we need to ask with regard to the corporatist model, what are the main ingredients in the model and how does that help us better understand distinct political systems?

One of the main ingredients in corporatism is a strong, directing state—either in actual fact or, most often in the developing nations, in aspiration. Along with the strong state, we find a variety of corporate interests: In emerging nations these would include the military, religious bodies, elite groups, and traditional units like the family, clan, or tribe; in developed nations, organized labor, big business, professional associations, modern interest associations, and the like would be included. Under corporatism, the state tries to structure, license, control, and even monopolize this group structure to prevent the competition among the groups from getting out-of-hand, to better integrate and organize state policy. At the same time, the corporate groups try to maintain some level of autonomy from the state and to bargain with, infiltrate, and/or capture it to promote the best interests of their members. This dynamic between state and society, this tension and struggle, lies at the heart of the theory of corporatism, just as individual freedom lies at the heart of liberalism and class struggle lies at the heart of Marxism.

If the state-society arena is the dominant arena in the theory of corporatism, then how does the corporatist framework help us understand comparative politics and public policy? At this point we are getting close to the usefulness and practicality of corporatism as a theory. Keeping in mind this state-society arena, I have found that using the corporatist framework is especially helpful in thinking about and analyzing such public policy issues as social security, labor relations, industrial policy, and wage policy. The corporatist framework in its neo-corporatist form is also useful in examining health care, education policy, housing programs, and a host of other public policy issues.

But more than these public policy issues, I find the corporatist framework assists in examining comparatively the balance of power in society, the relations between labor and management, the increase (or decline) in the power of the state, the interrelations of interest groups and their tie-ins with bureaucratic agencies, which interest groups are rising and falling in influence and power, and how change and development (social, economic, political) occur in society and how these are related to the dynamics of modernization, industrialization, and societal evolution. In short, most of the big issues in comparative politics, in both developed and developing nations, can be usefully studied by using the corporatist framework.[3]

ISSUES FOR CONSIDERATION

The above discussion has identified four types of corporatism: (1) natural or historical corporatism; (2) ideological corporatism; (3) manifest corporatism; and (4) neo-corporatism. In addition, we have set forth some preliminary ideas about corporatism as a model or framework for analysis. It is important to keep these four types, the suggested comparative framework, and the definitions and discussions of each clearly in mind as we proceed with the discussion. Building on the discussion of these four types and the framework presented, we now proceed to ask a series of questions and raise key issues that students of corporatism need to think about.

1. Where does corporatism come from? Does it emerge out of the history and culture of the society, out of political or institutional needs, from economic requirements, from crises, or from some combination of these and other factors?
2. What are the precise relations of corporatism to state-society relations and to such specific groups as organized labor, business, the armed forces, and so on? What are the implications of a corporatist system of state-society relations versus a liberal-pluralist one?
3. What are the dynamics of change within corporatism? This question implies two additional questions:
   a. How do societies move from one form of corporatism to another (from historical or precorporatism, to ideological corporatism, to manifest corporatism, to neo-corporatism)? Is there a progression and evolution involved, and what are the dynamic factors that account for the change? In other words, we are suggesting not only that the four types listed above are a classificatory outline but also that there is often a progressive evolution in society from one type of corporatism to the next.
   b. How do corporatist regimes respond to changed social and economic circumstances? For while some corporatist regimes prove to be static, others are able to respond to change just as effectively (in some cases more so) as liberal-pluralist regimes.
4. What are the specific implications of corporatism for labor relations, economic planning, social welfare, wage policy, and other social policies? And how does this differ from a liberal-pluralist or a socialist system?
5. Recently we have begun to see patterns of corporatist representation emerging at the international level—for example, in the structure of interest-group representation in the European Union (EU)—as well as at national levels. Is this a new stage of transnational corporatism, and what does it mean?

6. How widespread is corporatism? Corporatism is present, in different forms, in many European countries, throughout Asia and Latin America, and in many developing nations; the United States seems also to be practicing a form of "creeping corporatism." If corporatism is becoming ubiquitous, present in so many regimes and cultures, of what use is it as an explanatory device? Alternatively, can we distinguish more sharply among distinct types and forms of corporatism?

7. Finally, we wrestle with the big philosophical question: What are the implications of all this corporatism in terms of bigness and bureaucracy, interest-group competition, individualism versus collectivism, and even democracy itself?[4]

NOTES

1. Thomas Kuhn, *The Structure of Scientific Revolutions* (Chicago: University of Chicago Press, 1971).

2. Mihail Manoilesco, *Le Siècle du Corporatisme* (Paris: Felix Alcan, 1934).

3. The revival of interest in corporatism in the 1970s paralleled the revival of interest among comparativists in what was called the "relative autonomy of the state." Under liberal-pluralism the state was often seen as a mere reflection of the interest-group competition; in Marxism the state was supposed to "wither away." But clearly during the 1970s the central state and its bureaucracies were becoming more powerful, not less; hence, the interest both in corporatism, which posited a strong, directing state, and in the state's position as an autonomous, authoritative if not authoritarian actor independent from interest groups and the class system.

4. Some of the basic literature includes Martin Heisler (ed.), *Politics in Europe* (New York: McKay, 1974); Philippe Schmitter and Gerhard Lehmbruch (eds.), *Trends toward Corporatist Intermediation* (Beverly Hills: Sage, 1979); Peter Williamson, *Corporatism in Perspective* (London: Sage, 1989); and Howard J. Wiarda, *Corporatism and Comparative Politics* (New York: M. E. Sharpe, 1997).

6

Indigenous Theories
of Change

INTRODUCTION

In the 1950s and 1960s, many American social scientists thought that social, economic, and political development in the non-Western or Third
World would largely follow and echo that of the West. In both Marxian
and non-Marxian models, the modal patterns were the Western or already
developed nations; the developed nations showed to the undeveloped the
socioeconomic and political mirror of the latter's future.

Then in the 1970s the idea of indigenous or homegrown models of development caught hold in various areas of the Third World. Rather than
slavishly and retardedly imitating the West, the non-Western nations were
attracted to the idea of fashioning their own systems of politics, economics, and social organization based on native and recently rediscovered values and institutions. There would be, conceivably, an East Asian or Confucian model of development, a South Asian model of development, an
Islamic model of development, a sub-Saharan African model of development, and perhaps also a Latin American model of development. Latin
America presented a particularly difficult case because, while it was pre-
dominately Western, it represented a semifeudal fragment of the Western
tradition dating back to pre-1500.

Today the situation is more complex, more confusing, and therefore deserving of a serious study and updating. On the one hand, some groups
and individuals (the Iranian mullahs, former prime ministers Lee Kwan
Yew of Singapore and Mahathir bin Mohamud of Malaysia, Col. Mu'am-
mar al-Qaddafi in Libya, and various Islamic fundamentalists, among

others) continue to assert the advantages of non-Western theories of development. But many others in these same countries have become disillusioned with indigenous theories and institutions, seeing them as romantic visions, unrealistic, unworkable, and products of intellectual thinking but not necessarily in accord with their own people's wishes or practices. The argument has been tipped recently by the mammoth and probably irresistible impact of Western influences (Coca-Cola, McDonald's, blue jeans, rock music, consumerism, and, especially, democracy, human rights, and free-market capitalism) on the non-Western world. Meanwhile, the end of the Cold War means not only the collapse and discrediting of one of the main alternatives (Marxism-Leninism) to Westernization, but also the end of the Third World's ability to play the United States off against the Soviet Union and, thus, to preserve a larger degree of their own autonomy and independence.

All these changes, new currents and countercurrents, make it imperative that we reassess, in this new national and international context, the argument between local or regional and global or universal models of development. To what extent in today's circumstances can indigenous models and movements hope to survive? Will they not be overwhelmed by what MIT political scientist Lucian Pye once called the "world culture" of Western values and ideas? Or, paradoxically, might not the end of the Cold War, rather than producing only one model, provide opportunity for a great variety of indigenous ethnic, religious, and national groups in Asia, Latin America, Africa, the Middle East, Russia, and Eastern Europe to assert more strongly their own indigenous solutions, ethnic pride, and ideas of separatism? Could we not see a continuum of countries, ranging by degree from those with strong indigenous cultures, such as Japan, India, and China, able to borrow *selectively* from the Western tradition, versus countries with weaker, local cultures that are likely to be overwhelmed and/or submerged by Western influences?

This chapter wrestles with the question of whether there is now only one (mainly Western, democratic, capitalist) model of development, or is there still room for two (socialist), three (mercantilist, statist), or many (Islamic, African, Confucian, Latin American, etc.) more models of development? What kinds of blends and overlaps exist between the Western and non-Western models? With the end of the Cold War and the seeming triumph of the neoliberal model, is it still possible to envision multiple routes to development, or is there now only one path? Must indigenous groups like those in Mexico or Guatemala give up their struggle and resign themselves to being absorbed into Western ways, or can they still hope for some degree of autonomy?

The topic is fraught with heavy issues that resonate both intellectually in terms of the models we use to interpret non-Western countries, *and* practically and politically as regards the future development of Third World countries and the indigenous movements within them. In the cases of Russia, China, and Japan, the debate between Western and non-Western models involves important security issues as well.

BACKGROUND AND CONTEXT OF THE ISSUE

During the 1960s the fields of comparative politics, comparative sociology, and economic development studies were largely dominated by what came to be called "developmentalism." Developmentalism in turn derived from earlier studies in the fields of cultural anthropology and sociology and from greater dynamism and analysis of change processes in political science. Developmentalism encompassed the study of economic, social, and political development in the Third World of emerging nations. The study of development was further fueled by the emergence of a host of new, formerly colonial nations onto the world stage in the late 1950s and early 1960s, and by the rising preoccupation in American foreign policy to fashion an attractive, noncommunist model of development that would serve as an alternative to Marxism-Leninism.[1] In the 1960s the study of social, political, economic, cultural, even psychological development became *the* dominant paradigm in the social sciences.

The development model generally posited that all societies go through similar if not identical processes of economic development, social change, and political modernization—the latter not always well defined but usually implying greater pluralism, democracy, and social justice. Once the great motor force of economic development begins, it produces some quite predictable social changes: the rise of a middle class, a working class, and the mobilization of the peasantry. These social transformations in turn help produce greater political pluralism, more democratic politics, and the need for more effective public policy.[2]

The process was usually portrayed in nice, antiseptic phrases like these, implying a happy ending—thus ignoring the wrenching, often bloody disruption and chaos that accompany such major change processes. Moreover, the developmental approach suggested that hated fascism and communism were "diseases of the transition" that could be overcome or vanquished through development, and that the end product of this unilinear, presumably universal development process was a society that looked just like we do: happily democratic, pluralist, and socially just. How comforting that conclusion was both to the scholars of developmentalism and to U.S. foreign policy makers? Unfortunately, it was not an accurate portrayal either of development or of the Third World nations starting out on the development path.

Then came the war in Vietnam, the assassinations of John F. and Robert Kennedy and Martin Luther King, Jr., upheavals in American cities and universities, and Watergate. These events shook our faith in the inevitability and even the desirability of the American model on which so much of the development paradigm had been based. In addition, it turned out that much of the earlier development literature was written by theorists who had never visited the Third World. Furthermore, after a decade of actual experience with and study of development in Third World nations, policy makers and theorists realized that the main institutions and processes involved often failed to conform to the Western model. The result during the 1970s was strong criticism of the prevailing development model, the assertion of alternative approaches (dependency theory, corporatism, bureaucratic-statism), and the dawning realization that the Third World would not and could not imitate the developmental experiences of the West (the United States and Europe).[3]

One of the alternatives put forward in the 1970s and then blossoming in the 1980s was the notion of a homegrown or indigenous Third World model of development. After the numerous failures of Marxism as well as developmentalism, and the coming to power of a whole wave of repressive, human-rights-abusing regimes in Africa, Asia, the Middle East, and Latin America, the idea of a native or indigenous theory of development was enormously attractive. Presumably, these homegrown models would be more closely attuned to local conditions than the imported and often ill-fitting Western ones. There would, therefore, have to be an East Asian, perhaps Confucian, theory of development; an Indian and presumably Hindu theory of development; a sub-Saharan African theory of development; a Latin American theory of development; and—particularly after the Iranian revolution of 1979—a distinct Islamic theory of development. There were, probably, still universals in the development process but now each Third World region would do it, to use the title of the Frank Sinatra song, "My Way."[4]

During the decade of the 1980s, the idea of a homegrown theory of development was very popular among Third World intellectuals. Not only did it offer an attractive alternative to the often (in their contexts) dysfunctional Western model but it held promise of another way between democracy and authoritarianism, between capitalism and communism. Unfortunately, the countries where an indigenous theory of development was seriously embraced (Iran, Tanzania, Cambodia) turned out to be not very attractive places. There were other serious problems with indigenous theories of development as well, which are discussed at length later in the chapter. Suffice it here to say that these indigenous, homegrown ideas and models of development proved to be (except perhaps in East Asia) no more effective in actually promoting development than earlier theories had been, and they were often downright harmful.

Then came the collapse of the Soviet Union, the end of the Cold War, and a new international world where every basic foreign policy assumption of the preceding forty-five years required reexamination. This transformation in international politics took place at precisely the time in the 1980s and 1990s when the "Third Wave"[5] of democracy seemed to be triumphing worldwide and representing the wave of the future,[6] when free market or neoliberal economic policies acquired the cachet of a new orthodoxy and American cultural influence seemed to become universal.

So what then in this context becomes of the idea of an indigenous theory or several indigenous theories of development? Is this idea still viable and attractive or has it now been overwhelmed by Western influences? Is it possible to blend or to select, retaining what is good and useful of indigenous practices but also accommodating to powerful Western ways? Or are the Third World and its institutions bound to be submerged in the Western onslaught? Are there some countries (Japan, for instance) that are so important and powerful that they can successfully blend and fuse Western and indigenous ways, choosing selectively among the best features of each, while other countries less wealthy and less self-confident will simply be overwhelmed by Western culture? What kinds of blends and fusions are possible? And what implications do all these trends have for the social sciences, both for our theories of development and even for the notion of a universal social science?

INDIGENOUS THEORIES OF DEVELOPMENT

The idea of an indigenous, local, or home-grown theory of development is undoubtedly attractive. It proved to be enormously influential among intellectual elites and some political leaders in the Third World during the 1970s and 1980s—and in some countries it is attractive today. The fashioning of indigenous models of development was particularly attractive to Third World leaders given the apparent failures or unattractiveness of the main alternatives, both Marxism and the U.S.-favored developmentalist approach. Both the Marxian and the non-Marxian models are, after all, based on the particular developmental experience of a select group of countries in Western Europe (Germany, France, Great Britain) and the United States. But by the 1970s it was clear that *neither* of these two major alternatives was necessarily appropriate for or had much relevance for the Third World. Hence, the newfound interest in fashioning a homegrown model that *did* reflect indigenous cultures and institutions.

Think for a moment about how the main fields in the social sciences are organized, and that will provide a start in helping us understand why Third World leaders view them as biased and of limited relevance to their circumstances. Political theory begins with Plato, Aristotle, and Cicero; proceeds to the (European) Middle Ages; then takes in Machiavelli, Hobbes, Locke, Rousseau, and the Enlightenment; then Kant, Hegel, Marx, Hume, and Mill. All of these are *Western* thinkers; but where in our political theory courses is there attention to Confucian, Buddhist, Islamic, African, or Latin American political theory? Similarly with sociology: all the great classical sociologists—Weber, Durkheim, Parsons, Lipset—had *the West* as their research laboratory; and based on the Western implications of industrialization, urbanization, and social change largely assumed the non-West or Third World would follow the Western experience.

Likewise in economics. All the great models of economic development—whether Marxian or non-Marxian—were based on the European or American experiences. But why would we assume, without proof, that Third World countries would simply imitate the Western development experience? Hence, if one thinks about it, one might conclude that virtually our entire liberal arts education—political science, sociology, economics, history—is really a long course in Western civilization. That is good and valuable to know, but where does the non-West fit into this? The answer is, it doesn't—unless, of course, it imitates the West. But if the non-West can't or won't imitate the West (think of Afghanistan, Iraq, Haiti, Somalia, Sierra Leone, and other cases), where does that leave them? One can, therefore, given these biases in so much of the literature and, indeed, in our entire educational system, see why the idea of a local, homegrown, indigenous model or framework for development and modernization would be so enticing, especially if it worked better than the imported models which didn't seem to work at all well in the Third World.

Our purpose here is not to present a complete analysis of the indigenous, Third World models set forth in the 1970s and 1980s; we leave that for a future book. Instead, our purpose in this chapter is to provide the broader context in which these ideas and approaches emerged and to offer a brief synopsis of them.

In Africa, for example, following the hopeful and optimistic euphoria that accompanied independence in the early 1960s, political as well as economic collapse and disintegration set in. Neither the Marxian nor the developmentalist approach provided adequate answers. Both approaches seemed to suggest that getting rid of tribalism or ethnicity (seen as a "traditional" institution) was necessary for development to occur. But the tribe or the ethnic group provided one of the few institutions that helped hold African society together, providing security, police protection, education, and other essential social services that no other "modern" institution seemed capable to supplying. Hence, instead of eliminating tribalism as the earlier development literature suggested, many African leaders began to look on it more benignly. Instead of dysfunctional centralized

regimes, some African political leaders began to envision a more decentralized or even federal regime in which localized ethnic organizations
would be utilized rather than snuffed out. Incompletely, by fits and starts,
and not without misgivings, some African leaders began to consider a political system that dealt realistically with persistent tribalism rather than
trying to eliminate it in the name of "modernization."

In India some parallel developments occurred. Not only did India have
a long tradition of philosophical and religious thought quite different
from that of the West, but it also had traditional institutions that stub-
bornly refused to give way under the impact of modernization. Indian
caste associations, for instance, proved to be not just parochial, ascriptive
institutions in the Parsons-Almond mold fated to disappear, but adapt-
able and even modernizing forces, taking on many of the functions of interest groups and political parties. While India did not wish to jettison the
liberal-democratic institutions inherited from earlier British colonial rule,
it did need to adapt its imported models (by now including both democracy on the political side and more open markets on the economic side) to
Indian ways of doing things.

Much the same can be said of East Asia. Here we have an area that has
strong indigenous (Confucian, Shintoist, Taoist) traditions and culture. At
the same time, East Asia (Japan, South Korea, Taiwan, Hong Kong, Singapore, now China) has been the most successful non-Western area in
adapting Western ways to Asian practices and traditions. Japan, for example, produces cars, pianos, and all manner of high-tech instruments,
and plays Beethoven (even baseball!) often better than the West. Much of
Asia's success, in fact, has come not from abolishing traditional institutions but from adapting these to Western practices. More recently, Japan
and other East Asian countries have held up *their* development experiences, not America's or Europe's, as models of economic growth and governance for the world to emulate.

It is similar in the Islamic world. In Islam we have a long religious and
philosophical tradition comparable to Buddhism, Confucianism, or Christianity. The modernization literature argued that such traditional institutions as the Islamic religion should fade under the impact of development
and secularization; instead, it has flourished. Not only is Islamic fundamentalism growing and, especially since the Iranian revolution of 1979,
becoming more militant and aggressive, but increasingly whole societies
and polities are being recast in the Islamic mold. On the other hand—and
unlike East Asia—there are as yet *no* examples of a successful and specifically Islamic *economic* model; and in the political sphere, in non-Muslim
countries, there is little admiration for an Islamic theocratic state.

Latin America, Eastern Europe, and Russia represent variations on
these themes. Latin America is primarily Western in its main institutions,

but as an offshoot of Spain and Portugal of the Middle Ages, it represents a particular, semifeudal fragment of an earlier West and is now seeking to catch up both economically and politically. For decades Latin America has been searching for a political and economic model that reflects both its Westernness and its particularly Hispanic past—and has not found it yet. Some Latin American countries also have large indigenous, Indian populations, so when we speak of an "indigenous model" of that area we need to know if we are speaking of the assertion of Indian rights or of a distinctive Hispanic framework. For a time Latin American intellectuals also put forth dependency theory as their own creation but that assertion faded as democracy and integration into the world economy grew.

Eastern Europe is similarly divided. Some countries of the region (the Baltics, the Czech Republic, Slovakia, Poland, Hungary, Slovenia, perhaps Croatia) are mainly Western in their histories, peoples, languages, and religion; since the collapse of the Soviet Union and its communist satellite regimes in Eastern Europe, these countries have become increasingly interconnected with the West, both politically (democracy) and economically (free markets). But other countries of the region (Bulgaria, Romania, Serbia, Albania, Macedonia, Bosnia) are, by the same criteria of language, ethnicity, culture, and religion, more mixed, often both Western and Eastern. Unlike the other regions surveyed, however, a distinctly Eastern European model of development—or even much agreement on what "Eastern Europe" now means or if it has a separate identity—has not been seen here. Instead, we have witnessed, especially in southeastern Europe, a great deal of confusion, even chaos and instability in some countries, and uncertainty as to what precise directions to take either politically or economically.

Russia is an especially interesting case not only because of the divisions over its identity and future directions but also because it is such a large country with so many nuclear weapons. In that respect, the West has high strategic stakes in the outcome. Russia has long been divided between its pro-Western and Slavophile loyalties, divisions that were often hidden or submerged during its long, seventy-year period of communist dictatorship. But with the collapse of communism these divisions have resurfaced, made more complicated by the new forms of electoral politics as well as foreign policy considerations. President Boris Yeltsin was identified with democracy and the West and received strong support from the West; his opponents, both Vladimir Zhirinovsky and more moderate Gennady Zyuganov, had put forth an oftentimes anti-Western and Slavophile political agenda, complicated by the fact that they were the candidates of a revived Communist Party which the West (the United States and its NATO allies) sees as threatening. President Vladimir Putin has similarly resurrected autocratic ways. The Slavophiles often emphasize authoritarianism, top-down rule, a strong state and military, and a more collectivist economy; but it is as yet unclear whether this constitutes a full-fledged and distinctive, indigenous *theory* of development.

The idea of an indigenous or homegrown theory of development thus became very popular in the 1970s, 1980s, and on into the 1990s. In one form or another, the idea of building a development model on local or native institutions and practices—as distinct from imported ones, whether stemming from Western or communist practices—gained popularity in virtually all areas of the globe. These efforts to fashion a model based on native institutions reflected not only dissatisfaction with existing models but also nationalistic, cultural, and ethnic pride in utilizing "our own" institutions and practices.

ASSESSMENT

The idea of a distinct, Third World model, or series of models, of development is undoubtedly attractive. Who could resist such a notion, particularly after the disappointment and misery brought on by earlier failed models and the often heartfelt demand by Third World peoples and leaders to do it "our way"? Who could stand against the idea of a homegrown, indigenous, grassroots model of development? The idea of an indigenous or non-Western model of development is indeed so attractive that one wonders why so few political leaders and intellectuals failed to think of it earlier.

During the 1970s and 1980s such indigenous theorizing and model construction swept through much of the Third World. It took different forms in different areas: for example, renewed emphasis on the modernizing role of caste associations in India as they converted from traditional institutions into quasipolitical parties or interest groups; the rediscovery of the positive role of ethnicity and tribalism in Africa as providing useful social services, police, and other functions; and the formulation of a distinctive Islamic theory of law and social science finding dramatic if not particularly attractive expression in the Iranian revolution of 1979. In Latin America the emphasis on corporatism by one group of scholars and on dependency theory by another group represented rival efforts to fashion a distinct model appropriate for that area.

In Russia the collapse of the older Soviet system led to a reemphasis among some groups on Slavic and uniquely Russian ways of doing things, while Eastern Europe, after the fall of the Berlin Wall and the disintegration of the Warsaw Pact, split into those countries that moved closer to the Western economic and political model and those who, on religious, linguistic, ethnic, cultural, geographic, and socioeconomic grounds, remained divided and uncertain as to their future. In East Asia, the undoubted success economically of that region's countries gave added credence to their assertion of a distinct Asian model of development, but whether the Asian claim included a separate political model as well as an economic one remained open to question. Thus in *every* Third World or non-Western area—although obviously varying from area to area, a theme to which the discussion shortly returns—we have seen the articulation and increasing assertion of local, indigenous, nationalistic, and grassroots models of development to replace or supplement the earlier, often discredited, imports.

In addition to the inherent attractiveness of indigenous approaches to development, there are social and political factors, specific to regional, national, and local circumstances, that help explain why the indigenous approach was so attractive in the 1970s, 1980s, and, in different circumstances, 1990s. First, by the 1970s it had become clear throughout much of the Third World that the imported Western models, whether derived from capitalist or socialist countries, were not working very well in these non-Western contexts; hence, the idea grew of substituting homegrown models for the frequently dysfunctional imported ones. Second, after Vietnam and Watergate, the United States seemed almost to lose its way for a time, lost confidence in its own vision and purpose as a nation and turned self-critical, and failed to push hard for its own developmental model, thus allowing other alternatives to come to the fore. Third, the Cold War parity and apparent standoff between the two great superpowers of the 1970s and 1980s enabled Third World leaders to see the advantages of playing the two against each other while advancing their own indigenous or nationalistic models.

Fourth—and here we need to jump ahead to the 1990s—after the Soviet Union collapsed, local, ethnic, and nationalistic groups in Russia and Eastern Europe, long bottled up by Soviet totalitarianism, were able to gain greater autonomy and assert their own traditions and practices in ways denied them before. It may prove ironic that indigenous and strongly nationalistic ideas were put forward in Russia and Eastern Europe at a time when the attractiveness of indigenous solutions was already beginning to fade in most other areas of the developing world—although that may be getting ahead of our story. In any case, it needs to be emphasized that the rising popularity for a time of indigenous approaches to development was due not just to their inherent attractiveness but also to larger socioeconomic and political forces in the world.

THE DIVERSITY OF INDIGENOUS MODELS

While the popularity of indigenous theories of development was widespread in the Third World, it is striking how diverse the responses were in each of the areas here analyzed. We make a mistake if we believe that the Third World response either to the inadequacies of the imported Western models or to the opportunities for maneuvering that the Cold War rivalry between the superpowers afforded was the same everywhere. In fact, this book documents just how diverse the non-Western experience has been among geographic areas and their social, political, and cultural experiences. Moreover, even *within* these areas there is room for great diversity among countries in terms of the popularity of indigenous solutions, which elements within that experience were emphasized, and the willingness of elites to assert indigenous solutions as opposed to acceptance of Western ways. China is very different in this regard from Japan; Iran's sense of an Islamic state is very different from Saudi Arabia's; Nigeria is very different from Tanzania; and Mexico, very different from Brazil.

The East Asian case, for example, is sui generis. First, while there is a common Confucian tradition, it takes different forms and is overlain with different ingredients (Taoism, Shintoism, Maoism) in different countries. Second, the interpretation of Confucianism itself has changed: at one time its self-effacing admonitions were viewed as a barrier to development; now it is seen as providing the self-discipline, order, and emphasis on education necessary for development. Third, while in some cases the assertion of an "Asian model" is seen as a rationalization for authoritarianism and ongoing human rights abuses, in others it represents a widespread sense that the West has lost its way economically, socially, politically, and morally, while Asia has found it. Then too, while some countries and leaders (Lee Kwan Yew of Singapore, Mahathir Mohamud of Malaysia) have championed a distinct Asian model, others (Japan, South Korea, Taiwan), wanting to keep close commercial and other ties to the West and especially the United States, have been more muted both in their criticisms of the West and in their assertion of a separate Asian way of doing things. Finally, it is still not entirely clear what an Asian model would entail: is it an economic model of state-led economic growth, a political model of considerable top-down rule, a cultural and social model of clean streets and formalized politeness, or some combination of these?

Like China in a sense, India is a culture, a civilization, a billion people, and virtually an entire continent in itself. Since its birth as an independent nation in 1946, India has been—and remains—a liberal, representative democracy in the Western (British) mold; so far there is little desire to go in some other direction besides democracy. Second, *within* India and within its various states, there is a great deal of cultural and social diversity, including distinct religious and ethnic movements, and a wide range of opinion about the value of retaining India's current political and intellectual model or substituting or perhaps supplementing it with something else, including indigenous influences; but there is no consensus on what or how or even whether this should occur. Third, when India eventually changed its economic model in the 1990s, it did so not so much because the Soviet model had collapsed (a negative example) but because of the remarkable economic success (a positive influence) of such neighboring countries as Singapore. And fourth, not only is India today a vibrant society, a mix of indigenous and imported (Asian *and* Western) influences, but it and other parallel "culture areas" ought to serve as the focus of *regional* theorizing about development before we go on to grand, global models.

The Latin American case is equally fascinating. Here we have a case, first, of an area that is predominantly Western but a fragment of a semifeudal, premodern West (Spain and Portugal) circa 1500. Second, while Latin America has often been confused and/or divided about its destiny, the general trend over the centuries has been gradually increasing approximation to the Western political and economic model. Third, when Latin America did begin to flirt with the possibility of pursuing its own way, there were at least two rival claimants to that honor—corporatism and dependency theory—which in a sense canceled each other out. Fourth, in the present era we have seen in Latin America what might be called "dual indigenization": one model still trying to define the area's uniqueness in Hispanic terms (Catholic, Spanish-speaking, etc.) and the other representing the increasing assertion of nativist or Indian rights. Meanwhile, on both the political (democracy) and economic (neoliberalism) fronts, Latin America has edged closer to global (Western) trends.

Africa is one of the areas where interest in indigenous models of development has been most pronounced. To begin, Africa was the continent where Western colonialism and imperialism were most rapacious, imposing artificial boundaries that divided the continent's natural groupings and subjecting it to unspeakable atrocities. Second, when Africa finally achieved independence in the 1950s and 1960s, the models of political and economic development it used were all imported from abroad, were illadapted to African realities, and led to numerous breakdowns and calamities. So, third, it is not unexpected that Africa would subsequently try to rediscover its roots, to fashion new social and political systems based not on ill-fitting imported models but on native, homegrown, usually decentralized or even federal traditions and institutions, including ethnic organizations. Unfortunately these efforts at indigenization have proven no or little more successful at achieving development or improving the lot of the African peoples than did the earlier imported models. Moreover, even the efforts recently at decentralization were largely based on imported models, not necessarily native ones. Meanwhile, democratization in Africa has proceeded irregularly and in only a few countries; what may be promising are the efforts at economic privatization and state downsizing, which may reduce corruption and promote economic growth.

The attraction of indigenous theories has also affected the Islamic world—perhaps more so than anywhere else. Part of the reason for this attraction is the manifest failures, again, of the imported models and the powerful sense of frustration, even rage, in countries throughout the Islamic world over their lack of domestic or international success. Then too, in the Koran and the Shariah, Islam has a coherent body of beliefs, a legal system, and civic guidelines that could, conceivably, serve as the basis for a distinct, Islamic political, social, and cultural model. However, in the Islamic world, as well as within individual Islamic countries, there are deep divisions over these issues. For example, Iran, Iraq, Egypt, Saudi Arabia, Pakistan, and Indonesia are all Islamic states in one form or another, but they are also very different not just in their social, economic, and political directions but also in their attitudes toward and relations with the West. Moreover, both Islamic leaders and the *ulema* have readily used Islam for partisan political purposes. And, in an area where we hear a great deal about Islamic fundamentalism and where the idea of a distinct, indigenous (Islamic) model is perhaps strongest of all Third World areas, the success of the fundamentalist agenda is by no means certain.

In Eastern Europe and Russia some very different issues arise. The questions here are not so much whether to embrace a full-blown and separate theory of development, but how to deal with strong, often competing nationalisms and rival ethnic and religious loyalties, and where to draw the boundary between "the West" and something else ("the East," the Slavic world, Eastern Orthodoxy, the Islamic world). Using linguistic, religious, ethnic, and nationalistic criteria, we might conclude that such countries of Eastern Europe as Poland, the Baltic states, the Czech Republic, Slovakia, Hungary, and Slovenia will likely remain anchored to the West and to Western models, both politically (democracy) and economically (modern, mixed economies). However, using these same criteria, we are far less certain about the prospects for Romania, Bulgaria, Serbia, Bosnia, Croatia, Albania, and Moldova. While these latter countries are likely to remain politically uncertain, economically laggard, and ethnically divided, there are few serious efforts—unlike in Africa, Asia, and the Islamic world—to develop a distinct *theory* of development.

Much the same could be said for post–Soviet Russia. Once again, as in Eastern Europe, the problem is deep ethnic, religious, cultural, and national differences. Debate in Russia often rages over whether it belongs, or should belong, to the West or to something else (Slavophile, the East, Asia,

Eastern Orthodox). These tensions have been exacerbated by the collapse and disintegration of the Soviet Union, the formation of the Commonwealth of Independent States, and the powerful centrifugal forces in Russian society. In my own travels in Russia, I have been impressed that the western Ukraine, western Belarus, and Moscow and its environs are mainly oriented toward Europe and the West, but that east of Moscow the non-West (still not well defined but much more Third World) sets in very quickly. Hence, Russia, not unlike southeast Europe, remains divided and even torn apart over its future; but other than nationalism, statism, strains of authoritarianism, and pride in its Slavic distinctiveness, there is as yet no serious effort in Russia to construct a full-fledged and uniquely Russian theory of development.

As this review suggests, the theme of an indigenous theory or theories of development has elicited mixed reviews in various parts of the world. It has been embraced in some areas, rejected in favor of the Western model in others, and treated with decidedly mixed attitudes in most. The necessity or sense of doing it "our way" has been strongest in Asia, Africa, and the Islamic world, but only in a few countries has there been an effort to eliminate Western influences, trade, and contacts entirely. Despite some reservations and efforts at finding indigenous solutions, northeastern Europe (Poland, Hungary, the Czech Republic, the Baltics, Slovakia) and Latin America have largely joined the West—Europe and North America, respectively—while Russia and southeastern Europe have been all but torn apart over these issues. Not only is there considerable diversity among the world's cultural and geographic regions over these issues, but within regions, within individual countries, and even within individuals there are often conflicting sentiments about continuing local ways versus integration into global trends (capitalism, democracy, free markets).

WHAT'S WRONG WITH AN INDIGENOUS MODEL?

In the 1970s and 1980s the idea of indigenous theories of development seemed to offer much hope and promise. The idea was eagerly embraced by those who had become disillusioned with earlier development models, all Western and imported, that failed to work very well in non-Western contexts. Indigenous models of change were thus born out of both a certain despair with the earlier and often unsuccessful experiments with development, and a passion, almost a romance, often naïveté, that doing things "our way" would be better. But now we need to subject the idea of indigenous theories of development to the same kind of careful critique that we used earlier on Western developmentalist models.

In practice, indigenous models of development have not, for the most part, worked out very well. Attractive in theory (who, having spent time in the Third World, could not be sympathetic to the idea of a local, home-grown theory of development?), indigenous models have often been sub-ject to the same problems as other well-meaning development plans. Fol-lowing is a list of some of the major problems associated with indigenous models of development:

Who Decides?

Who should decide what an indigenous theory consists of, what are its main ingredients, how it should be defined? This issue is actually very controversial. Should it be the Iranian mullahs, the priesthood, or the peo-ple? Should it be intellectuals and political leaders or voters? The fact is that different groups and individuals in a society often have very differ-ent ideas on this subject, and advocates of an indigenous theory have pro-vided no mechanism for deciding between them.

Political Manipulation and Bias

Generalissimo Francisco Franco in Spain stressed what he called "au-thentic" Spanish values: discipline, order, authority, traditional Catholi-cism. But he used these values to justify suppressing dissent and keeping himself in power; others disagreed that these were the only or even main Spanish values. In like manner, Asian autocrats like Lee Kwan Yew of Sin-gapore and Mahathir Mohamud of Malaysia have used the veil of "Asian models" to disguise and rationalize their own authoritarianism. African leaders have talked eloquently of "authenticity" and local models, but fre-quently these have been smokescreens for corruption, favoritism for one group over others, and authoritarianism.

Class or Ethnic Favoritism

It is not just individual rulers who have used the smokescreen of indige-nous values to disguise self-seeking motives but often whole classes or ethnic groups. Latin American elites tend to emphasize their authoritar-ian, corporatist, and patrimonial roots as a way of justifying their contin-uation in power, but lower-class elements often have a different, more democratic view. In Africa one ethnic group's values have often been set forth as the values for the entire society but that seldom sits well with other ethnic groups, nor does the distribution of government jobs and fa-vors on the basis of ethnicity rather than merit.

Elites versus the Masses

Elites in the Third World have often favored aristocratic, top-down, and hierarchical social structures—and the indigenous theories that favor them. But for the common people this usually means their interests are repressed or forgotten. Elites and intellectuals may favor an indigenous theory of development because it protects their interests, but what if the masses prefer Coca-Cola, rock music, *Sex and the City*, and all the goods associated with Western consumerism?

Contested Beliefs

In *every* country and culture surveyed here, the idea of an indigenous theory of development was hotly contested. Attractive as an abstract idea, it is in practice very controversial. Does acceptance of an indigenous development theory imply acceptance of the murderous Pol Pot regime in Cambodia? Does it mean in Islamic society acquiescence in the subordinate place of women, a theocratic society, or excessive harshness ("cruel and unusual punishment") against criminals? In other words, an indigenous theory of development does not emerge full-blown, instantaneously, or with automatic acceptance; instead it is often contested—often violently—by diverse groups and classes in society.

Functionality

Does it work? An indigenous theory or model sounds nice—especially to outsiders—but does it deliver in the way of goods and services? And by this we mean not just Coca-Cola and other consumer goods but such fundamentals as jobs, education, health care, social services—a higher standard of living. If these are not forthcoming, then people may simply prefer the Western models which *do* have a track record in providing such goods and services. In fact, indigenous models do not so far have a proven history of providing what people want.

Conflicting Theories

In Latin America we could probably arrive at an agreed-upon definition of Hispanic culture, but what about the indigenous Indian or African groups that not only have different cultures but may also assert claims to autonomy that cross national boundaries? In southern Africa blacks may have one kind of political and social model in mind while whites have another—or else the different African ethnic groups may have several distinct models: Who then is to decide and on what basis? Should followers of Islam adhere to the Sunni or Shiite versions? As we can see, this idea of an indigenous model gets very complicated.

Cultural Relativism

If each global region has a distinct model and social science of development, then how do we make judgments among them? Are we really ready to say that all solutions and models—even the most abusive ones—are equally valid (cultural relativism) or that the United States has *nothing* to offer the rest of the world in terms of human rights, the practice of democracy, or economic performance? Few Americans are willing to go that far or to countenance regimes that, in the name of doing it "their way," abuse human rights, commit atrocities, or repress their own peoples. But if we are not willing to take a completely cultural-relativist position, where *do* we draw the lines between universal beliefs and rights, on the one hand, and local or indigenous ways of doing things, on the other?

Splendid Isolation?

Countries that opt for an indigenous model of development (e.g., Cambodia, Iran) run the risk of being cut off from the rest of the world. Is that wise? Other countries, particularly in Asia, that were initially attracted to the idea of an indigenous model of development have backed away from it. These countries, whatever their pride in indigenous ways, do not wish to be entirely cut off from Western social, political, and cultural influences, and certainly not from the international trade and commerce vital to their economies. So, as before, the issue may not be the either-or one of indigenous-versus-universal but of tough choices on specific issues of where precisely one draws the lines between what is valuable "out there" in the global village versus what is worth preserving of local traditions.

As we see, therefore, the idea of an indigenous theory of development—obviously attractive at some levels—also has in it romantic, naive, and perhaps overly idealistic elements. Indigenous theories were the product of a particular time and place of growing disillusionment with the older Western theories that in the 1970s and 1980s didn't seem to work well and of the opportunity provided by the parity between the superpowers to maneuver between them. But when faced with the harsh realities and tough choices listed above, many countries became less enamored of the indigenous route and backed away from it. This is not to say that the indigenous path to development represents a totally false start, only that it probably needs to be reined in, viewed more pragmatically, and combined with other useful models of development. Within the social sciences, similarly, indigenous theories of development are being treated less romantically now but nonetheless still seriously as *one* approach among several (the others being liberal developmentalism, political economy, Marxism, dependency, corporatism, organic statism, bureaucratic-authoritarianism) deserving both of detailed scholarly study and of consideration for adoption by Third World countries.[7]

But while criticism of the indigenous path gradually intensified in the 1980s and a variety of countries were moving away from it or combining it with other approaches, a series of cataclysmic events in the late 1980s and early 1990s completely changed the global situation and forced once again a reassessment of the indigenous route.

THE NEW WORLD ORDER AND INDIGENOUS THEORIES

Between 1989 and 1991—precisely when the idea of indigenous theories of development had come to be viewed more skeptically, as one possible solution among several—a series of cataclysmic events changed the world power balance and had a major effect on thinking about indigenous solutions. The fall of the Berlin Wall and the reunification of Germany, the dissolution of the Warsaw Pact, and then the collapse of the Soviet Union itself were among the most important, even ground-shaking, events of the late twentieth century. These events not only changed the climate, making indigenous theories of development seem less attractive; but, because the Soviet Union had disintegrated, also diminished the capacity of the Third World to maneuver between and play the two superpowers against each other. A new post–Cold War world order began to emerge.

These world-transforming international events came at about the same time that a world revolution took place in communications—VCRs, cable television, the Internet, satellites, electronic money transfers, new radio and television broadcasting systems, CNN, computers, e-mail, and faxes were coming into everyday use. The communications revolution brought even the remotest Third World villages within the range of global television and, accelerating a trend begun earlier, drastically changed the tastes and preferences of *billions* of people. Put briefly, once you've seen the attractive lifestyles portrayed on American and European television—nice homes, cars, affluence, consumerism—who wants to continue in a poor Third World lifestyle, however "indigenous" it may be?

A third factor, stemming from the mid-1970s, was the equally revolutionary spread of democracy throughout the globe. The democratic revolution began in 1974–1975 in Portugal, Greece, and Spain; it then spread to Latin America, influenced Asia, has by now spread to Russia and Eastern Europe, and includes some countries in Africa and the Islamic world. Polls in these areas indicate that democracy enjoys widespread support and legitimacy (85–90 percent, depending on the region). All other solutions—military authoritarianism, Marxism-Leninism, *and* indigenous models—seem to have fallen by the wayside. In contrast to the situation a decade or two ago, few people seem to want an indigenous political formula anymore. Democracy and the democratic idea seem to have triumphed almost everywhere, notwithstanding ongoing conflicts in Iraq and Afghanistan.

Not only has democracy become virtually the only legitimate political system globally, but with the collapse of the Soviet Union and other communist states coupled with the phenomenal success of the east Asian nations, capitalism seems to have become the only viable economic system. The neoliberal model of free, open-market economies seems to have triumphed everywhere. It alone, despite the problems and inequalities to which capitalism gives rise, seems to be capable of delivering the goods and services that people, including those in the Third World, want. Our purpose here is not to make moral, ideological, or political judgments about these developments, but simply to report what is happening, which is that free, open markets are now seen almost universally as the most effective way to achieve economic growth. So there we have it: democracy (mainly Western-style) has triumphed in the political sphere and open-market capitalism or neoliberalism has emerged victorious in the economic sphere. Where in this new globalism is there still room for an indigenous theory of development?

When these factors are combined, they add up to an even stronger picture of the triumph of the Western model—for good or ill. The spread of the global communications revolution, for example, means that what most people want is not some new and unproven indigenous theory but instead such "universals" as Coca-Cola, rock music, blue jeans, consumerism, along with democracy, human rights, and free markets. The collapse of the Soviet Union not only means less freedom to maneuver for the former so-called "nonaligned" nations but also demands a whole new set of terms because the "Second World" of developed communist states has ceased to exist and, therefore, the term "Third World" makes no sense anymore. Moreover, among developing nations we need to distinguish newly industrializing countries (NICs—China, South Korea, Taiwan, Singapore, Indonesia, Brazil, Argentina, Mexico) that are making it into the modern world from others that continue to lag. We also should understand that this is not just an abstract intellectual argument: The United States not only favors democracy and free markets but it is also prepared to use the force of its diplomacy, economic strength, and even military/strategic might, as in Iraq, Haiti, or Bosnia, to ensure these outcomes.[8]

The result of all these influences combined, notwithstanding the extreme anti-Westernism engendered among some groups, is to strengthen once again the impact of the Western model (democracy, free markets) and to reduce the influence and attractiveness of indigenous models. What then is left or salvageable in the idea of an indigenous theory of development?

MIXED FORMS AND FUSIONS

In 1996 Professor Samuel P. Huntington of Harvard University published his provocative *The Clash of Civilizations*.[9] In this book Professor Huntington argues that, with the Cold War over, future conflicts in international affairs would be more between major *cultures* and *civilizations* and less between nations. Huntington also seems to be arguing that, with the rise of a diversity of conflicting civilizations, the idea of a universalist global civilization based on the Western model is dead.

More likely than a full-scale clash between civilizations, however, is an incredible mix of blends, fusions, and combinations both of conflicting internal cultural currents and of combined Western and local influences. Despite the "war on terrorism" and the violent anti-U.S. or antiglobalization sentiments of some elements, almost all countries continue to exhibit mixes of outside and domestic pressures, institutions, and ways of operating. These are likely to take "crazy quilt" patterns of unusual, shifting, and crosscutting combinations, or to represent "halfway houses" located at various points between Western and indigenous poles. In other words, we will see particularly African, Asian, Islamic, Latin American, and Russian ways of doing things combined with foreign influences and models in all sorts of imaginative and unusual ways. Occasionally, these diverse pressures will produce conflict but not likely a full-scale civilizational *war*.

But some culture areas are stronger than others in these regards; or their economies or political power is of such importance—e.g., China, Japan—that we are obliged to consider their cultural claims seriously. Japan is the paradigm. It is not only the most successful of the non-Western countries but it also has a remarkably uniform and coherent internal culture that is uniquely Japanese. Among the many reasons that Japan is admired is its *selective* borrowing from the West. It has taken the best that the West has to offer (and often improved upon it) while also taking great pains to preserve Japanese culture and traditions. One suspects that parallel developments will occur in other powerful and important countries that have strong internal cultures: China, India, Mexico, maybe Russia, maybe Brazil, and some Middle Eastern countries.

Other smaller, weaker countries and areas present more mixed outlooks. In Africa there are frequent internal divisions over culture and ethnicity, few examples of successful economies (certainly not on the East Asian scale), and no countries of potential superpower status. So, while there will always be an "African" way (actually a great diversity of ways) of doing things, the capacity of African states to selectively resist or filter outside influences in the same way Japan has will be limited.

Similarly with Latin America. Here we have some large, important countries (Argentina, Brazil, Chile, Colombia, Mexico, Peru, Venezuela) but none of them as big or important as China or Japan. Here we also have Western cultures but often thinly institutionalized and representing a particular historical fragment of the West. While there will continue to be uniquely Latin American ways of doing things (Rousseauian, top-down democracy rather than Lockean, for example), at this stage Latin America seems to have thrown in its lot with the West and has little current interest in advancing its own, distinct theory of development.

An especially interesting test case is the Islamic world. Here we have perhaps the clearest instance of a separate, distinct, indigenous theory of development, grounded in Islam—and a certain aggressiveness in some cases in asserting it. But there are widely divergent conceptions of what an Islamic state or developmental model should look like (Iran versus Saudi Arabia, for instance) as well as great differences over the issues within countries (Iraq). In addition, we do not think of the Islamic models as being especially successful (unlike Japan), nor are there any current or future great powers among the Islamic states able to *enforce* their views on these issues. Moreover, even previously do-it-our-way nations like Iran recognize they cannot entirely go it alone in the world and are increasingly reaching out for trade and other purposes to other nations and culture areas, which almost certainly implies greater compromise with their own indigenous principles. Even the Islamic world is thus liable to end up as a mix with a variety of overlapping influences.

There will, therefore, always be distinct cultural differences among nations and particular, often culturally conditioned ways of doing things. Development and change will follow global patterns, but at the same time these changes will continue to be filtered through the prism of local or indigenous practices and institutions. Some countries and culture areas will doubtless continue to assert these differences and even advance their own "models" more strongly than others. But our prognosis is not so much for each global region to take up its own distinctive, culturally conditioned "model" of development but for varying mixes, blends, and overlaps of indigenous and global—e.g., caste or ethnic associations that function like interest groups, extended families and patronage networks that function like political parties, and so on. Meanwhile, at present and as far into the future as we can see, global currents appear to be ascendant, breaking down old cultural behaviors and stereotypes and often giving them radically new forms, insisting on universally recognized norms in such areas as trade and commerce, and combining and fusing with indigenous traditions in many confused, crosscutting ways.

This chapter and these comments also carry important policy implications. First, they suggest that future global leaders, if they are to succeed, must be adept at maneuvering both in their own societies and in the broader global one. Second, our study has implications for economic development. We now *know* fairly well the formula for economic development (open markets, an emphasis on education and infrastructure, legal guarantees, an honest and efficient state) but within that well-nigh universal formula there can still be some variation in state size and the public-private balance.

Third, our study has major implications for democracy and human rights. Democracy and human rights are no longer just Western creations but now enjoy near-universal popularity and legitimacy. It is no longer so easy for a regime to blatantly run roughshod over human rights; moreover, there is an emerging body of democratic human rights laws and sanctions which few countries can afford to ignore. But at the same time there are still numerous culturally conditioned differences over the precise meanings of *human rights, democracy,* and other broad terms, as well as different priorities in different culture areas among the several categories of rights. Democracy is the preferred political formula but within that system there is room for distinct, culturally shaped types and forms of democracy. Policy makers will still need to be both cognizant of these global trends toward democracy and free markets, and at the same time sensitive to the local, indigenous ways of organizing and running their political and economic systems.

NOTES

1. For an overview, see Howard J. Wiarda, *Introduction to Comparative Politics* (Belmont, CA: Wadsworth, 1993); also Irene Gendzier, *Managing Political Change: Social Scientists and the Third World* (Boulder, CO: Westview Press, 1985).

2. For some representative literature, see C. E. Black, *The Dynamics of Modernization* (New York: Harper and Row, 1968); and Robert J. Heilbroner, *The Great Ascent* (New York: Harper and Row, 1963).

3. The critical literature includes Sidney Verba, "Some Dilemmas in Comparative Research," *World Politics* 20 (Oct. 1967): 111–27; Mark Kesselman, "Order or Movement: The Literature of Political Development as Ideology," *World Politics* 26 (Oct. 1973): 139–53; Philip H. Melanson and Lauriston R. King, "Theory in Comparative Politics: A Critical Appraisal," *Comparative Political Studies* 4 (July 1971): 205–31; Geoffrey K. Roberts, "Comparative Politics Today," *Government and Opposition* 7 (Winter 1972): 38–55; Sally A. Merrill, "On the Logic of Comparative

Analysis," *Comparative Political Studies* 3 (Jan. 1971): 489–500; Robert T. Holt and John E. Turner, "Crises and Sequences in Collective Theory Development," *American Political Science Review* 69 (Sept. 1975): 979–95; R. S. Milne, "The Overdeveloped Study of Political Development," *Canadian Journal of Political Science* 5 (Dec. 1972): 560–68; Philip Coulter, "Political Development and Political Theory: Methodological and Technological Problems in the Comparative Study of Political Development," *Polity* 5 (Winter 1972): 233–42; and Ignacy Sachs, "The Logic of Development," *International Social Science Journal* 24, no. 1 (1972): 37–43.

4. Howard J. Wiarda, *Ethnocentrism in Foreign Policy: Can We Understand the Third World?* (Washington, DC: American Enterprise Institute for Public Policy Research, 1983); and A. H. Somjee, *Parallels and Actuals of Political Development* (London: Macmillan, 1986).

5. Samuel P. Huntington, *The Third Wave: Democratization in the Late Twentieth Century* (Norman: University of Oklahoma Press, 1991).

6. Francis Fukuyama, "The End of History," *The National Interest* 16 (Summer 1989).

7. For detailed treatment and assessments of these alternative models, see Howard J. Wiarda (ed.) *New Directions in Comparative Politics* (Boulder, CO: Westview Press, 1992); and, by the same author, *Introduction to Comparative Politics* (Fort Worth: Harcourt Brace, 2000).

8. David Sanger, "Playing the Trade Card: U.S. Is Exporting Its Free Market Values through Global Commercial Agreements," *New York Times*, February 17, 1997, 1.

9. Samuel P. Huntington, *The Clash of Civilizations and the Remaking of World Order* (New York: Simon & Schuster, 1996).

7

Political Development
Revisited—and
Its Alternatives

L ooking back over the last half century in comparative politics, one is
struck by how closely the dominant concepts and models in the sub-
field are related to actual events and the broad currents sweeping the
world of nations, to attitudinal and mood changes in the United States itself (where most, but by no means all, of the comparative politics literature is written), and to intellectual and methodological innovations
within the larger field of political science. It is not that comparative politics exactly follows the headlines (although it may do that, too), with their
almost daily and often fickle flights from one dramatic crisis or area to the
next; but it does tend to reflect the long-term trends in public and/or elite
opinion that help determine which geographic area or issue or which intellectual approach will receive priority. Such fluctuations in our attention
and priorities have also affected the field of comparative politics and its
changing emphases, research priorities, and conceptual perspectives over
the last several decades.

The purpose of this chapter is to trace in broad terms these developments and interrelations over the last fifty years, to show how comparative politics developed from its earlier formal-legal approach to a more
vigorous and genuinely *comparative* discipline, to review the rise and decline of the political development school, to assess the approaches that
supplanted it, to analyze the diversity of the field, and to assess its current
condition—most particularly, the comeback of the political development
approach. We seek to show how the field interacts with and is part of a
larger national, international, cultural, and political environment. As
United States (and maybe global) politics and policy making have become

increasingly divided, fragmented, and in disarray in recent years, comparative politics has seemed to follow these same trends. We ask whether this new ferment, diversity, and fragmentation is a pathetic sign of the state of the field or is it an indication of intellectual health and vigor?[1]

THE ASCENDANCE AND DECLINE
OF THE POLITICAL DEVELOPMENT APPROACH

Traditional comparative politics, we have seen, is universally thought to have been a parochial, formal-legal, and institutional approach. That is the charge, recall, that Roy Macridis, in his tub-thumping, flagwaving, and influential little book, raised against it in 1955.[2] Macridis, representing a new generation of comparativists, who were more influenced by the recent approaches in political science than by the older approach that had been heavily dominated by lawyers and legalists, wanted a comparative politics that concentrated on informal and dynamic aspects: public opinion, interest groups, political parties, process variables, input functions, decision making, and the processes of change. His proposed approach, which soon became the prevailing one, corresponded to other factors that we might call global. For our purposes, the most important of these were the Cold War in the 1940s and 1950s, the sudden emergence onto the world scene in the late 1950s and early 1960s of a host of new nations, and then the end of the Cold War in 1988–1991 and its aftermath.

By the 1960s, the political development approach, as outlined in chapter 3, had become dominant in comparative politics. Some scholars continued to labor in the vineyards of the more traditional institutional approaches and others continued to write first-rate books on Western Europe. But the developing nations were clearly where the action was, particularly so with the election of John F. Kennedy; the creation of the Peace Corps, whose mood was carried over into the effort to bring development to the emerging nations and not just to analyze it; the growth of the U.S. Agency for International Development, which sought to put development into concrete, realizable programs; the Cuban revolution; and the Alliance for Progress, which focused attention on Latin America and the Third World and reemphasized powerfully the Cold War considerations that undergirded the U.S. government's development efforts.[3]

Considerable variation existed among the leading writers and approaches to development—differences that have blurred in our memories over the years or that have been purposely subordinated to the goal of lumping all "developmentalists" together for the sake of more easily criticizing or discrediting them. There are the disciplinary differences: the more deterministic approaches of economists such as Rostow[4] and Heilbroner;[5]

the more sociological, but in their own ways also deterministic, approaches of Deutsch,[6] Levy,[7] and Lipset;[8] and to my mind the more sophisticated and subtle, political science approaches of Pye,[9] Apter,[10] Weiner,[11] and others.

What is required first of all, therefore, is a considerable sorting out of earlier development theory. There is a rich body of literature that deserves to be read and considered anew. It is not a monolithic "school" and its principal advocates were not all of one mind on the issues.

Rather, right from the beginning there were nuances, diverse views and approaches, and a wealth of scholarship and ideas. Far too often the developmentalist approach has been dismissed with a blanket condemnation and its principal figures have been lumped together in one amorphous category. While certain of its intellectual thrusts seem in retrospect to have taken us in some wrong directions, this early focus on the developing areas yielded rich insights and a vast literature. It is a shame that this literature is not paid more attention than it is at present because the information contained therein is still a marvelously fertile ground for the student of developing nations.

The second, related, factor to remember is that the criticisms of development theory (analyzed in the next section) were not necessarily applicable to the whole body of thought and research, but only some of its (I would say) most vulnerable published work. The criticisms have been most strongly leveled against the writings of Almond, Lipset, and Rostow, who are taken as the paradigm writers in the developmentalist school. But it seems to me their works are, in some of their particulars, the easiest works to set up as strawmen and to criticize; further, I am not sure that their writings are representative of the entire development approach. The field is far too rich and diverse for us to dismiss an entire body of work because a few of its leading writers went too far, said some things that can easily be criticized, or exaggerated the universality of their model.

CRITICISMS OF DEVELOPMENTALISM

During most of the 1960s, as we have already seen, the developmentalist approach was dominant in comparative politics. Although other comparative politics scholars continued to write from other points of view, the political development paradigm became the prevailing one. It appeared at the time to be the most intellectually stimulating approach; that was where the money was, in the form of research grants and opportunities; that was where the most prestigious publication outlets were (*World Politics*, Princeton University Press); and, since political development had also been accepted as a major goal of U.S. foreign policy toward the Third World, that was where the opportunity to influence policy was.

But eventually criticisms of developmentalism began to come from diverse directions;[12] their cumulative impact was devastating—so much so that today's graduate students are acquainted with the criticisms, but hardly know the original literature, no longer read it, and tend to treat it (if at all) dismissively in their seminars in one brief session. Before moving on to a discussion of the newer, alternative approaches in comparative politics, a brief review of these criticisms is necessary.

First, the political development literature is criticized as biased and ethnocentric, derived from the Western experience of development, and of doubtful utility in non-Western areas and only limited utility in the incompletely Western ones. For societies lacking the sociopolitical precepts of Greece, Rome, and the Bible, without the same experience of feudalism and capitalism, and not having experienced the cultural history of the West, the argument is, the Western developmental model is either irrelevant or of meager usefulness.[13] That is what helped give rise, as seen in the last chapter, to the indigenous theories of development and change.

Second, the timing, sequences, and stages of development in the West may not be replicable in today's developing nations. With regard to timing, countries whose development is occurring in the twenty-first century face different kinds of problems from those whose development began in the nineteenth century; with regards to sequences, it appears, for example, that rapid urbanization may precede industrialization in the Third World whereas in the West just the reverse occurred. With regard to stages, whereas capitalism followed feudalism in the West, the two have most often been fused in the Third World. Almost all our interpretations based on the Western developmental experience—the political behavior of the middle class, the presumed professionalization of the armed forces, the demographic transition, and other key indicators of modernity or the transition thereto—need to be rethought and reconceptualized when applied to the Third World.[14]

Third, the international context of today's developing nations is quite different from that of the earlier developers. That factor was ignored in most of the development literature, which in the 1960s focused almost exclusively on domestic social and political change. Few countries have ever developed autonomously and in complete isolation; but it is plain that today's developing nations are caught up in a much more complex web of dependency relations, international conflicts, alliances and blocs, transnational activities, and the "world culture" (Lucian Pye's term) of tastes, communications, and travel than was the case of the early modernizers. These international connections need to be factored into any theory of political development.[15]

Fourth, the critics argue, the political development literature often misrepresented the role of traditional or indigenous institutions. In much of the literature traditional institutions were treated as anachronisms, fated earlier to fade away or be destroyed as modernization went forward. But in most modernizing nations, we have seen, traditional institutions have proved durable, flexible, and long lasting, adapting to change rather than being overwhelmed by it. They have served as filters of modernization and even as agents of modernization. A much more complex understanding of the relation between tradition and modernity is required.[16]

Fifth, in the developing nations, the sense is strong that the early political development literature created unrealistic goals for these societies. Almond's original functional categories seemed reasonable and nonethnocentric enough, but in actual practice "rule adjudication" was taken to mean an independent judiciary; political parties and an independent legislature were required; and countries that lacked these institutions were too often labeled "dysfunctional." Hence, the development literature frequently skewed, biased, and distorted the political processes working in the developing nations, forced them to create Potemkin village-like institutions (such as political parties) that looked wonderful on paper but proved to be ephemeral, or that obliged them to destroy traditional institutions that might have been viable within their own contexts.[17]

Sixth, the political development perspective has been criticized as causing harm to the developing nations. The focus on political development sometimes had the effect of helping to destroy or undermine indigenous institutions within the Third World that were often quite viable, provided some cultural or social "cement," and might have helped these nations bridge some transitions to modern forms. Instead, because many intellectuals and government leaders within the Third World themselves accepted the developmental perspective and the seemingly inevitable progression from "traditional" to "modern," these traditional institutions (family and patronage networks, clan and tribal groups, and so forth) had to be eliminated in order for development to occur. The result in many developing nations is the worst of all possible worlds: their traditional institutions have been largely destroyed; their modern ones remain inchoate and incompletely established; and they are, hence, left not with development but with a political and institutional vacuum.[18]

These and other criticisms of the literature of political development were powerful and quite devastating. By the end of the 1960s not only were these criticisms widespread, but other factors were operating as well. So many case studies of developing nations had now been written in which the developmental approach was found wanting that the basic assumptions of the approach were questioned. Samuel Huntington weighed in with his powerful critique, suggesting that socioeconomic modernization and political development, instead of going forward hand-in-hand, might well work at cross purposes. The Vietnam War provided another blow since in some quarters the war was presented as what a misplaced emphasis on political development can get the United States into, with disastrous consequences; in addition, some of the early writers on development were viewed as supporters of the war or even its "architects."

A generational factor was also involved: the political development literature was largely fashioned by one generation of scholars and by the end of the 1960s there was a new generation of scholars who were critical of their predecessors or who simply had other ideas. And that gets us to the final reason for political development's demise: fad and fancy. Political development was in part a product of the early 1960s, of the enthusiasms of the Kennedy administration, the Alliance for Progress, and "the Peace Corps mood of the times" (Almond's phrase). But by the late 1960s both that spirit and that body of literature had largely come and gone. By then other approaches had come into existence: dependency theory, corporatism, political-economy, bureaucratic-authoritarianism, revived Marxism, and others.

NEW AND ALTERNATIVE MODELS

The decline in the consensus undergirding the political development approach brought a variety of other approaches to the fore. In part, these changes were related to logical and methodological flaws within the development approach; in part, they were due to broader changes in the larger society. One is tempted to draw parallels between the decline of the development approach in the 1960s and the decline of the societal and foreign policy consensus in the United States and to relate the rise of multiple approaches in comparative politics in the decade that followed to increasing division, even fragmentation, in the society as a whole.

The decline of the older consensus in the field need not necessarily be lamented. There *are* major problems with the political development approach, and the new approaches, for the most part, made a contribution to the discipline. However, as with development theory, there are "vulgar" as well as more sophisticated versions of most of these newer approaches which need to be sorted out. Furthermore, many of these newer approaches had run their courses by the 1980s and had begun to be supplanted. What is taking their place? What is the future of the field? Here we review dependency theory, bureaucratic authoritarianism, political economy, state-society relations, rational choice theory, and the new institutionalism. The corporatist and indigenous approaches have already been discussed.

DEPENDENCY THEORY

Dependency theory arose in the late 1960s and achieved considerable popularity especially—but not exclusively—among students on the left of the political spectrum. Indeed, that was part of the problem with dependency theory right from the beginning: it was not clear if dependency was a new and serious approach in comparative politics or simply a political position.

Dependency theory arose from two major sources, which helps explain the confusion as to what it represented. One strong influence was Marxian thought. Marxism was a small minority current in comparative politics, and for a long time it had wielded no influence because of the overwhelming dominance of the political development approach. However, with the U.S. military intervention in the Dominican Republic in 1965, the Vietnam War, and the student protests of 1969–1970, the Marxian approach began to attract more attention. It focused on the contradictions between U.S. interests in the developing nations and the interests of the developing nations themselves, as well as on the contradictions and conflicts within these countries. In contrast, development theory had stressed the peaceful, evolutionary process of modernization and the harmony between U.S. interests and those of the developing nations. An early statement of the dependency alternative and approach to development was André Gunder Frank's book *Capitalism and Underdevelopment in Latin America*, a book published at the height of the Vietnam War protests in 1969 and one that, while often misrepresenting facts and making erroneous interpretations, nevertheless set forth a strong Marxian position.[19]

The other influence in dependency theory came from non-Leninists who were interested in the politics of the developing nations but were critical of what the prevailing development theory had left out of its analysis. For example, development theory had not paid any attention to international actors in the field of development; it had not examined the role of international markets and capitalism in the processes of development; it had not addressed class conflicts or exploitation; and it had not talked about the role of multinational corporations. All of these are fundamental elements in the development process, or the lack thereof, and yet none of them was analyzed in the prevailing development theory. Hence, it was agreed that developmentalism must pay attention to these "dependency" factors—factors that make one country's development dependent on another's—and must analyze a country's or group of countries' "relations of dependency" to the industrialized world. These suggestions came often from writers in the Third World who had experienced such dependency—from social-democrats and independent Marxists (but not necessarily from Leninists). The most prominent book written from this perspective was Enzo Faletto and Fernando Henrique Cardoso's *Dependency and Development in Latin America*.[20]

The dependency approach was considered a serious corrective to the developmentalist approach. Instead of modernization in the industrialized world and the developing world going forward smoothly and inexorably as developmentalism posited, dependency theory posited that development in the Third World was *dependent* on development in the already developed nations. Unfortunately, these two processes may not always be in harmony. Indeed, the First World may exploit the Third World, may intervene militarily there, may allow its multinationals to drain Third World resources or attempt to control the government, and so on. In its more radical expressions dependency theory suggested that development in the First World came at the *expense* of development in the Third World, that First World development often exploited the Third World, and that Third World development was incompatible with First World development and could only take place when the First World and its capitalistic economic system was destroyed.

Dependency theory, therefore, is not one single school of thought. Rather, it presents a range of perspectives, some of which are neutral and scholarly and others of which are more partisan and ideological. Admittedly, the developing nations *are* often dependent on the developed ones, international market forces largely controlled by the developed world *do* sometimes retard Third World development, multinationals and other international actors *do* at times muck around in the internal affairs of other nations, and the United States has and *does* sometimes intervene militarily and in other ways in the Third World. One can pragmatically acknowledge these facts of life, however, as some writers about dependency have done,[21] without necessarily becoming an ideologue of *dependencia*. In other words, one can recognize that there are various relations of dependency in the world without elevating that into a single-causal explanation of all the world's ills or using dependency analysis simply to blame some scapegoat (the United States, multinationals, capitalism) for Third World underdevelopment.

More sophisticated dependency analysts have focused not just on the role of outside actors in internal Third World development but also on the interrelations between such outside influences and local elites within the developing nations.[22] For example, one might research the interactions of U.S. sugar companies, mining interests, or manufacturing concerns with local, Third World entrepreneurial groups, elites, and the government—all involved in an interlocking relationship. Or one might focus on the relations between the armed forces of a developing country who may happen to be in power, the civilian technicians who help manage the national accounts for them, and U.S. or other international investors who need a "favor" (tax breaks, import licenses, export permits) from these same groups. In short, dependency relations are often complex, including not just the actions of foreign concerns or governments but involving local actors and institutions as well.

The contributions and limitations of the dependency approach are several. First, the contributions: it obliges us to focus on international actors in ways that development theory did not; it emphasizes world market and financial trends over which the developing countries often have little control; it talks of multinational corporations and other transnational actors who sometimes have considerable influence in developing nations' internal affairs; it brings in U.S. intervention, the role of capitalism, and other international factors about which earlier development theory had little to say. These are all important subjects with which comparative politics ought to be concerned. These dependency factors ought to be seen as a supplement to earlier comparative politics work, however—elements that the earlier work left out—rather than as a complete, all-encompassing approach, which is claiming too much for it.

Next, the limitations: First, dependency theory takes the blame for underdevelopment off the shoulders of the developing nations and places it squarely on those of the already industrialized nations—surely an overstatement but a factor that helps explain dependency theory's popularity especially in the developing nations. Second, and related, dependency analysis tends especially to blame the United States for the world's ills— again a vast overstatement. Third, the dependency approach is not evenhanded: It tends to concentrate on countries that are dependent on the United States but to ignore countries that were dependencies of the former Soviet Union—for example, the former Soviet satellites in Eastern Europe, as well as Afghanistan, Ethiopia, Vietnam, Cuba, and Nicaragua.[23] And fourth, also related to these others, dependency theory has generally had a leftist, Marxist, or Marxist-Leninist thrust, which means that its utility as a tool of scholarly analysis is often limited by this heavy ideological baggage, especially now that Marxism has been so strongly discredited.

In serious, scholarly hands dependency theory can be a useful tool of analysis because out there in the "real world" there are genuine relations of dependence. But in less sophisticated hands dependency analysis has a tendency to spin off in ideological directions in order to criticize the United States.

BUREAUCRATIC-AUTHORITARIANISM

Bureaucratic-authoritarianism, or B-A as it is popularly called, is a second approach that grew out of the late 1960s' disillusionment with developmentalism. Developmentalism, recall, had posited a close correlation

between economic growth and political democracy; as economic development went forward, democracy was supposed to follow. But in Africa, Asia,
and especially Latin America in the late 1960s, one democratic regime after
another gave way to military-authoritarianism. The B-A approach was
launched as an effort to try to explain what went wrong, why development
produced not democracy but breakdown and authoritarianism.

As with the other approaches previously mentioned, the B-A approach
can be utilized at several different levels. First, there is the issue of *bureaucratic*-authoritarianism. This term was used to indicate that military
takeovers, especially in Latin America, are no longer just simple one-man
affairs but have become far more involved than that. In the new, more
complex societies of Latin America, coups d'état are usually carried out by
the military acting as an institution, not just by a single disgruntled officer.
Or, typically, they are carried out with both civilian and military participation, again implying a more complex process and structure than an old-
fashioned military takeover. For these reasons, the military regimes in such
more developed and complex countries as Argentina, Brazil, and Chile required analysis at a complexity level commensurate with their own level
of modernization—hence, the term *bureaucratic-authoritarianism*.

At a second level B-A as articulated by its foremost exponent,
Guillermo O'Donnell, was closely related to, and an extension of, dependency theory.[24] According to O'Donnell the dependent position of the
Latin American economies placed strong limitations on the region's capacity for economic growth. As economic expansion declines, discontent
grows, especially in the lower classes. The ruling elites, including the military, then have a clear-cut choice: they can curtail growth or they can continue to pursue it by squeezing and repressing the workers, through wage
reductions, belt tightenings, and general austerity. When faced with this
stark choice, the elites have consistently opted to continue growth. To control the lower classes, however, they have required a repressive military
regime in power. Hence, the alliance of civilian elites and the military
brought together in a concerted effort—bureaucratic-authoritarianism—
to control the lower classes.

At a third level B-A became a rather vague and unclear economic determinist argument that spun off into a kind of vague Marxism. In O'Donnell's argument B-A was produced by what he called the "crisis of import
substitution." He argued that Latin America's industrialization, which
took the form of manufacturing local products as substitutes for those historically imported from abroad (hence, the term "import substitution"),
had reached a point of saturation and could not be continued. Why this
was so was not clear in O'Donnell's writing. In any case, the crisis of import substitution led to a slowing of economic growth, rising discontent
from below, and, hence, a rash of military takeovers. In a subsequent for-

mulation, however, O'Donnell used the selfsame crisis of import substitution to account for the transitions away from authoritarianism and toward democracy in the region. Now, you can't have it both ways: either the crisis of import substitution leads to authoritarianism or it leads to democracy, but it cannot lead to both. In addition to containing this logical flaw, O'Donnell's analysis was now subjected to a polite but devastating critique that suggested powerfully that his economics were all wrong.[25]

The general assessment of most scholars at this stage is, first, that the focus on *bureaucratic*-authoritarianism is correct—these *are* (or were) more complex bureaucratic regimes than the one-man dictatorships of the past. Second, there *was* a mainly *political* crisis in Latin America in the 1960s that threatened the elites and middle class, who then turned to the military to protect their interests. But third, O'Donnell's attempt to impose a Marxian overlay and an economic determinist interpretation on these events will not stand up. Here the analysis is flawed both economically and politically. So let us accept the B-A phenomenon, and let us also accept that there was a sociopolitical crisis in the 1960s that threatened the governing elites and made them turn to the military for allies; but let us reject the economic determinist elements, which do not do the B-A theory any good and, in fact, detract from its usefulness.

In the meantime, most of the B-A regimes of record have since undergone transitions to democracy, a phenomenon that has by now rendered the B-A theory mostly of historical interest. These transitions to democracy and the literature they have spawned are taken up in chapter 8.

POLITICAL ECONOMY

Political economy (PE) as an approach has been around for a long time. Aristotle and Machiavelli, though known as political scientists, also paid close attention to economic factors; Adam Smith and Karl Marx, though economists, similarly saw the importance of political variables. The PE approach, essentially, tries to scale the barriers of our academic disciplines by focusing on both politics *and* economics, and particularly on the interrelations between the two.

A number of influences came together in the 1960s and 1970s that help explain the revival and rising importance of the PE approach. The first and simplest was the discrediting and decline of developmentalism as the main and, to that point, predominant alternative. As developmentalism appeared less attractive, the political economy approach gained more adherents.

The second reason was the rising influence of Marxism, for a time, in American college and university faculties during the period of the Vietnam War, the student protests of the late 1960s and 1970s, and Watergate.

Quite a number of the radical student leaders subsequently went on to earn advanced degrees and then to join university faculties. Whereas in the 1950s and 1960s Marxism had been such a minority strain in American colleges that its influence was about nil (despite the effort by some politicians to get political mileage out of investigating it), by the 1970s the Marxist influence had become considerable and was still rising.[26]

A third reason for PE's growing influence was simply pragmatic: the increasing importance of international economic issues in world affairs. With the rise of Japan to economic great-power status, the emergence of the other East Asian economic "tigers" (Hong Kong, Singapore, South Korea, Taiwan), the great oil crises of the 1970s, the increasing influences of multinational corporations, and the rising sense of the United States's own dependence on imports and trade, economic issues became more and more important. In some circles it seemed that economic issues were surpassing political, diplomatic, and strategic ones as the most important in international politics. As economic issues gained greater salience, students of comparative politics began to focus more on international economic interrelationships and on domestic economic policy making than they had previously.[27]

One other factor helped explain this new focus on political economy: professional economists seemed to be doing a poor job of analyzing these new international economic or political-economic forces. Whereas before, comparative politics scholars had largely concentrated on studying political institutions and had left economics to the economists, now, for the questions in which they were interested—the role of multinationals, the political implications of international trade, changing power relationships derived from economic rather than military might, the political role of labor unions, the international debt issue, central planning versus privatization, and many others—political scientists often discovered that they would have to do their own economic studies. Either there was no literature on these subjects from economists or else what there was proved less than useful for the purposes of comparative political analysis. So specialists in comparative politics began reschooling themselves in economics and employing the tools of economics to probe the issues they wished to explore.

The result was a flurry of studies by comparative politics scholars of various political economy issues. Some scholars studied the incidence and impact of labor strikes in such turbulent countries in the 1970s as Italy, France, and Spain.[28] Others examined comparative policy making in such areas as housing, health care, and social security.[29] Still others focused on the role of multinational corporations or—making the link to dependency theory—on the impact of changing terms of trade on different political systems.[30] The comparative study of socialist and capitalist economic performance was another main topic, as were government planning, the transition from socialism to capitalism (as in Eastern Europe and the former Soviet Union), and issues of privatization of state-run enterprises.[31] During the 1970s and 1980s a veritable flood of PE studies emerged in books and scholarly journals, and PE developed as one of the major approaches in comparative politics.[32]

The political economy approach is clearly related to some of the other approaches already studied. The explanation for bureaucratic-authoritarianism, for example, could be seen as a type of PE analysis, as could corporatism with its focus on socioeconomic interests and their relations to the state. Dependency analysis, too, is clearly a type of PE approach applied particularly to the developing nations. Political development and political economy are also related (economic growth is the motor force that helps drive political development); but because PE has often had a Marxist thrust and political development was conceived in part as a non- or even anticommunist approach, these two have often been at loggerheads.

That fact leads to our final comments about PE. On many university campuses and in quite a bit of the writing on the subject, political economy has often been identified with a Marxist approach. To the extent that is true, an ideological component and political bias have been added to PE analysis. Because many scholars do not find that particular ideology congenial or even useful, PE as an approach has suffered as a result of its association with Marxism.

But such an automatic connection between Marxism and PE need not necessarily be made, and in fact some of the most sophisticated work in comparative politics is now being done using a political economy approach. The argument is similar to that regarding dependency theory: both PE and dependency theory can take Marxist or non-Marxist directions. Shorn of its ideological blinders, PE (like dependency analysis) can be an exceedingly useful approach; but to the degree it takes on political overtones from either the Right or the Left, PE (again like dependency) becomes mainly a political instrument rather than a serious tool of analysis.

STATE-SOCIETY RELATIONS

State-society relations as an approach is in some senses akin to corporatism. That is, it is not meant as a full and complete approach but as a useful complement to some other approaches. At the same time, it is not as ideological or as controversial as some of the other approaches analyzed here. Rather, the state-society approach has been largely accepted within the field without giving rise to the academic brawls that some other of the other approaches do.

The state-society approach deals with the interrelations between the central state and the various units (classes, interest groups) that make up a society. This approach arose from the fact that in much of social science, both Marxian and non-Marxian, the state was not viewed as a major actor. In Marxian theory the state is seen as part of the "superstructure," which is determined by economic and class factors. In non-Marxian interest group theory the state is a kind of neutral referee that umpires the interest group struggle but is not itself a major player. In both of these conceptions the state is a minor player, relegated to the position of being a "dependent variable"—dependent, that is, on the classes or the interest group struggle.

By contrast, the state-society relations focus seeks to "bring the state back in" as a major factor.[33] The state is seen as being a key regulator of interest group activity, of political parties, and of the policy-making process. The state is now viewed as being an "independent variable," or at least mostly so. The state is pictured as having varying degrees of autonomy from the society and as having a dynamic relationship with that society. Of course, it must be noted that many scholars of comparative politics have always believed the state or government to be an independent variable. They did not need to be reminded of the state's autonomy and independence in making some decisions, and they argue it is mostly economists and sociologists—neither of whom have been prone to acknowledge the independence of political variables—who have been responsible for the *revival* of the state-society approach, when in fact political scientists have always recognized a leading role for the state.

Actually, several different approaches to studying state-society relations have been advanced. In Latin American studies, state-society relations have been usefully employed as a way of emphasizing the strong, integrative, often organic role of the state in that area, along with such strong societal groups as the Catholic Church and the armed forces, as well as the changing balance between them over time.[34] In other developing nations the state-society focus has been used to study the relations of the clan, the tribe, or the caste association with the state, and the ways these relations have changed as the society moved from a feudal-agrarian-rural type to an urban-industrial type.[35] In still other scholars' hands the state-society focus has been used to study revolutions, the disjunctions that may exist between state policy and societal needs or demands, and the processes of policy making—or breakdown—in the modern state.[36] In these areas the state-society focus often overlaps with the corporatism approach.

Most of us in comparative politics rather like the state-society approach. It claims neither too little nor too much. It is an important focus, but it does not presume to be a complete or all-encompassing one. At the same time, the state-society focus emphasizes political factors as well as social and economic ones. It provides important links to such other approaches as corporatism, dependency, and development. Thus the state-society approach has been largely accepted in the field without great fanfare.

RATIONAL CHOICE THEORY

Rational choice theory in comparative politics grew largely out of voting behavior studies in the United States and from the effort to explain politics in scientific, "rational" terms. This quest, in turn, derived from economics and the attempts by political scientists to fashion a universal science of politics that would parallel economics' focus on rational, self-interested actors operating to their own best advantage. Rational choice theory sought similarly to develop a model of political behavior based on rational or self-interest and to use that as a means to explain individual electoral choice, congressional voting behavior, interest group politics, and governmental decision making.

Most scholars of comparative politics have so far been skeptical of the rational choice approach. They argue that politics is too complex and multilayered to be amenable to any single causal explanation. They say that even if rational choice theory explains *some* aspects of *American* political behavior, the world is too diverse for *all* the world's political systems to be explained in this way. Comparativists, as we have seen, have given a lot of attention to the study of political culture; but if cultures vary widely from area to area, how can one single explanatory model apply to all of them? In addition, rational choice theory assumes a certain stability of institutions; but in many countries instability, revolution, and chaos characterize the political system, so how can a theory based on stable institutions be of use? The result is that in no other field of political science has the rational choice approach been less favorably welcomed than in comparative politics. To the extent comparative politics remains oriented toward interpretation and toward explaining cultural differences, it has not been very receptive to the rational choice approach.

More recently the advocates of rational choice, acknowledging the importance of cultural differences, have tried to advance the argument a step further toward their approach. They may grant that different cultures and different political systems have different institutions, different values and beliefs, and different ways of expressing political preferences—for example, through a coup d'état rather than through the ballot box. Even granting these differences, however, the rational choice approach suggests that such diverse events as coups d'état in Latin America, ethnic conflict in the former Yugoslavia, decision making on economic policy in a variety of culture areas, and interest group competition can all be explained using this method. Combining both cultural and rational choice approaches, it is suggested that one *first* become immersed in the culture so as to thoroughly understand the context and uniqueness of the case, and *then* use rational choice to give the study a greater scientific and comparative basis.

Comparative politics and rational choice theory have often been at loggerheads in the past, and even today there are major differences between them. But there are also trends toward compromise in the two positions and ways to accommodate rational choice to comparative politics and vice versa. Both the tensions as well as the efforts to fuse the two will likely continue into the future.[37]

THE NEW INSTITUTIONALISM

In recent years students of comparative politics have rediscovered institutions. The new approach is called "the new institutionalism," but no one is quite sure what is new about this focus or if it is mainly a case of "old wine in new bottles." After all, fifty years ago institutions were the main and virtually only thing that comparative politics studied—that is, before the attack on the institutional approach in the 1950s launched by Macridis. Have we now come full circle, or is there really something new about the "new institutionalism"?

Several influences are operating in this rediscovery of institutions by comparative politics. One is that, after nearly half a century of studying political process, political behavior, and decision making, political scientists have rediscovered that institutions and institutional arrangements—legislatures, judiciaries, executives, bureaucracies, elections, federalism, local government, and so forth—really do count. Second, the renewed emphasis on institutions reflects the resurgence in comparative politics in the study of developed nations—North America, Europe, Japan—where political institutions tend to have greater importance. Third, the new institutionalism is related to the focus on state-society relations, corporatism, and rational choice theory, all of which emphasize institutions. Fourth, the transition to democracy in so many areas of the globe in the 1980s and 1990s has meant a renewed emphasis on getting the institutions right. And fifth, there are numerous interesting issues out there—welfare reform, centralism versus local government, presidentialism or parliamentarism, many others—in which institutions play a key role.

Many of the issues and concepts in the new institutionalism were first raised in quite sophisticated form by the "old" institutionalists. Students of comparative politics may wish to go back and read some of these post–World War II classics, such as the books by Maurice Duverger, Herman Finer, Carl Friedrich, or Karl Loewenstein.[38] There one will find extensive treatments of such subjects as constitutionalism, federalism, elections and political parties, parliamentarian versus presidentialism, as well as state regulation of political party and interest group activity (now usually discussed under the heading of corporatism or state-society relations). Most of what is called the "new institutionalism" is there, in these classic but now obviously dated accounts.

At the same time, the new institutionalism has brought some new issues into prominence.[39] These include constitution writing in countries that have recently returned to democracy; issues of centralism versus decentralization in the carrying out of public policy; the role of congresses and courts; the importance of elections, political parties, and parliaments in deciding public policy; the role of bureaucracies in implementing change; and the impact of laws and legal systems on politics and public policy. In addition, the new institutionalism has also meant in some research the emphasis on economic or "structural" matters (political economy) in determining policy outcomes.

There is both old and new in the "new institutionalism." The renewed emphasis on institutions also brings us back to the points made in the introduction and to our model of the political process. That is, in studying comparative politics, it is important to study both structure and process, both institutions and more informal aspects of policy making, and to weave both of these as well as other factors into a coherent, unified view of comparative political systems.

POLITICAL DEVELOPMENT REVISITED

In the early 1960s, when the last major experiment in democratic development in Africa and Latin America took place, great hope existed that democracy, development, peace, and security would be closely correlated. Intellectual justification for such correlations was provided in the developmental literature of that period, and most particularly in the writings of Walt Rostow, Seymour Lipset, and Karl Deutsch. Using his famous aeronautical metaphor of the several stages of "take-off," Rostow demonstrated, based on the European and U.S. experiences, that as countries developed economically, they also tended to become middle class, pluralistic, democratic, stable, socially just, and peaceful.[40] Lipset and Deutsch in pathbreaking articles[41] at that time showed the close correlations between literacy, social mobilization, economic development, and democracy. An obvious foreign policy lesson also followed from this research: if we can help developing countries to be more literate, affluent, and middle class, they will consequently become more democratic and more able to resist the appeals of extremism.

But correlations do not imply causal relationships, and in Latin America as well as other developing areas in the 1960s a wave of military coups swept the civilian democratic governments out of power. Greater literacy and social mobilization did not lead to democracy and stability but to upheaval and, ultimately, under military governments, to repression. The middle class proved to be not a bastion of stability and democracy but deeply divided and very conservative, often goading the military to seize power from the civilian democrats. By the late 1970s, none of the correlations was correlating very well. Democracy had collapsed; seventeen of the twenty Latin American nations were under military-authoritarian rule; the developmentalist literature was rejected and in shambles; and the new, postdevelopmentalist interpretations (dependency theory, corporatism, Marxist explanations, bureaucratic-authoritarianism) were in their heyday.[42]

But since the late 1970s nations as diverse as South Korea, Indonesia, the Philippines, Brazil, and Mexico have embarked on some remarkable transitions to democracy. In Latin America the figures of a decade ago have been reversed: twenty of the twenty-one countries and over 90 percent of the population are either democracies or en route to democracy. This transition in so short a time has been nothing less than amazing. Not only has this given rise to a whole new approach and body of literature ("Transitions to Democracy," see chapter 8) in comparative politics, but it may also force us to reconsider and maybe resurrect the older, discredited developmentalist approach.

The democratization, development, and modernization that have occurred in many Third World areas in the last decade force us to reassess the Lipsetonian and Rostowian theories in the light of these new circumstances. Lipset, Rostow, and the entire development approach and school were thoroughly discredited in the 1960s and 1970s—and often for good reasons. They and their followers, as well as many U.S. government officials, tended to portray development in ways that proved far too simple, implying a causative relationship between development and democracy that did not exist, basing their theories of development too heavily on the Western and European experiences, and thus helping to misdirect development theory and the policies that flowed from it.

But we now need to consider that while Lipset and Rostow (and their schools) were wrong in the short run, they may still prove to have been correct in the long run. That is, although there is no necessary, automatic, or causative connection between development and democracy (as some of the early developmentalists themselves pointed out), there are tendencies, correlations, and long-term relationships that cannot be denied. It is, therefore, necessary, I believe, to begin a serious reexamination of the earlier development literature to see what should be saved and what jettisoned. There may well be more worth saving than we might have guessed a decade or two ago.[43]

For example, we learned in the 1960s that there was no necessary correlation between democracy and the size of the middle class; indeed, in many countries it was the middle class that plotted to overthrow democracy. But in the 1980s it was the middle class that led the opposition to military authoritarianism in many countries and became convinced, having tried other models, that democracy is much to be preferred. Employing other indexes yields further correlations. The armed forces in much of the Third World have become both more professionalized and more in favor of democracy than they were in the 1960s. Literacy has increased and so has the spread of democracy. Despite the depressing circumstances of many Third World countries today, economic development over four decades has gone forward and in many others the desire for democracy has increased. The correlations that did not correlate in the 1960s now seem to be correlating very well indeed.[44]

These strong correlations raise the possibility that, while Lipset, Rostow, and others were too optimistic and, hence, mistaken in the short run, in the longer term their correlations (and the predictions that went with them) may yet prove to be correct. One decade (the 1960s) was simply too short a period for the developmentalist propositions to be tested adequately. The more sophisticated theories of development recognized that these were long-term processes, that the transitional period was almost by definition likely to be chaotic, and that there were bound to be many setbacks on the road to development. By the year 2006, with a longer period of observation and considerable experience with development, the correlations and assumptions of the development approach have begun to look better and better.

The fact is that the base for democracy in Latin America as well as in Asia, and maybe in Africa and the Middle East, is bigger, more solid, and more promising now than it was in the 1960s. The middle class is larger; there is far greater affluence; bureaucracies are better trained and more experienced with development; the associational and institutional life has grown and become better consolidated; literacy is far higher; vast social changes have led to pluralism; the military is better educated and more professional; per capita income is higher; more persons are better educated; the private sectors are larger and more active; and so on.[45] These changes may well mean that the current openings to democracy in much of the developing world may prove more than just cyclical, popular now but subject when the next crisis comes to a new round of coups. When civil society was weak and the process of development just beginning for many countries in the 1960s, an authoritarian regime might have seemed to some a possible alternative; but as development and pluralism have gone forward, a new wave of military coups seems increasingly unlikely, at least in the better institutionalized and more economically advanced countries. It may be that the developmental changes in the last three decades have been sufficiently profound that not only can many countries look forward to a more stable future based on development and democracy, but the processes involved force us to reconsider the main premises of the development approach in a newer and more positive light.

IMPLICATIONS FOR THE FUTURE

The criticisms and subsequent decline of the developmentalist approach, the prevailing approach in comparative politics in the 1960s, paved the way for the rise of a variety of other approaches. Dependency theory, corporatism, bureaucratic-authoritarianism, political economy, state-society relations, rational choice, the new institutionalism, and indigenous theories of change all emerged as alternatives to the developmentalist approach, or as amendments to it. Like developmentalism, the new approaches had their chief spokespersons, their apostles, their groupies, or camp followers in the form of graduate students and young faculty, their theories, and their "bibles"—literature that was considered fundamental. The appearance of all these new approaches set comparative politics to debating as to which approach or combination of approaches was the best and most useful.

We have also seen that within each approach there are "vulgar" as well as more sophisticated versions. Some of the approaches, or at least some practitioners of them, are weighted down with heavy ideological or political baggage. Students should be careful in sorting through these various approaches as well as the separate schools of thought within them. If one wants to practice partisan or ideological politics, so be it. But if one wants to be accepted as a serious scholar and to have one's research and writings considered seriously, then one should try to be as balanced and neutral as possible, and not try to disguise partisanship or ideological pleading in the language of some academic approach. In short, the approaches outlined in this chapter are useful tools of analysis, but one must be exceedingly careful in utilizing them.

Among the older schools of formal-legalism and developmentalism, the appearance of all these new approaches was upsetting. The new approaches challenged familiar ideas—and persons—in the field. Most scholars of comparative politics, however, welcomed these approaches as adding diversity and new insights to scholarship. The new approaches, even though they upset the unity of the field and deprived it of a single set of "truths," were not at all a sign of sickness, but rather a sign of the health of comparative politics.

Comparative politics now has a variety of approaches from which a scholar can choose. The next set of tasks, it seems to most of us who practice in the field, is to refine these approaches, separate their vulgar and dogmatic components from their more useful ones, and carry out our individual or collaborative studies employing those approaches that pragmatically offer us the greatest usefulness. At the same time, comparative politics needs to begin building bridges among these several "islands of theory." Many scholars would like to see, for example, theoretical connections made between corporatism and dependency theory, or between developmentalism and state-society relations, as well as other combinations. When such connections are made, comparative politics can begin rebuilding a more unified theory for the field as a whole as contrasted with the present situation of a considerable variety of sometimes overlapping, sometimes competing approaches.

NOTES

1. For an earlier discussion of some of these themes, see Howard J. Wiarda, ed., *New Directions in Comparative Politics*, 3rd ed. (Boulder, CO: Westview Press, 2002).

2. Roy Macridis, *The Study of Comparative Government* (New York: Random House, 1955).

3. For some reflections on the "political culture" in which political development studies began and flourished, see Gabriel A. Almond, *Political Development: Essays in Heuristic Theory* (Boston: Little Brown, 1970), Introduction.

4. Walt W. Rostow, *The Stages of Economic Growth: A Non-Communist Manifesto* (Cambridge, UK: Cambridge University Press, 1960).

5. Robert Heilbroner, *The Great Ascent* (New York: Harper & Row, 1963).

6. Karl W. Deutsch, "Social Mobilization and Political Development," *American Political Science Review* 55 (September 1961): 493–514.

7. Marion Levy, *The Structure of Society* (Princeton, NJ: Princeton University Press, 1952).

8. Seymour Martin Lipset, "Some Social Requisites of Democracy: Economic Development and Political Legitimacy," *American Political Science Review* 53 (March 1959): 69–105.

9. Lucian W. Pye, *Aspects of Political Development* (Boston: Little, Brown, 1966).

10. David E. Apter, *The Politics of Modernization* (Chicago: University of Chicago Press, 1965).

11. Myron Weiner, ed., *Modernization* (New York: Basic Books, 1966).

12. See, among others, Sidney Verba, "Some Dilemmas in Comparative Research," *World Politics* 20 (October 1967): 111–27; Mark Kesselman, "Order or Movement: The Literature of Political Development as Ideology," *World Politics* 26 (October 1973): 139–53; Philip H. Melanson and Lauriston R. King, "Theory in Comparative Politics: A Critical Appraisal," *Comparative Political Studies* 4 (July 1971): 205–31; Geoffrey K. Roberts, "Comparative Politics Today," *Government and*

Opposition 7 (Winter 1972): 38–55; Sally A. Merrill, "On the Logic of Comparative Analysis," *Comparative Political Studies* 3 (January 1971): 489–500; Robert T. Holt and John E. Turner, "Crises and Sequences in Collective Theory Development," *American Political Science Review* 69 (September 1975): 979–95; R. S. Milne, "The Overdeveloped Study of Political Development," *Canadian Journal of Political Science* 5 (December 1972): 560–68; Philip Coulter, "Political Development and Political Theory: Methodological and Technological Problems in the Comparative Study of Political Development," *Policy* 5 (Winter 1972): 233–42; Geoffrey K. Roberts, "Comparative Politics Today," *Government and Opposition* 7 (Winter 1972): 38–55; and Ignany Sachs, "The Logic of Development," *International Social Science Journal* 24, no. 1 (1972): 37–43.

13. A. H. Somjee, *Parallels and Actuals of Political Development* (London: Macmillan, 1986); Howard J. Wiarda, *Ethnocentrism in Foreign Policy: Can We Understand the Third World?* (Washington, DC: American Enterprise Institute for Public Policy Research, 1985).

14. Reinhard Bendix, "Tradition and Modernity Reconsidered," *Comparative Studies in Society and History* 9 (April 1967): 292–346; S. N. Eisenstadt, *Post-Traditional Societies* (New York: Norton, 1974).

15. Fernando Enrique Cardoso and Enzo Faletto, *Dependency and Development in Latin America* (Berkeley: University of California Press, 1978).

16. See Lloyd I. Rudolph and Susanne Hoeber Rudolph, *The Modernity of Tradition* (Chicago: University of Chicago Press, 1967).

17. Somjee, *Parallels*; Wiarda, *Ethnocentrism*.

18. Huntington, *Political Order*; A. H. Somjee, *Political Capacity in Developing Societies* (New York: St. Martin's Press, 1982).

19. André Gunder Frank, *Capitalism and Underdevelopment in Latin America* (New York: Monthly Review Press, 1969).

20. Enzo Faletto and Fernando Henrique Cardoso, *Dependency and Development in Latin America* (Berkeley: University of California Press, 1979).

21. See Theodore H. Moran, *Multinational Corporations and the Politics of Dependence* (Cambridge, MA: Harvard University, Center for International Affairs, 1975); or Howard J. Wiarda, *Dictatorship, Development, and Disintegration: Politics and Social Change in the Dominican Republic* (Ann Arbor, MI: Xerox University Microfilms Monograph Series, 1975), chapters 11–12.

22. Peter Evans, *Dependent Development: The Alliance of Multinational, State, and Local Capital in Brazil* (Princeton, NJ: Princeton University Press, 1979).

23. An exception is Robert Packenham, "Capitalist Dependency and Socialist Dependency: The Case of Cuba," paper presented at Annual Meeting of the American Political Science Association, New Orleans, LA, August 29–September 1, 1985.

24. Guillermo O'Donnell, *Modernization and Bureaucratic-Authoritarianism: Studies in South American Politics* (Berkeley: Institute of International Studies, University of California, 1973).

25. David Collier, ed., *The New Authoritarianism in Latin America* (Princeton, NJ: Princeton University Press, 1979).

26. Fun reading, though by no means a complete picture, is Roger Kimball, *Tenured Radicals: How Politics Has Corrupted Our Higher Education* (New York: HarperCollins, 1990).

27. Some of the better literature includes Stephen D. Cohen, *The Making of United States International Economic Policy* (New York: Praeger, 1988); and Joan

Edelman Spero, *The Politics of International Economic Relations* (New York: St. Martin's Press, 1977).

28. Douglas Hibbs, "On the Political Economy of Long-Run Trends in Strike Activity," *British Journal of Political Science* 8 (1978): 153–75.

29. Arnold Heidenheimer et al., *Comparative Public Policy: Policies of Social Choice in Europe and America* (New York: St. Martin's Press, 1975).

30. Stimulating reading is Mancur Olson, *The Rise and Decline of Nations* (New Haven, CT: Yale University Press, 1982).

31. Raymond Vernon, *The Promise of Privatization* (New York: Council on Foreign Relations, 1988).

32. The leading journal of political economy studies is *International Organization*.

33. Theda Skocpol, ed., *Bringing the State Back In* (Cambridge, UK: Cambridge University Press, 1985).

34. Alfred Stepan, *State and Society: Peru in Comparative Perspective* (Princeton, NJ: Princeton University Press, 1978).

35. Joel Migdal, *Strong Societies and Weak States* (Princeton, NJ: Princeton University Press, 1986).

36. Theda Skocpol, *States and Social Revolutions: A Comparative Study of France, Russia, and China* (New York: Cambridge University Press, 1979).

37. George Tsebelis, *Nested Games: Rational Choice in Comparative Politics* (Berkeley: University of California Press, 1990); Robert Bates and Barry Weingast, "A New Comparative Politics: Integrating Rational Choice and Interpretivist Perspectives," Center for International Affairs, Harvard University, Working Papers No. 95-3, April 1995.

38. Maurice Duverger, *Political Parties* (London: Methuen, 1954); Herman Finer, *The Theory and Practice of Modern Government* (London: Methuen, 1961); Carl Friedrich, *Constitutional Government and Democracy* (Boston: Ginn, 1950); and Karl Loewenstein, *Political Power and the Government Process* (Chicago: University of Chicago Press, 1957).

39. James G. March and Johan P. Olsen, *Rediscovering Institutions* (New York: Free Press, 1989); Sven Steinmo et al., *Structuring Politics: Historical Institutionalism in Comparative Analysis* (Cambridge, UK: Cambridge University Press, 1992).

40. Rostow, *Stages of Economic Growth*.

41. Lipset, "Some Social Requisites"; Deutsch, "Social Mobilization."

42. Howard J. Wiarda, ed., *The Continuing Struggle for Democracy in Latin America* (Boulder, CO: Westview Press, 1979).

43. Ronald Scheman, ed., *The Alliance for Progress–Twenty-five Years After* (New York: Praeger, 1988); also Howard J. Wiarda, "Development and Democracy: Their Relationship to Peace and Security," paper presented at the Conference on Regional Cooperation for Development and the Peaceful Settlement of Disputes in Latin America, International Peace Academy and the Peruvian Center for International Studies, Lima, October 27–29, 1986. But see also, for an earlier statement, Apter, *Politics of Modernization*.

44. The outstanding study is Diamond, Linz, and Lipset, *Democracy in Developing Countries*.

45. The most substantial report is *Democracy in Latin America: The Promise and The Challenge*. Special Report No. 158 (Washington, DC: Bureau of Public Affairs, U.S. Department of State, 1987).

III

HOT ISSUES

8

Comparative Democracy and Democratization

INTRODUCTION

Along with the disintegration of the Soviet Union, the collapse of the Warsaw Pact, and the fall of the Berlin Wall and the reunification of Germany, the transition to democracy in many areas of the world has to be one of the most significant transformations of the late twentieth century—maybe even more important than the others mentioned. Beginning in the mid-1970s in Southern Europe (Greece, Portugal, Spain), then continuing through Latin America, spreading to much of East Asia, then exploding in Russia and Eastern Europe, and now encompassing parts of Africa and the Middle East, the march of democracy has become a global phenomenon. Sweeping away authoritarian-corporatist regimes on the right and Marxist-Leninist regimes on the left, democracy has now become the only form of government that enjoys universal legitimacy—even if not yet universal adherence (Afghanistan, Iraq, China, others).

The themes and events of these democratic transitions make for exciting reading: the collapse of such long-time dictatorships as those of Franco in Spain and Salazar in Portugal, the sweeping away of human-rights-abusing authorities in Latin America, the profound transformations first economically and then politically in East Asia, the "Moscow Spring" and an earlier, happier vision of Boris Yeltsin holding back the forces of renewed Russian repression, and the early stirrings of civil society, democratic elections, and more participatory politics in sub-Saharan Africa and the Middle East. All of this is high drama with major issues and major stakes involved, relating to both the domestic politics and international relations of all these areas and the world.

The issues are important conceptually as well as for the individual countries and areas affected. How do we explain and account for these democratic transitions? What factors are involved? Are there common patterns that these countries and regions have gone through? Have these new democratic regimes been institutionalized and consolidated? Is the process of democratization now complete or might it still be reversible? Do these countries and areas all mean the same thing by "democracy," and what accounts for, and what are the implications of, the differences? Are these democratic transitions due mainly to domestic forces or international pressure, or to some combination of both? Does the triumph of democracy worldwide mean that the great systems debate of the twentieth century (Marxism, authoritarianism, and democracy) is over? Has history, as Francis Fukiyama famously argues, ended? These larger issues lie at the heart of the theoretical considerations and the region-by-region analysis in this chapter and give it both underlying unity as well as the "meat" for stimulating class discussions.

ISSUES AND COMPLEXITIES

Three major types of political systems, we have said, have been dominant in the world in modern times. There are: *liberal democracy*, prevalent in Western Europe, North America, the members of the British Commonwealth (Australia, New Zealand, etc.), and some countries of Asia and Latin America; *Marxism-Leninism* or *Communism*, present in the former Soviet Union, Eastern Europe, China, as well as North Korea, Vietnam, Cambodia, and Cuba; and *authoritarianism*, often found in the developing or Third World nations. The division of the world's political systems into these three major types not only dominated the textbooks most often used in political science courses but seemed to reflect quite realistically the main political systems by which the countries of the world were actually governed.

But in the 1970s and 1980s this three-part division of the world's political systems began to change rapidly. First, beginning in the mid-1970s in Southern Europe (Greece, Portugal, Spain), then spreading to Latin America, East Asia, and some parts of the Middle East and Africa, a large number of formerly authoritarian regimes began to transition to democracy. Second, during the period 1989–1991, the Berlin Wall came tumbling down, the Iron Curtain fell, the Soviet Union collapsed along with a host of Marxist-Leninist regimes in Eastern Europe, and a large number of formerly communist countries began their transitions to democracy. The results: a *huge* decrease in the number of both authoritarian and communist countries in the world, a large increase in the number of democracies, and the seeming triumph of democracy and the democratic idea as the sole legitimate type of political system.[1] See table 8.1.

The apparent triumph of democracy globally, however, does not end the debate; history, contrary to author Francis Fukuyama, has not "ended."[2] For one thing, there are quite a number of both authoritarian and Marxist-Leninist regimes still in power, most of which show few signs of disappearing quickly. For another, some authoritarian regimes have instigated just enough "democracy" to earn the world's approval (and quality for international loans) but not enough to be considered genuinely democratic. More than that, many of the recent transitions to democracy have been partial, incomplete, leaving mixed or hybrid forms of democracy and authoritarianism in a variety of combinations. But most importantly for the purposes of this book, we have discovered that many countries have different meanings and understandings of democracy, accord it different priorities, and have quite different philosophical underpinnings and institutional arrangements of democracy.

We need to explore the distinct philosophical, cultural, and political-theoretical bases of democracy in different countries. For example, we know that the philosophical and theoretical bases of American liberal democracy lie in the English writer John Locke, and then the writings and statements of Thomas Jefferson, James Madison, Abraham Lincoln, Woodrow Wilson, Franklin Roosevelt, and others. But what of Continental Europe, where the basis of understanding derives more from French philosopher Jean-Jacques Rousseau and not Locke, and where the meanings of such terms as liberalism, pluralism, and democracy are often quite different from in the United States? Or how about Russia, a country that was, and remains, only partly Westernized, and still seems to want sometimes to follow its own path; or Latin America which long represented a less-developed, sixteenth-century (scholastic, semifeudal, counter-reformationary) fragment of the West carried over by Columbus and the Spanish and Portuguese *conquistadores* to the New World.

Table 8.1.   Freedom Ratings 1974–2004

Year under Review	Free Countries	Partly Free Countries	Not Free Countries
1974	41 (27%)	48 (32%)	63 (41%)
1984	53 (32%)	59 (35%)	55 (33%)
1994	76 (40%)	61 (32%)	54 (28%)
2004	89 (46%)	54 (28%)	49 (26%)

Source: Freedom House, "Freedom in the World, 2005."

The issues are compounded when we move to non-Western areas. To what degree is Asian democracy based on historic Confucian theories, or is Asia now in a "post-Confucian" era? What is the influence of Islam in shaping Middle Eastern democracy (or in explaining the lack thereof); how does one explain the persistence and apparent viability of democracy in India, despite the country's underdevelopment and wrenching social and economic problems; and to what extent does Africa have an indigenous or homegrown tradition of institutions that can serve as an African theory of democracy?

The main question we wrestle with here is whether democracy is one and universal (similar to the U.S. model) or particular and based on very different local, regional, and cultural traditions and institutions. Is democracy everywhere the same or fated to become that way as countries become wealthier and better integrated into globalization, or is it present in *various* forms depending on distinct philosophical and political backgrounds, as well as having different levels of socioeconomic and political development? Americans tend to believe that ours is the best and virtually only form of democracy, but in fact there are many and diverse kinds and foundations of democracy. We need to understand and appreciate these diverse forms not only for a better comprehension of different countries and traditions but also because many policy considerations having to do with democracy and human rights hinge on whether democracy is everywhere the same or has distinct meanings and priorities in different countries.

This analysis takes a generally middle and consensus position on these issues. It recognizes realistically that different countries and cultures mean different things by, and have different institutions and philosophical foundations of, democracy. At the same time it argues that there are certain minimum core requirements, such as competitive elections and basic freedoms, that all countries must have if they wish to be called "democracies." Just because some tyrant calls himself or his system "democratic" or runs rigged elections is no reason why we cannot use more objective standards to verify the truthfulness of his statement. A sense of cultural difference is useful as a way of enabling us to understand diverse countries and cultures, but we also need to recognize a means to gauge whether a country is in fact democratic or not.

But then we take the argument a step farther, suggesting that globalization is now forcing *all* countries to come closer to a U.S. or Western understanding and practice of democracy, whether that is in accord with their own philosophical traditions or not. Modern communications (television, satellites, VCRs, etc.) are bringing the advantages of modern Western life, including democracy, into every living room. Democracy and human rights Western-style are now becoming the norm to which all countries aspire—or to which they must conform if they want international aid and investment. The issue is fraught with controversy because it suggests a single standard of democracy—largely defined in U.S. or Western terms and with U.S.-style institutional arrangements—which many countries, because of both lack of development *and* distinct political traditions, are not able to fully live up to. Or, which may ultimately destabilize them either because the standard is set too high or because their philosophical traditions are very different from our own.

It is a major issue which speaks to questions of ethnocentrism (whether we can understand other societies on their own terms rather than only through our own rose-colored lenses), whether democracy and the U.S. model are truly universal, and what effects globalization is now having on these controversies.

THE MEANING(S) OF DEMOCRACY

Democracy was born and even "invented" in the West by the ancient Greeks, and it has long been closely associated with the development and institutional arrangements of the West, including both Western Europe and its extension in North America. Democracy, including its several definitions, seems to be a good "fit" in the West, tied in as it is to Western culture and institutions. Implied in the above is the notion that democracy is more than a "mere" set of institutional arrangements (regular elections and the like) which presumably any country could imitate with minimal constitutional engineering. Instead, democracy is embedded in the culture of the West, the society, the economy, indeed as a whole way of life. And that makes it much harder to imitate or to reproduce in societies where the history, culture, society, and economic relationships are much different from our own.

It is hard, for example, to conceive of democracy apart from the Renaissance, the Enlightenment, and the sense of individualism, pragmatism, tolerance, and rationality to which these movements gave rise. Similarly, at the social level, it seems difficult to conceive of democracy without some degree of equality or egalitarianism among the citizens. For countries that are deeply riven by class, racial, and ethnic divisions; where the gaps between rich and poor are so large as to be all but insurmountable; or where the upper classes do not believe those below them on the social or racial scale are even fully human, it seems hard to imagine that some formula of institutional tinkering (creating political parties or parliaments, for example) could magically transform them into democracies. Democracy, in short, is usually correlated to some degree with a sense of egalitarianism and the rise of a strong middle class.

In the economic sphere, although the correlations are not always one-to-one, most of us understand that at some level freedom in the economic

marketplace is related to freedom in the political sphere, and that at some
points in history the rise of economic individualism, entrepreneurship,
and capitalism was and is related to the rise of political democracy. It is
possible to have democracy without free and open markets and a system
of individual private property rights, but in general a system of strong
rights including property rights has served to limit oppressive government and bolster democracy. Parallel comments apply in broad terms to
the role of religion; without ascribing any particular good or bad points to
any one religion, it seems likely that the rise of a sense of individual
choice and responsibility in the polling booth is related to the rise of individual choice and responsibility in matters of religion, to the breakup of
the theocracy and absolutist religion of the Middle Ages, and to the
growth of religious pluralism and tolerance that accompanied the rise of
political pluralism.

There are other features that need to be emphasized to have a full understanding of democracy and its meaning, as well as its possibilities in
diverse societies. For example, can you have democracy in countries
where the levels of literacy or of socioeconomic development are so low
that people have no sense of national politics or are so preoccupied with
scratching out a daily subsistence that they have no time, energy, or interest in politics? Can you have democracy in countries where the gaps
between rich and poor are so vast that the notions of egalitarianism or
one-person, one-vote are a laugh, a farce? Can you have democracy where
the armed forces or religious authorities intervene in the political process
to nullify the popular vote?

In other words, democracy is more than a narrow and particular
arrangement of political institutions. It is embedded in the history, culture, sociology, economics, philosophy, and even religion of the West, and
it may be inseparable from these. The question, therefore, becomes: if democracy is tied up closely with the history, culture, sociology, economics,
and religion of the West, how can the non-West, which lacks this same history and traditions, be expected to develop Western-style democracy?
How can societies that never experienced the Renaissance, the Enlightenment, the Protestant Reformation, the Industrial Revolution, and the rise
of capitalism, the British (1689) or French (1789) revolutions, or the scientific revolution ushered in with Galileo and Newton, develop the same
kind of democracy as that of the West? If all these ingredients and more
were necessary for the growth of Western-style democracy, then surely
countries that lacked these ingredients will have to enact their own systems of democracy, with their own institutional forms, and their own ingredients and priorities.

Democracy, therefore, is not an export commodity; it cannot be transplanted like a rose bush from one cultural flowerbed to another. Rather,

it requires careful nurturing and adjustment to local conditions. One country can offer to another specific institutional suggestions about electoral systems or parliamentarian versus presidentialism. But without similar historical, cultural, social, economic, or even religious conditions and philosophical traditions, democracy—and even the possibility of establishing democracy—is going to vary considerably from country to country. Democracy may take many different forms in many different societies—or, as in Haiti, Somalia, or Kosovo, it may be unlikely to flourish at all. We need to recognize these differences realistically, even while we continue to hope and work for democracy's spread.

And yet the familiar definitions of democracy, almost all of which derive from the Western experience, tend to ignore and take for granted the special historical, cultural, and socioeconomic conditions on which Western democracy rests, even while assuming that the West's institutional arrangements can be easily transferred to the non-West. Take Joseph Schumpeter's classic definition of democracy as a system "for arriving at political decisions in which individuals acquire the power to decide by means of a competitive struggle for the people's vote."[3] Similarly, Harvard professor Samuel P. Huntington in his pathbreaking study of democratization echoes Schumpeter in his emphasis on competitive elections as *the* essence of democracy.[4] Now, of course, competitive and democratic elections are absolutely necessary in any acceptable definition of democracy; the question is: are they the only thing? And particularly with regard to the Third World, note that the Schumpeter-Huntington definition makes no mention of the particular cultural, social, and other conditions enumerated earlier which make democracy possible. In other words, their definition *takes for granted* the broader Western tradition that allows democracy to flourish and within which a narrow, *institutional* definition of democracy can be offered. But, of course, in the non-West these conditions cannot be taken for granted and, therefore, a broader, ampler definition of democracy would be necessary in order for it to apply there.

In the political science literature the best-known definition of democracy, or what he calls polyarchy, has been offered by Robert Dahl.[5] Dahl's definition amplifies that of Schumpeter and Huntington but is very much in the same tradition and, again, closely tied to the Western experience. Dahl's definition emphasizes these aspects: (1) organized contestation through regular, free, and fair elections; (2) the right of virtually all adults to vote and contest for office; and (3) freedom of press, assembly, speech, petition, and organization. Note Dahl, like Schumpeter and Huntington, also emphasizes competitive elections in his first two criteria, but then expands the definition in his third criterion to include the

[handwritten: also = attitude + behaviour]
[handwritten: but = tolerance, civility etc.]

classic, nineteenth-century, Western freedoms. Later, Dahl expanded his definition to include the following eight criteria:

1. Freedom to form and join organizations.
2. Freedom of expression.
3. The right to vote.
4. Eligibility for public office.
5. The right of political leaders to compete for support.
6. Alternative sources of information.
7. Free and fair elections.
8. Institutions for making government policies depend on votes and other expressions of preference.

No one could quarrel with this broadened definition; the problem is it still does not go far enough. It is still tied, in its emphasis on elections and political rights, exclusively to the Western tradition, takes for granted once again the broader Western social and cultural tradition that makes democracy possible, and completely ignores non-Western ideas of democracy or the broader non-Western traditions whose ingredients are very different from the West's and that cannot be simply taken for granted.

Let us illustrate these points with some examples from the Third World. For instance, we all understand that democracy has not often been successful in the Islamic countries of the Middle East. *One* solution to this problem—a not-very-feasible one, in my view—is to tell these countries to forget about Islam, develop their economies and societies, and become just like us. Of course, that will not work; countries cannot change that fast, dump their entire history and culture, and take up something new; and certainly we cannot tell other countries to forget their religious, cultural, and historical roots any more than they can tell us to do so.

Another solution, therefore, even while encouraging the social, economic, and political development of the Middle East, is to emphasize in the Koran, the Shariah, and the writings and interpretations of the Muslim clergy those passages that justify consultation between ruler and ruled, the rights of communities and individuals, the necessity of pluralism, honest and responsible government, and democratic representation. These criteria may not fully satisfy Dahl's and others' strict and narrow *Western* definition of democracy but they certainly provide a start *and* they have the added advantage of being rooted in Islamic culture, history, and beliefs. Such an approach has the benefit of enabling democracy to grow and develop genuinely indigenous roots rather than—as all too often happens—the United States *imposing* its definition of democracy on the region and expecting the Islamic countries to imitate our institutions even though their entire culture, history, and tradition are quite different from our own.

Or, let us take the case of Africa, another area with only a brief and often unhappy experience with democracy. The solution on the part of the outside powers has usually been to insist on free and democratic elections in the Western fashion—or to wring our hands and ignore Africa altogether. Once again, we all understand Africa's problems: poverty, underdevelopment, disease, the legacy of the colonial powers, ethnic and tribal conflict that sometimes tears society apart, violence, crime, and war. And we all recognize that social, economic, and political development is absolutely necessary if Africa is ever to achieve stable democracy. But is the way to achieve that to impose prematurely American- or European-style elections on countries that have no such democratic traditions? Wouldn't it be better to build up the African economies and societies, and at the same time—similar to our suggestions for the Islamic countries—try to find in African *indigenous* culture and society institutions and practices that help mitigate authoritarianism, provide for consultation and pluralism, strengthen homegrown civil society and help deliver sorely needed public policy goods and services. Meanwhile, we should strive to nudge these countries, if not toward full democracy, at least in a more democratic direction. Such a needed strategy will obviously not bring instant democracy (impossible to achieve in any case) but it does have the advantage of *providing* a grassroots and indigenous base on which democratic practices can be nurtured and brought along.

The issue here is not just a hair-splitting definitional one of what we mean by democracy. Nor is it purely a problem of development: the idea that if we provide enough foreign aid, economic growth, and investment, the Islamic world, China, Africa, and other global regions will eventually come to have a democracy that looks just like our own. Nor is it even sensitivity to cultures and societies other than our own, although we should be in favor of that idea, too. Rather the issue is purely pragmatic: if we are committed to democracy and believe that it is the best system extant for the diverse countries of the world, then what is the best way to achieve that goal? Is it by running roughshod over local institutions, cultures, history, and ways of doing things by imposing our own narrow and particular, U.S.- and Western-based definition and institutions of democracy on countries and areas where the traditions are different and American-style democracy doesn't fit very well? Or is it by slowly nurturing homegrown, local, and indigenous institutions, which are often the only viable ones in the society, and carefully cultivating them—meanwhile encouraging economic, social, and political growth—until they have a chance to flower into full-fledged democracy?[6] The latter course, since it implies vast cultural, social, and political change, may require two or three generations—fifty to a hundred years—but it has a much better chance of success than the current policy, which is to try to impose a pure, American-style democracy (is our own democracy really so pure?) on countries that are ill-prepared for it and whose history and traditions are quite different from our own.

These examples illustrate that the debate over democracy, its meaning(s), and the best way(s) to achieve it is not limited to academic or intellectual debates. Rather, a large part of post–Cold War foreign policy has a democracy component to it; indeed some scholars and policy activists believe democracy should be *the* basis of U.S. foreign policy. In addition, there are now offices of democracy enhancement in the Department of State, the U.S. Agency for International Development (AID), and even the Defense Department and the Central Intelligence Agency (CIA). Outside the government but often overlapping with it, the Carter Center in Atlanta, the National Endowment for Democracy (NED), the International Foundation for Electoral Systems (IFES), the National Democratic Institute (NDI), and the International Republican Institute (IRI)—*all* have democracy promotion at the forefront of their agendas. Democracy is, therefore, not just an abstract, theoretical, or philosophical issue anymore; instead, it has become a major policy issue with large interest groups, money, government, bureaucracies, and international actors and personnel involved.

Slop

X **DISTINCT PHILOSOPHICAL/CULTURAL BASES OF DEMOCRACY**

Democracy does not have the same meaning, the same socioeconomic, cultural, or institutional base, or the same priority in every society. We believe that there *are* certain universals that democracy requires—regular and competitive elections, political freedoms, periodic changeovers of governments—but at the same time the precise meaning, implications, importance, and cultural understandings of democracy may vary considerably.

In this section we present a summary statement of the main traditions of democracy (or its absence). At least five agendas or scenarios seem to be operating here:

1. Variations among well-established, democratic regimes; for example, the different types of democracies prevailing in the United States and the countries of Western Europe.
2. Partial rejection of the Western democratic model by a significant proportion of the population, but without a viable alternative—e.g., Russia.
3. Aspiration for Western-style democracy but a weak socioeconomic base and alternative traditions that may compete with democracy—India, Latin America.

4. Successful economic modernizers but now with Western cultural traditions and political systems that are experimenting with their own hybrid forms of democracy for the first time—East Asia.
5. Non-Western countries that have neither the socioeconomic base for democracy nor a clear and strong democratic historical and cultural tradition—the Islamic countries, sub-Saharan Africa.

Let us take up each of these variations—and the areas or countries represented—in turn.

We begin with American democracy, not only because that is the system most of us know best but also because the United States is often presented as a model for the rest of the world to emulate, a "beacon on a hill" as early Americans expressed it. However, the American experience is so particular, so unique ("American exceptionalism") that it is difficult to believe our democratic traditions and experiments could be readily exported to the rest of a world that lacks such traditions. First, we are a frontier country that could absorb expanding population as well as discontents; second, we are a product of religious nonconformity and eventually religious and political pluralism; third, we are the offshoot of the Enlightenment, the English legal tradition, and the notion of government as a contract between rulers and *consenting* citizens. Fourth, we have multiculturalism and a diversity of racial and ethnic strains; fifth, although we had slavery in the South, we had no real feudal tradition to overcome to achieve modernity; sixth, we are a country of enormous wealth, natural resources, and favorable climate and geography. Seventh, we have a homegrown (and constantly evolving) system of checks and balances and representative government; eighth, as de Tocqueville demonstrated, we have this incredible infrastructure of grassroots civil society; ninth, we are the world's richest and most powerful nation. There are undoubtedly many other unique features of American democracy and doubtless each of us could readily come up with our own list of special characteristics; but the point is how fortunate, and at the same time how distinctive, the United States is. Can any of these beneficial features or combination of features really be replicated in other societies? Is it, therefore, realistic to expect that U.S. democracy can be transplanted in other countries that lack all our advantages?

When we "cross the pond" to Europe, we confront another set of issues. First, Europe is itself exceedingly diverse with many forms and types of democracy in the several countries, so when we speak of "the Western model" of democracy, we will need to know if it is British, French, German, Scandinavian, Italian, Spanish, Polish, or another form of democracy we are speaking of. Second, and as implied above, the European experience by itself is the best evidence for the main argument of this book: that democracy can take a great variety of forms depending on time, history, level of socio-economic development, religion, political culture, institutional arrangements, and international forces.

Third, the historic tradition and even meaning of European democracy has evolved over time and is very different from that of the United States. For one thing, Europeans mean something quite different by "liberalism" than do Americans: for Europeans liberalism generally means a nineteenth-century, laissez-faire, economic philosophy akin to that of former Conservative British prime minister Margaret Thatcher and with a very small political following that is on the right of the political spectrum, not the left. For another, "socialism" or social democracy in Western Europe carries far fewer negative connotations than it does in the United States; the European political and party spectrum is thus generally wider and more to the left than is that of the United States. Following from the above, when Europeans nowadays speak of democracy, they have in mind modern "social democracy" (the welfare state) and no longer just the formal institutions of democracy. Increasingly, Eastern and Central Europe now aspire to this same social-democratic model.

But as we proceed even farther east in Europe, the issue of democracy becomes more and more problematic. Indeed, some have argued that with the end of the Cold War the old Iron Curtain separating East from West in Europe has been erased; a new divide—somewhat farther east and corresponding closely to the borders of the Russia-dominated Commonwealth of Independent States (CIS)—has emerged separating the democratic (including the newly democratic states of Eastern Europe) from the non- or only partially democratic. Russia is our primary case, although such newly independent and still only partially democratic states as Belarus, the Ukraine, Moldova, Chechnya, Georgia, Armenia, Azerbaijan, Turkmenistan, Uzbekistan, Kazakhstan, Kyrgyzstan, and Tajikistan might also be included.

Russia is an especially interesting case for us because, while it is a (mainly) Western country, it has long been isolated from the West and from its key intellectual currents, including the Renaissance, the Enlightenment, and democracy itself. Russia has at present a democratically elected government and many of the classic freedoms, but it also has a powerful antidemocratic and authoritarian tradition, whether that appears in Czarist or Marxist-Leninist versions. Moreover, Russia's attitudes toward the West and Western democracy are ambivalent: At some times (and among some people) it admires the West and wants to imitate and be accepted by it; at other times, it seeks to reject the West and to elevate and laud its own Slavic institutions, sometimes seeking in the Slavic tradition a model of development and governance of its own. Unlike some of the other areas with which we shall be dealing, Russia does not have its own or Slavic theory of democracy; but Russia is still sufficiently ambivalent about the West and democracy, and with such powerful authoritarian traditions, that it merits separate treatment in this book.

When we analyze Latin America, we find—and the statement may be surprising—many similarities to Russia. Both are poor, underdeveloped areas, although with many dynamic sectors. Both have long traditions of authoritarianism. In both cases authoritarianism in the political sphere was undergirded by a body of religious beliefs and institutions—in the Orthodox Church in Russia and the medieval Roman Catholic Church in Latin America—that emphasized authority, discipline, hierarchy, and top-down decision making. Both areas are (mainly) a part of the West but also apart from it, geographically, psychologically, and politically. Russia is contiguous to Western Europe and the latter's democratic traditions, while Latin America is separated from it by thousands of miles of oceans; nevertheless, Latin America's main intellectual and political traditions have been predominantly Western for over five hundred years.

Latin America, however, was founded as a *fragment* of the West, circa 1500. That is, it is Western but premodern. Beginning with Columbus's discovery of the Americas in 1492, Latin America was founded on principles and institutions that were feudal, scholastic, and medieval in origins. The Spanish/Portuguese conquest of the Americas was largely completed by 1570, half a century before the North American colonies were settled on the basis of representative government. In contrast, Latin America emerged from feudalism from the Middle Ages, from a system that was authoritarian, hierarchical, top-down, elitist, two-class, nonegalitarian, nondemocratic. Founded on premodern principles and institutions. Latin America never experienced until recently the modernizing trends that we associate with the modern age, the Renaissance, the Enlightenment, the Protestant Reformation, the Industrial Revolution, the rise of capitalism, and liberal, representative government.

Hence, Latin America lagged behind, trapped in the Middle Ages, while the United States forged ahead. Even when Latin America began to move toward independence and republicanism, moreover, it did so on a basis that was different from that of the United States: scholastic rather than empirical arguments, Rousseau rather than Locke (implying heroic "saviors" like Castro or Pinochet instead of democratic elections), Comtean positivism (order and progress) rather than genuine freedom and liberalism. So as Latin America now democratizes, really for the first time, and moves toward a free-market economy, we will want to know if that is genuine liberal democracy as we know it or if it is still in keeping with Latin America's own organic, corporate, top-down tradition of democracy. Complicating the issue in Latin America is the emergence of indigenous Indian groups who are increasingly demanding their own system of political organization.

The discussion now moves from semi-Western areas (Russia, Latin America) to non-Western areas, beginning with East Asia. East Asia, of course, is non-Western and had none of the modernizing, democratizing experiences with which Westerners are familiar: Renaissance, Enlightenment, Industrial Revolution, and so on. Instead, the dominant, historic tradition in East Asia is Confucianism, although Buddhism, Taoism, Shintoism, and others are also present and important. Confucianism should be thought of not so much as a religion in the Western sense but as a body of ethical principles: discipline, order, obedience, honor, education, family obligation, consensus, group solidarity, and community. For a long time these principles were thought to be conservative, traditionalist, and to hold back East Asian development and democratization. But as, first, Japan took off, then the "Four Tigers" of South Korea, Taiwan, Hong Kong, and Singapore, eventually China, Malaysia, Thailand, and the Asian region as a whole, the principles of Confucianism came to be seen in a new light: as providing the work ethic that undergirded Asian economic development and the consensus and stability that enabled democracy to grow and become institutionalized.

We need to be careful in making these assertions for they do not apply to all Asian nations across the board. First, while much of East Asia has moved toward democracy, Burma is still a military dictatorship and the People's Republic of China, though modernizing economically, is still Marxist-Leninist politically. Second and particularly relevant for our discussion here, the part of Asia that is democratic seems to practice a form of democracy that is different (more Confucian?) than that of the West, with more emphasis on consensus, group solidarity, continuity, and interlocking elites. Third, as Asia has developed and become more self-confident, it has asserted the ascendancy of "Asian values" over Western values (which it often sees as decadent and distinctive) and expressed resentment over U.S. efforts to lecture them about democracy and human rights. But here again we need to be careful, distinguishing those countries that practice democracy but are nevertheless sometimes critical of the West (Japan, Taiwan, South Korea) from those countries that hide behind "Asian values" as a way of rationalizing some frankly authoritarian practices (Malaysia, Singapore, the People's Republic of China).

The analysis now turns to India. Here we have another fascinating case. First, India is a very old culture and civilization (far older than the United States) with a great variety of religious and ethical traditions: Hindu, Buddhist, Sikh, Muslim, among others. Second, in large part because of the English colonial legacy, but also by now with India's own institutional development, the country has been a functioning democracy (the world's largest) for over half a century—although we will surely want to know how much Indian democracy reflects that of the West versus how much is homegrown, especially now that the Hindu Nationalist Party (BJP), which mixes religion and politics, has taken power. Third, while India is and has been a practicing democracy, the economic model it followed for a long time was that of central planning, state-led industrialization, autarky, and socialism. Only after the collapse of the Soviet Union, and having in front of it the incredible economic success stories of Singapore and other East Asian nations, did India move toward a more open-market economy. India, therefore, provides us with an interesting test case, not only of a mix of imported and indigenous elements in Indian democracy but also whether it is possible, for more than the short term, to separate democracy in the political sphere from liberalism in the economy. Keep in mind also that India's democracy is still precarious, that it is an underdeveloped country, and that by mid-century India may surpass China as the world's most populous and "crowded" country.

In the Middle East the main question is: why have so few of the Islamic countries, in contrast to Russia, Eastern Europe, Asia, and Latin America, embraced democracy? Is there something in Islamic culture or religion that retards democratization? Why has the Middle East (except Israel) not become a part of the great wave of democratization that swept over much of the globe in the late twentieth century?

To begin, there *are* powerful admonitions and currents within Islam that seem to legitimize authoritarianism and top-down rule, just as there were in medieval Catholicism. These currents are so strong that frequently the question is raised: are Islam and democracy compatible? But at the same time, both the Koran and the Shariah (Islamic law) contain passages that require rulers to govern justly, to consult with their own people (elections?), and to reflect and respond to the pluralism of their societies—all of which may provide a basis for democracy. Moreover, nowhere in the Koran or the Shariah is democracy expressly ruled out or prohibited. A third factor to keep in mind is the economic and social underdevelopment of most of the Islamic countries, so that, while democracy there is not widespread now, they may well repeat the experience of other countries: as economic growth and social modernization occur, the chances for democracy to expand are enhanced. Finally, as with Asia, we need to be careful with our judgments and avoid stereotypes or simplistic assessments, for in such predominantly Islamic countries as Indonesia, Iran, Jordan, Algeria, and Turkey, the strength of democratic sentiment and institutions is increasing.

Finally, we turn to Africa. If there is any continent where the prospects for democracy have not been propitious, it is Africa. First, the colonial legacy of Africa and its colonialist political institutions all but guaranteed that Africa's experience with democracy would be less than successful. Second, as with the Middle East, we need to be aware of Africa's incredible poverty and underdevelopment, which suggests that much of the continent lacks the social, economic, and institutional foundation on which successful democracy can be built. Third, there was a time in the 1970s and 1980s when some countries of Africa experimented with indigenous or homegrown models of democracy, but often these were based on naive, romantic, and unrealistic visions that lacked credibility and stood little chance of success. Hence, today, some of the more grandiose visions have been abandoned and more modest (and realistic) plans put in their place: some decentralization, better human rights, some privatization, investments, greater transparency in the public accounts, education, etc. The goal of democracy has not been abandoned (South Africa is a functioning democracy; other countries function more or less democratically and/or have had democratic elections), but a more realistic assessment of democracy's prospects and possibilities is needed; further, these modest steps now will help lay the groundwork for a more solid and widespread democracy later on.

DISCUSSION

Democracy is both universal—in the sense that all people (*almost* all) want it and that it has certain core requirements that give it global applicability—and particular, in the sense that all countries and culture areas practice democracy in their own way.

No doubt most people, if they are able to choose, want democracy. Democracy and the political freedoms and basic human rights that it implies are well-nigh a universal aspiration. Public opinion surveys tell us that in country after country, most of the population prefers democracy. Particularly with the decline, overthrow, and discrediting of authoritarianism on the one hand and Marxism-Leninism on the other—the two major alternatives to democracy of the twentieth century—democracy seems to have the global playing field all to itself. In the modern world, no other system of government enjoys the legitimacy that democracy has; indeed, one can go further and say that democracy is now the *only* form of government that has global legitimacy. Today, democracy has triumphed in the world; Winston Churchill's backhanded compliment that "democracy is the worst form of government except for all the others" seems to have been borne out.

Furthermore, there is substantial agreement on the core requirements of democracy: (1) regular, fair, competitive elections; (2) basic civil and political rights and liberties; and (3) a considerable degree of political pluralism. In Western Europe the definition of modern democracy has been expanded to encompass social and economic democracy, the welfare state; but in other countries that may not necessarily be the case: either as a poor country you cannot afford all the elaborate and costly provisions of full economic democracy or, as in the United States, such provisions are seen more as a matter of voter choice rather than integral to democracy.

Note again that the definition and "core requirements" of democracy listed above largely apply to Western, developed democracies; they tend to assume and take for granted the culture, history, and overall high socioeconomic development of the West. They assume that a country has experienced the Renaissance, the Enlightenment, the Industrial Revolution, the movement toward limited government; in fact, the *whole panoply* of Western experiences, history, culture, and high socioeconomic development. But in many poor and non-Western countries, this history, experience, and foundation for democracy have been lacking. That is why we suggested the need for a broader definition of democracy, one that encompasses some level of literacy and socioeconomic development, some degree of tolerance and civility, some degree of egalitarianism, military subordination to civilian authority, a functioning and independent legislature and judiciary, a considerable degree of probity in the management of public funds. We use the terms "some level of" or "a considerable degree of" because no democracy is ever perfect and we need to be realistic about the level of democracy we can expect—including in the United States!

Here we have at least a working definition of democracy. But then we also have all those distinct political, philosophical, religious, and cultural traditions surveyed here. Many of these are not only different from but at variance with the Western conception of democracy. And even *within* the West, we have seen, both the practice and the philosophical basis of democracy may be quite different. The question is: can these two ever meet? That is: can we find some concordance between our general definition of democracy (largely Western-based) on the one hand, and all those myriad and diverse cultural, regional, philosophical, and historical differences and distinct countries and regions, on the other?

Let us take the easiest case first. U.S. democracy is highly individualistic, grounded at least historically on Anglo-Dutch Protestant conceptions, organized on the basis of separation of powers, and highly pluralistic. But can that be the basis for a universal model? European democracy tends to be based on solidarity and communitarianism more than individualism; does not have, in its parliamentary systems, the same conception of separation of powers as in the United States; is less oriented toward interest group lobbying; and has a broader sense of socioeconomic democracy. Even in the contrasts among the United States and its close allies and culturally related democracies in Western Europe, therefore, there are some major differences that require at least a certain degree of cultural relativism.

Russia, or at least those areas west of the Ural Mountains, is European in geography; but in its history, religion, sociology, politics, and culture it is only partly European. Since the collapse and overthrow of communism in the period from 1989 to 1991, Russia has embarked on a democratic, more capitalistic or mixed-economy course, and it wishes to be incorporated into the prosperity, affluence, and consumerist culture of the West. But Russia is divided over its commitment to democracy and a Western-style economy. Particularly when the political and economic going gets tough, Russia tends to repudiate that which comes from the West, including democracy. Instead, it emphasizes its "Slavic traditions," which is a code phrase for nationalism, authoritarianism, top-down decision making, concentrated power, and even anti-Americanism. But because it is desperately poor and needs Western capital, Russia accepts Western influence even while resenting it; at the same time, Russia now has institutions and public opinion supportive of democracy, and even its Slavophiles have no alternative *system* to offer, only criticism of the existing system. So Russia is a mixed bag: a country that is formally democratic but with weak democratic institutions and a political culture that is still only partly democratic.

Much the same, interestingly, could be said of Latin America. Latin America is *partly* Western, a fragment of feudal, medieval Spain and Portugal circa 1500 that is still struggling to modernize and democratize. Beginning in the 1970s Latin America commenced an impressive transition to democracy that resulted in nineteen of the twenty countries (all except Cuba) now being counted in the democratic camp (defined in most cases as formal or electoral democracy). However, Latin America is still, like Russia, only partially democratic; its democracy, grounded in ancient and medieval Christianity, is quite different from U.S. democracy; Latin American democracy demonstrates a curious, often confusing, sometimes chaotic, blend of U.S., European, indigenous, and Hispanic traditions. Democracy in Latin America is also development related: As socioeconomic modernization has gone forward, the foundations of Latin American democracy have also been strengthened. Latin America is, again like Russia, currently in transition; and its political institutions, therefore, often exhibit curious blends and hybrids of democracy and authoritarianism.

Next, we consider East Asia, the first of our non-Western areas, and the Confucian tradition. Here the political trajectories, traditions, and current situations are complex and varied, so complex that it may be difficult to generalize across countries. First, Japan: defeated, occupied, and strongly influenced in its political institutions by the post–World War II U.S. occupation forces, formally a democracy but with its culture, work habits, family system, and all-powerful bureaucracy still dominated by not-very-democratic Confucian traditions of order, hierarchy, and obligation. Second, Taiwan and South Korea, which may be treated together for our purpose. Both had long and strong Confucian traditions; both had authoritarianism for long periods, but then both democratized in the 1980s and 1990s. The reasons for democratization are significant: outside (U.S. and others) pressures, internal demands for greater freedom, the end of the Cold War which made security issues less important, and developmental transformations. In the early stages of their development (1950s–1970s), Taiwan and South Korea felt they had to keep the authoritarian lid on in order to prevent social upheaval and disintegration, but in the last two decades they became affluent, secure, and self-confident enough that they felt they could loosen up—democratization.

The Philippines had four centuries of Spanish colonialism followed by a half century of U.S. occupation on top of a long but fragmented indigenous tradition; its democracy is a mix of all three of these influences. China is, of course, the paradigm case: *the* center of Confucianism, a powerful, autocratic, and authoritarian tradition, then a communist revolution, now a gradual loosening up. China, at least in the coastal trading areas, is becoming more capitalistic but its political system is still Marxist-Leninist totalitarian, and it shows few signs of gravitating in a democratic direction. But the possibility exists that China as well as other Southeast Asian nations will follow the South Korea/Taiwan model: economic development first, followed by a gradual liberalization that leads to democracy. Meanwhile, we also need to wrestle with the fact that *all* of Asia is becoming *post*-Confucian: more affluent, more pragmatic, globalist, less shaped by its ancient traditions and more by interdependence.

Our analysis shifts to South Asia, specifically India. India is a big and important country (one billion people), an emerging world power, with (like its neighbor and rival China) a long history and rich cultural heritage (mainly Hindu) of its own. It was colonial master Great Britain that brought democratic institutions to India and, unlike other former colonies, once independent, India did not feel compelled to repudiate everything from its colonial past. Rather, its democracy has proved to be healthy and vigorous, although in its own special fashion (rather like Japan). However, India's economic system for a long time remained autarkic; only in recent years has it begun to liberalize. So here we have a case that is the opposite of the East Asian examples; in India it is political democracy that has come before economic liberalization and growth rather than the other way around. The result is a paradox: the absorption of Western theories but a non-Western democratic experience.

Of all the areas surveyed here, the Middle East has been among the least hospitable to democracy, with only five or six governments out of forty that could be termed even partially democratic. Recall also Professor Samuel P. Huntington's conclusion from his study of "the clash of civilizations"[7] that it was Islamic civilization with whom the United States was most likely to clash in the twenty-first century. It *is* true that there is much in Islam, as in Confucianism, that can be used to justify autocratic, authoritarian, despotic government, and that has certainly been the predominant practice so far. However, one can also find in Islam justification for democratic consultation between ruler and ruled, for pluralism, and for a government limited by social norms and popular values. Additionally, we must take seriously the statement that there is nothing in Islam, neither in the Koran nor in the Shariah, that expressly prohibits democracy. So is it something inherent in Islamic culture and religion that has proved inhospitable to democracy, or is it instead frustration, a feeling of powerlessness in the face of Western (U.S., European, Israeli) power or perhaps—like China or, earlier, Taiwan and South Korea—underdevelopment? The answer: probably some combination of all of these.

Finally, Africa. Despite the optimistic official rhetoric coming out of Washington recently, Africa seems to be on the edge of a precipice. War, pestilence, disease, starvation, AIDS, underdevelopment, corruption, bloodshed, natural disasters, dictatorship, thuggery, ethnic conflict, bad government, donor fatigue, Western indifference—all these and other ills plague Africa. In almost every country the situation seems well-nigh hopeless. And yet in a handful of countries there are some rays of hope: democratic elections, reduction of the corrupt state sector, greater transparency in the management of public affairs and funds, a nascent civil society, decentralization of public services and their administration through local or indigenous agencies. Africa is also the poorest area surveyed, so again the question arises: if Africa were more economically and socially developed, would its chances for democracy be improved? Africa's problems are presently so overwhelming and the conditions so bad that no amount of economic pump-priming is going to do the trick anytime soon; nor can we hold out much hope for an indigenous African model of democracy if war, revolution, disease, and the myriad other problems listed above constantly wipe out or threaten to eliminate the gains made.

ANALYSIS AND CONCLUSION

This brief survey supports several conclusions. First, the desire or aspiration for democracy is virtually universal, particularly since the other main alternatives, authoritarianism and Marxism-Leninism, have declined, collapsed, or lost legitimacy. Second, that this universal drive for democracy runs up against an incredible diversity of countries and societies that have very different histories and cultures, mean different things by democracy, or accord it different priorities. Matching people's aspirations for democracy, therefore, with these distinct cultural traditions is a real problem if our goal is the advancement of democracy.

But we have also seen that the frequent mismatch between democratic aspirations and the realities of political culture can change over time. East Asia is a prime example: a Confucian tradition that in the past often supported authoritarian or autocratic rule has now been transformed in several key countries into support for stable democratic government. What accounts for such changes? We identify five factors: (1) war and military occupation, (2) the changing balance of international forces and power, (3) social and economic development, (4) globalization, and (5) changing political culture. We take up each of these factors below, but first we need to examine more closely the argument over whether democracy is universal or not.

There is a growing consensus at least in the West that democracy and human rights are universal.[8] Those universal goals are incorporated in the United Nations charter, to which all member states are signatories, and in the Universal Declaration of Human Rights. No one wants to live under dictatorship or suffer torture or abuse under tyrants, either left or right. Instead, if given a choice, all peoples everywhere would opt for democracy. And, if one looks at the world over the last three decades, there is strong support for this position: quite remarkable transitions to democracy in many parts of the world, the collapse of both authoritarianism and communism paving the way for democracy, a sharp increase in the number of democracies globally, and overwhelming public support for democracy across cultures as *the* best form of government.

The contrary argument is also strong. It asserts that few things are universal, that all rights, values, and political institutions are defined and limited by cultural perceptions. If there is no universal culture, there can be no universally accepted criteria of democracy. For example, the United States has a strongly individualistic culture, but how can one talk about individual rights or one-person, one-vote in societies that are communitarian and emphasize group rights, not those of individuals? Similarly, in the Confucian and Indian traditions, the emphasis is on duties more than rights; how can *that* be reconciled with an American or universal conception of democracy and human rights? Hence, the argument runs, it is both ethnocratic and self-defeating for the West to try to impose its definition and criteria of democracy on the rest of the world. Indeed, many in the Third World suggest that the concept of "universal" human rights or democracy is a smokescreen for the West to impose its values on them and to continue dominating them. Additional arguments include that democracy is too divisive and polarizing for poor and weak countries to afford, and that authoritarianism is more efficient in establishing stability and achieving economic growth, particularly in its early stages.

The viewpoint and conclusion of this analysis are that there are certain *core principles* that all countries, regardless of culture, need to have to qualify as democracies: honest and competitive elections, basic political and human rights, some degree of pluralism and egalitarianism, military subordination to civilian authority, honesty and transparency in the administration of public funds and programs. But beyond that there is a great deal of variety, depending on culture, history, tradition, and level of development, in the form, institutions, and practice of democracy. As long as a country has the core principles listed here, we are prepared to call that country democratic. The result is that not only are the *institutions* of democracy often different as between the United States and Europe, for example, but the actual *practice* and *functioning* of democracy in such diverse countries as Japan, India, South Africa, and Argentina may be quite different as well. So long as we agree on the democratic basics, we are prepared to accept considerable variation on the particulars.

Moreover, we argue here for the acceptance of degrees, gradations, and "halfway houses" of democracy. Authoritarianism and democracy need not be seen as polar opposites but as involving a spectrum, a continuum; in this sense all countries including the United States are incomplete democracies or democracies-in-progress, with some countries further along on the journey than others. That also means we may have to settle on the fact that some countries are incomplete democracies, partial democracies, that they lack the foundations and infrastructure of democracy and, therefore, often blend some degree of democracy with some degree of authoritarianism. These are often the hardest countries to deal with in a policy sense, giving rise to the dilemma of whether you reward them for their democratic accomplishments or punish them for their democratic failures. For example, some African tyrants have held elections that are just democratic enough to avoid international sanction but not democratic enough to allow the opposition to win. Peru's Alberto Fujimori was democratically elected but the election was tainted; he ruled as an autocrat but was particularly effective and popular in terms of combating drugs, achieving economic growth, and eliminating a terrorist guerrilla threat. For policy makers, these are the tough cases.

But even if we accept gradations, degrees, and varieties of democracy, we need not say that is the end of the story. For, in fact, countries change, evolve, and are transformed. We now take up the question raised and briefly outlined earlier of how countries do in fact evolve and how democracy may be established or enhanced in the process.

1. War and military occupation. In the mid-1940s the United States defeated and militarily occupied both Germany and Japan. During the occupation, the United States eliminated or abolished numerous

older and authoritarian institutions, *forced* these countries to write new and more democratic constitutions, and oversaw the transition to democracy in both. More recently the United States and its NATO allies have militarily occupied parts of the former Yugoslavia and sought to instill democracy there. Haiti is another example of a country whose democracy was restored at the point of U.S. bayonets. Obviously one does not want to recommend this solution for very many countries of the world but one must also admit that such key countries as Germany and Japan are democracies today in significant part because of wartime defeat and subsequent military occupation.

2. The changing balance of international forces and power: diplomacy and pressure. U.S. and international influence can often be decisive in pressuring countries toward democracy or in preventing a coup or backsliding in an already existing democracy. President Jimmy Carter initiated a foreign policy heavily influenced by human rights considerations; under President Ronald Reagan the emphasis was on democracy, both as a way of influencing wobbly authoritarian regimes and of undermining communism. And now, particularly since the end of the Cold War, the United States stands as a democratic beacon for many nations with unprecedented influence in world affairs. Obviously the United States has to be careful when, where, and how it promotes democracy (sanctions or quiet diplomacy, overt pressure or simple persuasion), but no doubt the United States can use its international force, power, and pressure to advance democracy. Some analysts want the United States to go so far as to use force to impose democracy on the rest of the world; others are skeptical of that tactic. Nevertheless U.S. diplomacy and pressure can be and is often used to advance democracy abroad.[9]

3. Social and economic development. A large body of literature suggests a rather close correlation between levels of socioeconomic development and democracy. As literacy, education, urbanization, levels of economic development, and overall modernization go up, so do the odds for democracy. This is not to imply direct causation (economic growth does not *cause* democracy), nor is it to suggest that democracy requires rigid prerequisites (e.g., a fixed rate of literacy before democracy becomes possible). But it is to say that as countries become more affluent, middle class, and educated, the chances of their having and sustaining democracy increase. Other things being equal, if you want democracy it is better to be wealthy than poor. By the same token, while no country needs to be dismissed as hopeless, we must recognize if we wish to be successful that the odds of the United States successfully bringing democracy to Cambodia, Haiti, Afghanistan, or Somalia are pretty low. And from a foreign policy

point of view where you need to point to accomplishments for the
policy to succeed, be funded, and have popular support, it is better
to notch successes on your belt than a string of failures. Hence, while
we may *wish* for democracy to be successful everywhere, we also
need to be realistic in deciding where and when the policy can be
successful.

4. Globalization. Globalization is a hotly debated topic these days; it
has its effect on democracy in the following ways. First, with authoritarianism discredited and Marxism-Leninism having collapsed
in most countries, democracy enjoys unprecedented, near-universal
legitimacy and is "the only game in town." Second, the spread of the
mass media, the Web, music, television, and the freedom and choices
they convey all enhance the possibilities for democracy. Third, large
numbers of businessmen and governments, even if they are not necessarily enamored of democracy, recognize that, if they want capital,
investment, and economic growth, they must put in place regular
and honest elections, transparency in the handling of public funds
and programs, pluralism, responsibility, and accountability—i.e., democracy. Globalization is, therefore, not just an economic or Internet
phenomenon; it has profound and generally positive implications
for the spread of democracy as well.

5. Changing political culture. We have learned in this discussion that
some political cultures (Russian, Confucian, Islamic, Latin American) have not historically been very supportive of democracy. But
political culture is not fixed forever and unchanging; there can be
divisions over political culture, the evolution of political culture,
and changing interpretations of the political culture's basic precepts. For example, Confucianism, which was once thought to
stand in the way of democracy, is now thought to be an ally of democracy; similarly, both Russia and Latin America have long had
authoritarian political cultures but these are now changing in favor
of democracy or at least mixed forms. The political culture of the Islamic countries has been less favorable to democracy, but recall
there are no express provisions against democracy in Islam; at the
same time, African political culture(s) may prove to be malleable
with the main problem being lack of economic development to
support democracy. And, of course, in all countries political culture is often altered as a result of economic development, rising literacy, and changing social structures, as well as the global forces
noted above. So while some countries and some regions have not
in the past had a political culture supportive of democracy, over
time new interpretations and new forces may cause such attitudes
to change as well.

While democracy, therefore, is not necessarily universal, it is becoming increasingly more so. Moreover, the dynamic factors analyzed above—changing political culture, globalization, social and economic development, foreign policy influence and pressure, even sometimes war and military occupation—are all pointing in a direction that makes democracy more likely. The organization Freedom House that charts democracy's progress on a daily basis reports that 118 countries are now democracies, a record high number. Democracy is the only system of government that presently enjoys global legitimacy.

Although democracy as a system of government now has near-universal legitimacy, it is also mediated through local, national, and grassroots organizations that make its form distinctive from country to country and region to region. Moreover, the meaning(s), the emphasis, the priorities, the institutions, to say nothing of the practices of democracy, vary significantly around the globe. In addition, we must recognize the fusions, the halfway houses, the crazy-quilt patterns that may exist. For instance, Japanese democracy with its emphasis on consensus and harmony is quite different from the partisan and adversarial democracy of the United States. Indian democracy rooted in ethnicity, caste, and identity is very different from West European continental democracy. And Latin America with its centralized, organic, and corporatist traditions seems at present to be finding a set of new equilibria with most countries strung out at various points between autocracy and authoritarianism on one side and democracy on the other. East Asia, Russia, Latin America, and Eastern Europe all seem to exhibit variations of these mixed forms.

Yet over time these mixed forms are also undergoing transformation; meanwhile, local ways of doing things are themselves being changed. The mixed forms that exist in Russia, East Asia, Latin America, or Eastern Europe, for example, are by no means static; rather, they continue to change under the ongoing impact of internal and external pressures: the same pressures that pushed them in a democratic direction in the first place continue to pressure them toward *greater* democracy. Similarly with the argument concerning local institutions: while Indian caste associations, African ethnic groups, and Islamic tribal leaders are all performing political functions and delivering public programs that can be described as pre- or protodemocratic, the very local institutions that are often lauded as providing homegrown forms of democracy are themselves also undergoing modernization. Indian caste associations often operate as actual or would-be political parties, African ethnic groups deliver rudimentary public policy, and Islamic tribal leaders are performing consultative and representational functions. In short, while we laud these local and grassroots forms of democracy, they themselves are also changing in the process of overall modernization. Few things are static anymore and the direction of the evolution is mainly toward democracy or democratic openings.

We find both this variety and this dynamism of democracy to be healthy. After all, different cultures and different societies at different levels of development do practice democracy in their own ways, and we should celebrate this diversity. Few countries practice democracy in the same exact way as in the United States; first, because their histories and cultures are different; second, because their level of development only permits democracy at a certain level; and third, because they may actually prefer their own form of democracy, their own ways of doing things. Just as many cultures, societies, and economies are different, so we can also expect different forms and practices of democracy. As long as the *core ingredients*—elections, rights, pluralism, and the like—are present, democracy can encompass many different varieties.

All countries will continue to filter the concept, institutions, and practices of democracy through the lenses of their own social, cultural, historical, and political values, priorities, and understandings. At the same time, all countries will increasingly be influenced by U.S. and Western culture, which is rapidly becoming a global culture and, therefore, by U.S. and Western concepts of democracy. But some countries have stronger cultures and societies than others. Japan, China, India, Iran, Argentina, Brazil, and Mexico are all examples of countries with strong political cultures of their own. Their political systems, while clearly influenced from the outside and by the pressures of globalization, will continue to try to shape the outside currents, including those of democratization, to their own realities. Japan is perhaps the best example of a highly successful and developed country that has absorbed *some aspects* of Western-style democracy even while continuing to follow its own path. In other words, big and strong countries, with their own powerful cultures, are able to selectively absorb what is useful from the West and its form of democracy even while retaining their own distinctive ways of doing things and of practicing democracy.

Other smaller, weaker countries and cultures—for example, those of Central America and the Caribbean—are less able to resist the outside pressures. They may simply be overwhelmed by the pressures emanating from the outside, from the global culture, from the United States. Their own cultures and institutions are often too weak to assert their independence, to perform the winnowing or filtering functions that the Japanese culture does. Some of these countries may simply be overwhelmed by the pressures of globalization, by the insistence that they conform to U.S. and Western standards of economic and political practice. American-style democracy, or capitalism for that matter, may be "too rich" for these countries to afford, certainly quickly and all at once; attempts to push them too rapidly toward democracy could result not in democracy but in destabilization, which would set back democracy still further. And yet, even small countries often have an amazing capacity for flexibility, to absorb outside pressures (including democracy) while at the same time continuing to practice politics in their own ways which may involve compromises with full or complete democracy.

That is why we need to recognize mixes, gradations, and distinct varieties of democracy, to acknowledge that democracy in many countries is not an either-or proposition but a continuum, a journey, an ongoing process. We need a set of categories—limited democracy, partial democracy, incomplete democracy, and the like—that enable us to comprehend and come to grips not only with the many gradations of democracy but also with the unique, culturally conditioned forms that democracy may take. Not only will that give us a useful and realistic way of measuring the condition and status of global democracy but it also provides us with a base to encourage further evolution toward democracy in the future.

NOTES

1. Samuel P. Huntington, *The Third Wave: Democratization in the Late Twentieth Century* (Norman: University of Oklahoma Press, 1991).

2. Francis Fukuyama, *The End of History and the Last Man* (New York: Free Press, 1992).

3. Joseph Schumpeter, *Capitalism, Socialism, and Democracy* (New York: Harper, 1947).

4. Huntington, *The Third Wave.*

5. Robert Dahl, *Polyarchy: Participation and Opposition* (New Haven: Yale University Press, 1971); Dahl, *Democracy and Its Critics* (New Haven: Yale University Press, 1989).

6. *They Know How* (Washington, DC: Inter-American Foundation, 1977).

7. Samuel P. Huntington, *The Clash of Civilizations and the Remaking of World Order* (New York: Simon & Schuster, 1996).

8. The analysis here follows Shashi Tharoor, "Are Human Rights Universal?" *World Policy Journal* (Winter 1999–2000), 1–6.

9. Thomas Carothers, *Aiding Democracy Abroad* (Washington, DC: Carnegie Endowment for International Peace, 1999).

9

Is Civil Society Exportable?

PROVOCATION

Civil society may be defined as that vast web of intermediary associations (labor unions, farm groups, business associations, Boy and Girl Scouts, religious bodies, etc.) that occupy the ground between individual citizens and the state and that serve as transmission belts between them. Civil society has long been thought of as essential to democracy.

The concept of civil society has a long and distinguished history in Western political thought and practice.[1] And therein, right at the beginning, lies the first and most important set of issues with which we must deal: (1) while civil society is indisputably part of the Western tradition, its meaning and implications have varied enormously over time, in different historical contexts, and from country to country; and (2) while civil society is tied to and closely a part of the distinctively Western tradition, with its emphasis at least in modern times on individualism, absence of feudal or semifeudal restraints, freedom of association, liberty, participatory and pluralist politics, and middle-class, entrepreneurial, and free-market economics, we must question whether and how much it has relevance in many Third World countries with their quite different histories, cultures, societies, economies, and political traditions. Or is civil society now such a genuinely universal concept that it is applicable to all countries in approximately the same form? Those are the issues we wrestle with in this chapter.

Many countries of the Third World have not in the past had strong civil societies or been very liberal; instead, they have for most of their recent histories been corporatist and often authoritarian. Whereas liberalism means a system of free and unfettered associability, pluralism, and largely unregulated civil society, interest group or nongovernmental organization (NGO) activity, corporatism (not to be equated with one of its variants, fascism) means state regulation and control of interest group/NGO activity and even the creation of official, state-run associational life.

Now as the economies of many Third World countries are being deregulated, and as authoritarianism is giving way to democracy, numerous societies and political systems are similarly transitioning from corporatism to free association, civil society, and greater societal and political pluralism. But in many countries that process is still incomplete and partial. There are often still limits on NGO/civil society activities. Or the new groups must compete, often unfairly, with official, state-sponsored organizations. There is fear in many developing countries that unfettered, unregulated interest-group activity will produce chaos and breakdown. Many governments, while dismantling corporatism formally, are nevertheless continuing its practices; or, even though repudiating corporatism at the national level, governments are re-creating corporatist controls at the local level—precisely where many NGOs and civil society groups operate. There is a delicate balance between wanting democracy and pluralism, and the reality that many Third World countries may unravel, break down, and prove ungovernable if that process proceeds too rapidly.

Liberalism and free associability have not been the sole, inevitable, or universal outcome of recent modernization processes; instead, corporatism and various mixed forms of state control/freedom have predominated. But while economic reform and democratization (parties and elections) have received a great deal of attention from scholars, policy makers, and the NGO civil society community, almost no one is analyzing the equally important phenomenon of the transition in the interest-group arena from corporatism to free associability. For if democracy is to flourish beyond the mere formal level, free, unfettered associability, genuine social and political pluralism, and civil society must also be encouraged, enhanced, and nurtured. If we are wise, that transition can be managed smoothly; if we are not, it can produce upheaval, instability, fragmentation, and a likely return to authoritarianism.

This chapter explores the political processes involved as Third World societies transition from authoritarianism and statism to democracy, and from corporatism to free associability. It is specifically focused on the legacy and frequently still present reality of state or government controls over NGO/civil society activity during the transition process. The research not only examines these controls in an academic sense, but it is also interested in the practical policy implications: how can the dismantling of authoritarianism and corporatism be speeded up (if that is what is needed) and made more complete; how can we be sensitive to local mores, institutions, and ways of doing things during the crucial transitional stage; how can NGOs/civil society operate more effectively in the transitional phases and in the interstices between corporatism and liberalism or democracy; what can be done when governments seek to *re*-establish statist controls either at national or local levels; how can civil society be made more effective and democracy, therefore, hopefully strengthened?

POLICY FOCUS

This is a critically important focus on an important policy issue. The author's interviews indicate that few persons in the NGO/civil society community, or in policy making in the United States government (USG) or international agencies, have sufficient background on corporatism to understand, let alone deal with in a policy sense, this phenomenon. The assumption usually is that, since Marxism-Leninism has been discredited and authoritarianism in many countries undermined, democratic, pluralist, civil society will automatically and universally follow. But the issues and processes are not so simple. The process is not necessarily inevitable, unilinear, or universal. There are many gaps, glitches, overlaps of traditional and modern, and halfway houses *between* corporatism and free associability. The Tocquevillian model of free, multiple, laissez-faire associability that is at the heart of American political and public life does not apply, or applies only partially and in mixed form, in much of the Third World.

For NGO/civil society agencies to be effective in the Third World, and particularly in countries now undergoing transitions, they must understand the context in which they are operating and be prepared to adapt their universalist programs to local, national, or regional conditions. Numerous earlier reform programs aimed at the Third World—agrarian reform, community development, family planning, judicial reform, and others—have foundered by failing to adapt to the social, political, and cultural conditions in which they found themselves. At present, however, many NGO/civil society sector leaders, although buoyed by the early success of democratization, are increasingly frustrated by their inability to expand their programs. Or they are facing hurdles caused either by the reassertion of state controls or by the reluctance of Third World leaders to go faster or farther toward a free society. Or they are encountering newfound hostility or increased host government suspicion, regulation, and controls over their own activities. Some NGOs have been booted out of the countries in which they were operating; others have been forced to curtail their activities; still others have been obliged to accept increased scrutiny of their finances, foreign connections, memberships, and internal procedures—that is, a reassertion of corporatism.

This analysis seeks to enlighten the NGO/civil society community in dealing with and overcoming these new restrictions and in understanding the political processes involved. In order to function effectively, NGOs must comprehend how Third World governments, fearing unrest and instability, are extremely hesitant to move to unfettered freedom of association, use the process of regulation and licensing of civil society groups to control and/or co-opt them, and try to incorporate rising social groups under official state auspices. The result is that NGOs must often navigate very carefully in these waters so as to remain effective, avoid being shunted aside into irrelevance or expulsion, and continue advancing their agenda.

The analysis here is, therefore, directed at these audiences: the NGO/civil society community, which is often not fully aware of corporatism's continuing and pervasive influences and implications in many Third World areas, U.S. policy makers in AID and other development agencies who must deal with the same phenomena, and scholars and agencies concerned with democratic transitions—such agencies as the National Endowment for Democracy (NED), National Democratic Institute for International Affairs (NDI), and National Republican Institute for International Affairs (NRI), who must wrestle with these issues. We all need to keep the goal in mind of a democratic, pluralist system of free associability, but to operate effectively we need to recognize and deal realistically with the various transitional regimes, the mixed systems involved, and the various steps or halfway houses along the way.

BACKGROUND AND MAIN QUESTIONS

In much of the theoretical literature on developing nations as well as in policy analysis, three main routes to development were usually posited: an authoritarian route, a liberal-pluralist route, and a Marxist-Leninist one. Authoritarianism has been vanquished in many countries and now, with the end of the Cold War and the demise of the Marxist-Leninist alternative, it is generally thought that liberalism and pluralism will triumph universally. That may still happen in the long term, but in the meantime analysts, activists, and policy makers alike have largely ignored or not been cognizant of the other great systems outcome and alternative, particularly attractive in the unstable political systems of the Third World: corporatism.

Corporatism, organicism, and integralism have long histories in Western thought as well as political practice. Corporatism was particularly attractive in those key Third World countries (Egypt, Indonesia, Iran, South Korea, Taiwan, Brazil, Mexico) where political elites favored economic development but were often fearful of its social and political consequences (pluralism and democracy). Hence, they erected elaborate corporate structures of institutions and regulations to control, manage, co-opt, and even suppress the rising new social forces of civil society: organized labor, peasant groups, women, indigenous elements, neighborhood- and community-based groups, NGOs of all kinds, social movements, and civil society generally.

In the past two decades, there has been an explosion *worldwide* of civil society, NGOs, and private-interest associations in general. In addition, particularly in the last decade, many developing nations have reformed, privatized, and moved toward neoliberalism in the economic sphere. And though many have moved toward electoral democracy, genuine liberal and pluralist democracy has proved more difficult and elusive. Many Third World nations, fearing disorder and breakdown, are reluctant to let go of the political strings, to relax or eliminate entirely the vast web of corporative regulatory controls that still remain in place. The result is a mishmash of confusion and contradictions with NGO/civil society groups and advocates caught in the middle, uncertain as to how to operate. Although a handful of developing nations have abolished corporative controls as part of a broader democratization strategy, in most the corporative controls remain in place, or else official interest associations and accompanying regulatory mechanisms exist alongside and in a conflicting, overlapping, *competitive* relationship with the newer groups and NGOs oriented toward free associability.

Here we explore some fundamental questions that must be addressed by the emerging NGO/civil society policy community:

1. What is the theoretical, sociological, and political basis of the systems of corporatism that are so widespread in the Third World but are almost entirely unknown (including among the leaders of international NGOs seeking to operate in these countries) in the United States?

2. What are the *processes* and dynamics by which corporatist systems are now being dismantled or giving way to more liberal systems of free associability; how extensive are the remaining controls on free associations; what kind of mixed systems exist, how do they change, and how do NGO/civil society groups learn to navigate around these controls?

3. What regulations and controls (legal, constitutional, political) must NGO/civil society groups still conform to and how does that inhibit their activities? What can be done to ameliorate these restrictions?

4. How can the international community (IC) and NGOs, in particular, assist the process of devolution from corporatist to genuinely liberal, open, and pluralist societies and politics? How can the IC put pressure on countries to deregulate NGO activity, as they are already deregulating economic activity, and move more quickly to a system of free associability?

5. In the present context, corporatism is being dismantled in many countries at the national level but recreated at the local level—precisely where many NGOs operate; how best can NGOs and civil society groups resist, work around, or reverse this tendency?

6. How can American-based NGOs, in particular, in their enthusiasm for free and democratic pluralism, avoid pushing Third World countries too far and too fast in this area, and thus causing the very instability and chaos that having a strong civil society infrastructure is designed to prevent?

7. Can American NGOs and civil society advocates understand forms of civil society other than our own and thus develop the empathy necessary to deal with Third World countries on their own terms rather than through the narrow, particular lenses of U.S. pluralism and free associability?

MAIN ISSUES AND CONTROVERSIES

Civil society has become a topic of increasing interest in recent years. Scholars have examined its historic theoretical and philosophic foundations; the U.S. government has built civil society requirements into many of its foreign aid programs as well as overall foreign policy; and the foundations and international lending agencies have settled on civil society as their latest "discovery" to solve the problems of the world. Many nongovernmental organizations are similarly integrating civil society concepts into their programs; civil society is being touted by the Third World as holding great promise for assisting democratization and national development efforts; still others see civil society grandiosely as "saving the world."[2]

One can readily understand why the notion of civil society is so attractive, particularly to scholars, foundations, policy advocates, and the NGO community. First, it has a nice ring to it: civil society as a term sounds lofty, nonpartisan, citizen-oriented, participatory, and democratic; and who could argue with those attributes? Second, civil society conjures up images of Madisonian, Tocquevillian pluralism, town meetings, grassroots participation, checks and balances, and countervailing yet ultimately harmonious interest-group competition and democratic public policy. The images most of us have of civil society include bowling leagues, PTAs, soccer moms, Girl and Boy Scouts, neighborhood associations, town meetings, and peaceful, harmonious collective bargaining.[3] All of these evoke favorable images to the American Congress, public, and policy makers.

A third reason why civil society is so attractive is that it holds the promise of taking policy making out of the hands of often corrupt, venal bureaucracies, governments, and "evil" international organizations like the World Trade Organization (WTO) or the International Monetary Fund (IMF), and placing it directly in the hands of popular organizations, or "the people." Fourth (and this by no means exhausts the list), civil society is popular because it looks "just like us" or at least what we imagine ourselves to be: democratic, grassroots-oriented, participatory, pluralist. It seems as a concept to avoid all of America's bad attributes (the influence of money on politics, gridlock between the executive and legislative branches, large, impersonal bureaucracy, and so on) and to restore an earlier, more pristine form of citizen participation, interest-group balance, and direct democracy. Civil society has thus taken on aspects of a civic renewal, the apparent rediscovery of our long-lost and better attributes, even in some quarters a quasi-religious crusade and reconversion.[4]

Over the last two decades, policy makers have also recognized the importance of civil society and have seized upon it as an instrument of foreign policy. For example, in the 1980s and 1990s the U.S. government and others used emerging civil society organizations to assist in the ouster of discredited authoritarian regimes (Marcos, Duvalier, etc.) as well as, through Solidarity and other organizations, in the overthrow of communist regimes in Eastern Europe. Recognizing the incapacity and/or corruption of central governments, civil society organizations have been used to carry out policies in the areas of family planning, education, environmentalism, and democratization. Civil society has proved a means to "think globally but act locally" on a variety of policy fronts; civil society has also proved to be a useful conduit for U.S. and other foreign assistance programs. Where civil society has not existed in many Third World nations, the United States, including the government, AID, foundations, and American civil society groups, has created, aided, and even invented it, obviously for its own national interest purposes as well as because we believe it assists democracy in the Third World. Already in these comments we can find several reasons to begin to worry about the civil society approach.

This last aspect raises a familiar Washington issue. Whenever a concept like civil society has so many positives, achieves widespread popularity and consensus, and seems to accomplish so many positive goals (overthrowing both authoritarianism and communism) at once, its attractiveness to politicians becomes irresistible. The concept then becomes politicized and is used for purposes other than those intended. Already AID, the State

Department, the Defense Department, the CIA, the White House, Congress, and sundry others have latched onto the concept. In addition, the National Endowment for Democracy, the Republican and Democratic international affairs institutes, the Ford and MacArthur Foundations, the Washington think tanks, and numerous human rights and religious groups have similarly seized on the concept. "Civil society" has become a growth industry. And when that happens, the concept itself and its purposes run the risk of being hopelessly distorted. It also runs the risk of falling victim to the same policy cycle that so many other well-meaning programs in the past—agrarian reform, community development, family planning, basic human needs, sustainable development—have gone through: initial excitement and enthusiasm, followed by politicization and distortion, resulting in disillusionment, disappointment, and eventual petering out (but never complete *disappearance*; remember, these are *government* and *bureaucratic* programs). My reading is that civil society, parallel to these other panaceas, has now about exhausted its romantic and enthusiastic phase and is presently on the cusp of either decline or a more realistic assessment.

The issues are compounded once the concept travels abroad. First, as we have seen, different societies and cultures mean different things by civil society than do Lockean, Tocquevillian, Madisonian Americans. Second, the *form* that civil society takes in different countries may vary greatly from the U.S. model—and not all of these by any means are liberal, pluralist, and democratic. Third, money is involved—now often big money—and legions of opportunists in the United States and abroad are waiting to take advantage of the largesse now going into civil society projects. Often these are the same opportunists who had earlier milked other AID and U.S. government panaceas—agrarian reform, community development, etc.—dry, without producing much in the way of reform. And fourth, when host governments observe civil society activities, which by their nature are often oppositionist, outside of state control, and liberal-pluralist in the U.S. mold, the temptation is powerful to control, regulate, co-opt, and expel, or repress them. Elites and national governments in Latin America, East Asia, and elsewhere have used, and continue to use, *corporatism* as a way to harness and control pluralist interest groups.[5] Now, since corporatism at the national level is being gradually replaced in many countries by a form of neoliberalism, it is being resurrected at the local level where civil society groups are increasingly being required to register, divulge their members' names, disclose their financing, and seek recognition or "juridical personality" from local authorities, which also carries with it the possibility of nonrecognition and, therefore, suppression if the group persists in its activities.

When my research project on comparative civil society was first proposed, its thrust was aimed at suggesting ways to dismantle the corporatist structures we have found so prevalent in the various Third World areas studied, and to move quickly toward democratic, genuinely pluralist civil society. Those remain the long-term objectives. But in the course of the research it became plain that dismantling corporatist controls over interest-group activities too quickly or precipitously would in most countries produce instability and possibly chaos and disintegration. The research instead suggests that corporatism ought to be seen as a transitional regime between authoritarianism and democracy. As in South Korea, Taiwan, Brazil, Mexico, and hopefully Egypt, corporatism in its more benign forms should be viewed as a way of gradually bridging the transition to democracy and civil society but without producing ungovernability and breakdown. Most countries need to e...a...s...e their way to democracy and civil society, to establish a solid socioeconomic foundation, and then to gradually let up on the controls. Rather than dismantling corporatism, therefore, in most Third World countries it needs to be viewed as an intermediary stage on the road to democracy and pluralism, the delicate balance of which requires deft handling, mainly by officials and politicians within these countries who know their own often delicate political situations better than the American or international officials advising them.

These preliminary conclusions suggest the need for caution in our enthusiasm for civil society. What began as a noble and ennobling concept seems to go through, as with the other policy panaceas previously noted, a familiar life cycle: initial popularity and enthusiasm, widespread acceptance, then politicization, distortion, and decline. I judge that civil society is just now on the verge of these more realistic but otherwise disillusioning, downward-sloping transformations. Hence, a cautious and prudent approach to civil society rather than an excessively enthusiastic one may be called for.

FINDINGS FROM THE CASE STUDIES

The larger book[6] on which this chapter is based contained case studies of civil society in Africa, Asia, Latin America, and the Middle East. The case studies contained in the book stand by themselves with their own conclusions; what may be more useful to the reader at this stage is the *general patterns* that emerge from the cases presented.

The first conclusion is that in all the countries/areas studied, there has been over the last twenty to thirty years an impressive growth in the number and density of civil society and that, on balance, this has been good for the establishment and spread of democracy and pluralism.

Second, the case studies revealed tremendous variety in the kinds, types, priorities, cultural and philosophical bases, developmental levels, and systems of civil society and of state-society relations. History, culture, religion, as well as levels of socioeconomic development, were all important factors in explaining the varieties of civil society. No one size fits all, nor are all civil society organizations automatically, universally, or by definition beneficial for democracy, stability, and pluralism. More on this below.

Third, civil society growth has been general and universal but it received particular stimulus during times of crisis or challenge: the struggle for democracy in Latin America, the antiauthoritarianism movements in Asia, the antiapartheid struggle in South Africa, and the struggle for freedom and democracy in Eastern Europe. It is usually the case that, since other groups (political parties and the like) are proscribed, oppositionist civil society constituted the only or main opposition to dictatorial rule, and it attracted widespread support.

Fourth, in the early stages of the emergence of civil society, foreign support and finances are often crucial. Foreign donors and aid agencies are not only critical in assisting civil society, but often they literally create civil society to serve their own foreign policy goals as well as those of the local society, and therein lies a major problem.

Fifth, once that early crisis or challenge had been met and the goal (democracy, freedom, the end of apartheid) accomplished, civil society growth tends to drop off precipitously. The issue fades; international donors and supporters lose interest; the leaders and many members of the formerly opposition groups get patronage jobs in the new government; and the previously proscribed political parties and more institutionalized interest groups reassert themselves and often take over the agendas and followers of the earlier civil society movements.

Sixth, there are clear correlations between political culture and civil society: the United States and other nations that are products of British institutions and political culture tend to have strong societies and weak states; in contrast, Asian, Latin American, and African societies tend to have, at least by aspiration, strong state systems but weak civil society. Civil society in Islamic states tends to be weaker still or almost nonexistent.

There is also a correlation, seventh, between civil society and levels of socioeconomic development: countries that are more developed socially and economically tend to have stronger, more robust civil societies.

Eighth, there appears to be a class bias in civil society development: in the early stages a number of lower-class or mass movements are mobilized; at later stages, middle-class and elite elements tend to dominate civil society.

Often parallel with this last development, ninth, comes a tendency for state reassertion of limits, controls, and co-optation of civil society groups. In other words, corporatism, now of a more open kind, tends to reassert itself, often at the expense of free associability.

Nevertheless, tenth, even with the reassertion of corporatism, there tends to be a considerably greater level of freedom, pluralism, and openness than under the earlier authoritarian regime. Corporatism and pluralism, statism and free associability, may *both* be present, co-existing in an often uneasy but always dynamic relationship.

Eleventh, what one finds at present is an incredible mix of civil society groups: some genuinely autonomous from the state and supporting democracy and human rights, others manifestly hostile to these goals, still others co-opted and controlled corporatist-style by the state, as well as new, complex public-private or state-society partnerships.

TWENTY REASONS TO BE CAUTIOUS ABOUT CIVIL SOCIETY

While the idea of civil society has a nice ring and reputation, its practice in the Third World, and particularly the efforts of the U.S. government as well as NGOs to export it abroad, have produced decidedly mixed results. Here we report on the numerous problems in seeking to export civil society; in the last section of the chapter we return to more hopeful themes and seek to assess what we should do, or not do, in promoting civil society.

1. Civil Society as Panacea

Over the decades since we first started to pay attention to the developing world, American foreign aid and the international donor community have settled on a variety of "solutions" to Third World problems that later on prove to have been panaceas. The list of these panaceas is familiar to anyone with experience in foreign aid programs since the 1960s: the Alliance for Progress, infrastructure development, agrarian reform, community development, family planning, basic human needs, sustainable development, now civil society. Typically these programs begin with great hope and fanfare, are well funded for a time, then run into the harsh realities of politics and social structure in Third World countries or the fleeting, fickle interest of the American public and Congress, prove less successful than expected, start to run downhill, are effectively abandoned but are never quite dismantled because whole networks of bureaucratic and private interests grow up around them, and eventually are replaced by a new panacea. Is "civil society" about to go through the same life cycle? My own sense is that it is, that it currently, as a relatively fresh new idea, still has *cachet* with the Congress, foundations, intellectuals, and activists; but that the first serious studies are starting to come in with disappointing results, and that, therefore, this concept will soon (may have already) begin its downward slide as have so many of these other cure-alls in the past.[7]

2. Theory versus Reality

Civil society sounds wonderful in the abstract: democratic, pluralist, private-sector oriented, Tocquevillian, nonbureaucratic, Madisonian, participatory, like a New England town meeting full of yeoman citizens. The reality, however, is often considerably less than that. In practice in too many countries, "civil society" has been conceived in statist and corporatist terms, as a way to siphon money out of international donors without providing much in the way of reform, as a facade for authoritarian practices, as a way to control and limit new social and political groups rather than as an avenue for genuine democratization. Egypt is a case in point—greater authoritarianism rather than less—but there are many others.

3. Risks and Benefits

Civil society is undoubtedly beneficial where it works. But suppose, as in Indonesia and possibly India, the growth of civil society and the pluralism it engenders weaken governmental authority and policy making in countries where the state's ability to deliver public services is already too weak? Or it leads to the breakup of the state, with disastrous, disintegrative, anarchic consequences? Suppose civil society emerges as a substitute for, and, therefore, weakens political parties, which most analysts believe to be absolutely essential for democracy? Suppose civil society undermines traditional but time-tested modes of interest articulation and aggregation (tribes, clientelist relations, caste associations, ethnic coteries), leaving societies with the worst of all possible worlds: old interest associations undermined before the newer civil society ones have had a chance to take root.

4. Varieties of Civil Society

Most of us know what we have in mind by civil society: liberal, pluralist, Tocquevillian, democratic, participatory. But our theoretical survey has highlighted the variety of conceptions of civil society: totalitarian, authoritarian, corporatist, Rousseauian, Lockean. Only the last conforms to our preferred liberal model. In the developing world the most prevalent form is still corporatist (state-regulated, officially controlled), with some preference for the Rousseauian solution (direct rule, no intermediaries) combined (often under foreign pressure) with some, usually grudging, acquiescence in the Lockean-Madisonian model. In addition, there are Confucian, Buddhist, Islamic, and a variety of non-Western and indigenous forms of civil society, and various mixes and overlaps of these with the Western imports. The variety of outcomes should give us pause before we too precipitously pursue the civil society route. And in many countries liberal, corporatist, nondemocratic, and separatist forms of civil society exist simultaneously in a potentially potent, explosive, disintegrative mix.

5. Nondemocratic Civil Society: A Diversity of "Civil Society" Conceptions

The preceding point is so crucial that it deserves reiteration in another framework. Civil society development will not necessarily, inevitably, or universally lead to more democratic, liberal, or socially just outcomes. At least equally plausible are authoritarian, statist, corporatist, and Rousseauian outcomes. To say nothing of nondemocratic Islamic, Confucian, ethnic, clientelistic outcomes. Even more likely are mixed or combined systems in which elites and those in power maneuver and manipulate to satisfy diverse constituencies, allowing just enough civil society to keep international donors and domestic social groups satisfied, but not so much that the elites' own power and position are threatened.

The research points to the conclusion that this is one of the key problems of the effort to export civil society. My interviews revealed that almost all of the American government and NGO officials involved in promoting civil society abroad have in mind a very narrow, parochial, and particular notion of civil society based on the U.S. experience. That is, naturally enough, the Lockean, Madisonian, Tocquevillian, and very American concept of civil society with which we are all familiar because it is part of the American tradition in which we all grew up. But when it is suggested that we need to be familiar also with Confucian, Islamic, clientelistic, Rousseauian, corporatist, and other "strange" forms of civil society, American officials are often completely lost. They cannot conceive of a form of civil society other than our own American version. So when faced with non-Western or various mixed forms, they do not know what to do other than falling back on the American model, which may be inappropriate in various Third World settings, and blaming the country involved for not living up to the American-style system we have designed for them or for not moving fast enough toward the desired goal. This is not only a response certain to produce failure and frustration on the part of all parties (U.S. *and* host country officials) but also to run the risk of damaging and destabilizing the very countries we are seeking to assist.

6. Limited Pluralism: Ambiguity and Different Meanings in the Term *Civil Society*

As Latin America, Asia, and other Third World areas have developed, new social and political groups have emerged, including business and commercial elements, a larger middle class, trade unions, women, peasants, indigenous elements, and others. But in most of these countries this is still often limited, controlled, regulated pluralism, not the unfettered, freewheeling, unregulated, virtually anarchic pluralism of U.S. political society. Even in newly democratic regimes, civil society groups still must often be recognized, legitimated, and licensed by the state, which, of course, is not very democratic. Nor does most of the developing world practice the kind of pluralist interest-group lobbying found in the United States. So while we applaud the ofttimes greater pluralism of these societies, we still need to recognize that there are degrees and gradations of pluralism, that some groups are better organized and more influential than others, and that some, often very large, social sectors are not organized or represented at all.

The above paragraph emphasizes a key problem: the ambiguity and the many distinct meanings in the concept of civil society. Americans are in agreement, à la Madison, Tocqueville, and interest-group pluralism, that it means a web of associational life autonomous from the state and intermediary between the state and the family or individual, groups competing vigorously in the public sphere. But other societies mean something quite different by the term. The various definitions range from "the rule of law," "competitive elections," "separation of powers," to "tribalism," "ethnic identity," "clientelism," and many others. So when we talk about "civil society," Americans and the rest of the world are often talking about quite different meanings, concepts, and understandings. Other cultures also give civil society a different—and usually lesser—priority than do Americans. A final and critical point is that most other societies see a greater role for state regulation of interest-group activity than do Americans and do not see such an overriding need for "autonomy from the state" as in the U.S. definition. Clearly, given these differences, it will be hard to arrive at a common understanding of civil society, let alone a common policy agenda to promote such a vague, ambiguous concept.

7. Biases of Civil Society

There are many biases in the civil society literature and in the actions of civil society groups; here we enumerate only a few of them. First, the foreign foundations, donor groups, and strongest apostles of civil society are overwhelmingly liberal, activist, and associated with the U.S. Democratic Party, although Republicans may support the concept as well. There is, of course, nothing wrong with partisanship as long as we recognize that's what it is. Second, the movements abroad that these groups support tend not only to be similarly liberal, often radical, activist, and on the left, but also, almost by the definition of civil society itself, oppositionist and antigovernment. To be identified with such antigovernment activism, which may or may not be justified and is usually some fuzzy combination of the two, is very dangerous for outside groups and may lead to suppression, suspension of program activities, expulsion, and, overall, the overpoliticization of program activities. A third bias is the actions of these outside groups, often naive and well meaning but sometimes destructive as well, when they get involved in the internal affairs of other nations. A dramatic case in point is in the Mexican state of Chiapas, where many foreign NGOs have identified with and aided the revolutionary Zapatista movement; the Mexican government has sought to regulate and control them in classic corporatist fashion (hard to do with foreign-based groups while undergoing democratization and liberalization, and under media scrutiny at the same time), and finally threw up its hands in disgust and expelled many of the organizations from the country. This is not a forward step for civil society. There are *numerous* instances of foreign NGOs or the U.S. government using local, almost always U.S.-financed groups, to intervene in the internal affairs of other nations, and almost always as a way to influence political events in these countries.[8]

8. Whom to Include

Most of us have a conception of civil society that includes peasant groups, labor unions, women's groups, maybe political parties, neighborhood and community groups, human rights organizations, and—of course—bowling leagues.[9] But if we define civil society, as we must, as *all* those associations that are intermediary between state and citizen, we may have to include business groups, oligarchic sectors, paramilitaries, guerrillas, drug barons, and certainly in Latin America the Roman Catholic Church (historically more than a "mere" interest group, part of the state structure) as well as the rising Pentecostal movements. Now let us complicate the issue even more by including such unlovable groups as the European skinheads and the North American militias or the Ku Klux Klan, South African racists, terroristic Islamic fundamentalists, and violent and separatist ethnic movements.

An even more complex issue is presented by African ethnicity and tribalism, Indian caste associations, and Latin American patronage networks. Each of these is "parochial" and "traditional" in some senses, and we would probably prefer in terms of promoting modernization to confine them to the dustbins of history. Yet African tribalism often provides the only public and social services that many communities have; India's caste associations have become rather like modern interest associations and political parties; and without patronage networks to "grease" the machinery of government much of Latin America, the Middle Eastern states, Africa, and Southeast Asia (plus Louisiana, Arkansas, and a few other states) would collapse. In short, there is a large variety of civil society groups including many that we don't particularly like politically or consider passé or that are violent, destructive, and hateful. Civil society must be viewed like democracy: if that is what you want, then you have to be prepared to accept the outcome of the process even if it produces results in the form of groups that you may find objectionable.

9. Weakened States?

The concept of civil society implies limits on state authority; indeed, that is its purpose: to develop intermediaries between the state and its citizens that rein in the potential for the exercise of dictatorial power. However, the problem in many developing countries is no longer excessive state power (as it was in the 1970s under authoritarianism) but a state that, like other institutions in society and civil society itself, is weak, underdeveloped, and thus ineffective. Many Third World states, ostensibly strong and powerful, cannot make their writ felt in remote areas and are ineffective in carrying out the policies most of us would approve.[10] The problem in these societies may not be a too-strong state and, therefore, the need for the mediating influence and checks and balances of civil society, but a too-weak state that cannot govern or carry out effective public policies. Alternatively, the growth of civil society in ethnically divided (Indonesia) or fragmented (Argentina) societies may lead not to democracy but to divisions, ungovernability, and breakdown. My own view is the balanced one that we need both a strong and effective civil society and a strong and effective state; but with the current emphasis almost entirely on civil society, we run the risk of rendering states powerless and thus contributing to further fragmentation and ungovernability, already a major problem in many Third World nations.

A related issue involves the possible *reassertion* of state authority under threat of new challenges and provocations. We should not view the growth of civil society as necessarily inevitable, universal, irreversible, or as a result of inexorable development—although in the relatively peaceful 1980s and 1990s it might have appeared that way. From the perspective of post–September 11, 2001, and the terrorist attacks launched against the United States and other countries, many governments, threatened by ethnic, separatist, Islamic fundamentalist, terrorist, and disintegrative forces, are reversing past trends and strengthening statist and coercive forces. In the process, many civil society groups are being disbanded, harassed, and broken up, or having new restrictions placed on their activities. So while in the short run strengthened civil society seemed to be leading to weaker, less authoritarian, more democratic states, in the new circumstances we may be seeing a weakening of civil society and the corresponding strengthening of state structures, including reimposed authoritarian controls.

10. Ethnocentrism

Much of the literature on civil society seems to be based on the perception that one model fits all. And that one model, not surprising since that is where the modern version of the concept originated, almost always bears a striking resemblance to the Lockean, Madisonian, Tocquevillian, Hartzian liberalism and interest-group pluralism of the United States. But we have already seen that there are different models of civil society and state-society relations in the West; when we get to the non-West the differences become even more striking. Japan, South Korea, and Taiwan are all democracies and developed nations but with only weak civil society; the Islamic world similarly has weak civil society but almost no democracy at all. It seems to me the height of arrogance and ethnocentrism for the United States to proclaim that one size fits all, especially where that one size is modeled on ourselves and our own often *particular* history and society. Such a perception will in any case not work; we cannot export our model to societies where it does not fit and where the history, economy, sociology, and political culture are so much different from our own.[11] Meanwhile, Japan and quite a number of other nations seem to be doing quite well economically and as democracies without having a strong civil society. Civil society may, therefore, not be the critical variable in either democracy or development that is often suggested.

11. Sharks and Opportunists

In both the donor countries and the developing recipient ones, there are sharks and opportunists waiting to pounce on the latest program emanating from Washington and turn it to their own private financial or political advantage. I have been following the life cycles of these various programs since the beginning of the Alliance for Progress in the early 1960s, and it is striking how often the same people, whether on the U.S. contractor or consultant end or the developing country recipient end, are consistently involved. This cannot be sheer coincidence, nor is it simply that the same people will consistently have an interest in parallel progressive policies. In the developing countries that I know best, whether the issue is agrarian reform, community development, basic human needs, family planning, sustainable development, and now civil society, the same people always seem to form the local commissions and agencies that show the aid donors how and where to spend their monies. It is not merely love of public policy issues that motivates these persons; having been in quite a number of their homes, I can report that, as in political Washington, they have learned to "do well by doing good"; that is, to profit personally and/or politically by jumping quickly on the bandwagon of every new U.S. initiative that comes down the pike. Indeed, quite a few of these individuals are widely admired in their own countries on nationalistic grounds for having, over a forty-year period, milked and hoodwinked the (usually) American donor agencies while enriching themselves and rising to positions of prominence in the process. Of course, most of us will respond that "my friends and contacts would never do that and in any case there are controls in place"; but my experience is that the locals are at least as practiced as the donors at political machinations and are adept at taking advantage of these programs for private gain.

12. A Weak Popular Base?

The figures we have for all of Latin America indicate that only 13 percent of the population are members of civil society in any form; for other areas the numbers are even smaller. This figure includes political party, labor group, peasant group, women's group, community group, religious and other group members of all kinds. First, this is an incredibly low density number as compared with Western Europe or North America and offers scant evidence for the prospect of a mushrooming civil society in Latin America—or elsewhere in the developing world—anytime soon. Second, persons in Latin America tend to be members of one group and one group only; one does not find the webs of multiple and crosscutting group memberships that one finds in U.S. society that tend to moderate the citizen's position on any one issue. Rather, in Latin America one tends to go "all out" for the singular group of which one is a member, thus producing a society of almost stock types—*the* oligarch, *the* cleric, *the* military officer, *the* unionist, *the* student, etc.—whose behavior must conform to the stereotype. Such stereotyping and the rigidities of the categories, which probably go back to the social hierarchies of Saint Thomas, are not supportive of the moderating and stabilizing tendencies that civil society is supposed to engender.[12] Third, "civil society" in *all* of the areas investigated, particularly after the more immediate crisis (e.g., the struggle for a democratic election) has passed, is usually limited to elite and upper-middle-class groups, while the organization of the mass population is usually weak and inchoate.

13. A Product of Political Leaders and Intellectuals?

"Civil society" now has a certain *cachet*. Everyone among *our* friends and colleagues seems to agree it's a good thing. But are these sentiments widespread or are they only the preferences of government officials, party leaders, bureaucrats, and intellectuals? Has anyone yet checked with the mass of the populations of the developing world to see if they believe in civil society as much as we do? The few survey results we have indicate that, when it is explained to them, people often have a favorable view of civil society; at the same time, it remains vague, distant, and divorced from everyday realities. At the local level people may be reluctant to get involved; traditional fatalism is still widespread; and in those many countries based on the Napoleonic Code, one waits for guidance and direction from the central ministries, not relying on grassroots mobilization at the base. The issue may be parallel to that of "sustainable development," a concept to which the Brazilian government with considerable reluctance eventually agreed; meanwhile, Brazilian peasants, often with that same government's approval, continued to cut, burn, and "pave over" the Amazon basin, which supplies 40 percent of the world's oxygen. So with "civil society": government and political leaders and intellectuals approve at least in the abstract, but meantime overriding material interest and self-preservation often take priority.

14. Divorced from Power Realities?

Civil society cannot be seen as some magic formula that, as the title of a recent conference puts it, will "save the world." Instead, civil society must be seen in a broader political and power configuration. No government is going to favor civil society if in the process it sees its own power base eroding by the mobilization of new social sectors. Instead, it will try to co-opt, control, regulate, and maybe even repress civil society, to offer carrots or sticks or maybe both at once. At the same time, civil society groups will try to mobilize international public opinion and support to maintain their autonomy and freedom of action. These are political processes that will produce multiple outcomes and mixed results.

Let us take Mexico, whose complexities we can only barely begin to unravel. On the one hand, there is the official or state-run corporate structure of civil society (organized labor, business, farmers, professional associations), whose leaders in the face of a disintegrating state system and an opposition electoral victory are frantically scrambling to renegotiate their relationship with the state, the official Revolutionary Institutional Party (PRI), and the new government. On the other hand, there is the new, freer civil society widely credited with helping Mexico democratize over the last thirty years and now entering into a new relationship with the government and the citizens. These respective groups are renegotiating their relations not only with the state but also with each other, where conflict between the official labor, peasant, Indian, and business groups and the independent or civil society groups is intense and sometimes violent. Within these conglomerates of groups, negotiations and political relations are proceeding at different speeds; and in the south of Mexico the Zapatistas and other "civil society" groups have opted out of the co-optation game to pursue a radical agenda and guerrilla tactics. They are opposed by both the regular armed forces and police and by paramilitaries—another unlovely but often effective civil society group. Meanwhile, there are a host of foreign or foreign-sponsored groups whose relations with the government are complicated precisely because they are often nonnational. I count at least six state–civil society arenas here with multiple possible outcomes. To me this is all political process and interest politics with only limited relation to some idealistic goal of advancing civil society.[13]

15. Outside Sponsorship and Control

A related problem is that of outside, or foreign, sponsorship, control, and manipulation of civil society groups. In the Dominican Republic, for example, the U.S. Embassy had concluded that the aging and increasingly infirm President Joaquín Balaguer was not only corrupt, but that his continuation in office might be destructive of democracy and stability. Hence, the Embassy and U.S. AID provided massive support to a so-called citizens' group, the *Red Ciudadaña* (Citizens Network—many of the same opportunists who had earlier been involved in agrarian reform, family planning, sustainable development, etc.), to oppose Balaguer, find alternative candidates, and rally oppositionist sentiment. It brought in the National Endowment for Democracy (NED), the National Democratic Institute (NDI), and a host of well-paid civil society, political party, and elections experts to help support this campaign. Depending on one's politics, of course, one can approve or not approve of the Embassy's actions, but one should not confuse these embassy fronts and their political machinations with genuine indigenous, homegrown, or grassroots civil society, let alone with democracy. Moreover, once the Embassy had accomplished its short-term political goal, the funds for this ostensible "civil society" organization quickly dried up, leaving the Dominican groups high and dry and without sufficient support in most cases to survive. Many of their leaders then accepted high positions within the succeeding government (perhaps their goal all along in mobilizing civil society), thus leaving the fledgling civil society groups bereft of both funds and leadership. Such manipulation of "civil society" by governments and foreign embassies happens all the time, and we need thus to distinguish between genuine civil society of the homegrown kind and that sponsored by states and outside powers.[14]

16. Is Civil Society Self-Sustaining?

The above discussion touches on an important point: Is civil society sustainable after the foreign support and funds are gone? The answer is, no one knows and it is likely to be a mixed bag of outcomes. The issue is important and fraught with policy implications because, if civil society is not sustainable once the outside support dries up, the political system may well fragment, disintegrate, and collapse—precisely the outcome that the civil society initiatives were designed to prevent. But it is just as likely that another scenario will play out and that quite a number of countries may be left with the worst of all possible worlds: traditional civil society (tribes, caste associations, patronage networks) undermined and destroyed under the impact of both modernization and U.S. pressures, but a fledgling modern civil society—political parties, interest associations, opposition groups—floundering because of popular indifference and a withdrawal of critical foreign funding. Here we need to distinguish between countries: Mexico may be sufficiently well developed and institutionalized that its civil society can survive U.S. embassy machinations and funding shortfalls, but in the less developed, less well-institutionalized Dominican Republic, in sub-Saharan Africa, in the Philippines, Indonesia, and East Timor, and in the small countries of Central America, the decline or withdrawal of outside funding for civil society groups, in the absence of much homegrown associability, may well lead to societal unraveling and political breakdown.

17. "Civil Society" as a Reflection of the United States

It is striking how often, when we speak of civil society, we have in mind a society that looks just like we do. And when foreign funds are involved, the types of "civil society" supported tend to look just like their sponsoring groups in the United States. Take the case of the National Endowment for Democracy. For partisan reasons and to get the bill through Congress, NED consists of four constituent groups: the Republican and Democratic Parties' international affairs branches, big labor (the AFL-CIO), and big business (as represented through the U.S. Chamber of Commerce). This structure is, of course, a reflection of internal U.S. political power and interest-group relations, but whether a similar or imitative structure is appropriate for all other societies, cultures, and political systems is unlikely.[15] Similarly with other, more narrowly focused groups: what the Population Council, the National Wildlife Fund, and others have as their agendas may be quite appropriate in the United States but I am not sure the exact parallels, even mirrors of these groups, need to be established abroad. Civil society, it seems to me, needs to be variable and appropriate for diverse societies and cultures; patterning civil society in other countries exclusively or nearly so on our own model and society may be inappropriate and self-defeating, and ultimately lead to failure.

18. Central versus Local Controls

As liberalization and democratization have expanded in recent decades, we have seen a gradual dismantling—at least at the formal, legal, or constitutional level—of the authoritarian, corporative, or regulatory controls by which states control civil society. Democracy, in short, means not just parties and elections but a freeing up of associational life in general. For in most countries one cannot just go out as in the United States and organize an interest group; instead, the interest group must seek recognition and "juridical personality" from the state, and there is a vast web of regulations and corporative controls that is used to co-opt, control, and limit such group activities. But while in many countries these corporative controls are being repealed at the national level, they are being reenacted at the local level (where most civil society groups operate) as local authorities force civil society groups to register, show their membership lists and sources of financing, and gain recognition from local officialdom. Of course, the power to grant recognition to a group also implies the power *not* to grant it. So while corporatism is often in decline at national levels and democracy triumphant, at local levels corporatism is often reemerging. Democracy in its formal form may thus not be incompatible with a high degree of illiberalism at both national and local levels, but then, is that truly democratic?

19. Civil Society as Romantic Vision?

Are the focus and hopes that have come to be centered on civil society realistic? Or are they the product of unwarranted idealism and romance? Is civil society another one of those concepts that inflate expectations, provide short-term employment for thousands of consultants, and then fall to earth again? So far, the results of all civil society efforts have been disappointing: slightly over 10 percent organized in any fashion in all of Latin America, far less so in Africa, the Middle East, and Southeast Asia. Surely civil society has done little so far to enhance democracy or development in Africa or the Islamic countries, and East Asia appears both not to want *or need* much in the way of civil society. In Peru and Venezuela, under authoritarian-populist leadership, civil society has all but been destroyed; Cuba has no or minimal civil society to speak of apart from the state; and, particularly in the small, underdeveloped, weakly institutionalized countries of Africa and Central and South America, the Rousseauian model of direct identification between leader and masses, *sans* civil society, continues to be attractive. Is civil society, which seems to many to be an agency of hope, really just clutching at straws?

20. Can Civil Society Be Exported?

So far, there is *not a single case* of the West being able to export its model *en toto* to other lands and cultures. By this, I mean not just the Western model of civil society but, more basically, the cultural and social norms that undergird it, derived from the Renaissance; the Reformation and particularly its economic and political ramifications; the Enlightenment and its rationalist way of thinking; the Industrial Revolution; and the revolution of democracy in its Lockean, Madisonian, Jeffersonian form. *Parts* of the model—usually easily imitated institutional arrangements such as elections or parliaments—may be exported, both because people want them and because we put pressure on and leverage them; but usually not the underlying values of democracy (tolerance, egalitarianism, mutual respect) nor the vast webs of associability that de Tocqueville described. Those are peculiar, particular, a part of our unique history, culture, and tradition; they cannot be packed up and shipped over in a container carton to countries where the culture, society, and traditions are distinct. Of course, we can get thin and pale imitations of civil society and democracy (democracy with adjectives: "limited," "controlled," "organic," "delegative," "Rousseauian," "Islamic," "Confucian," "corporatist") but not often the real thing. That takes two or three generations, as in Russia, not two or three years; and other than in only superficial ways it remains doubtful if civil society is transplantable from one model country to another. The result in most of these countries is what has come to be called "formal democracy" (regular elections and the like) but not "liberal democracy."

TOWARD THE FUTURE

Having said all of these skeptical things about civil society, let me also say that I tend to be in favor of the concept and what it implies in a policy sense. For most (not all) countries, a web of intermediary associations between the citizen and the state serves both to limit state power and authoritarianism and to serve as a transmission belt by which citizens can make their interests known to government officials. To the degree civil society is present, it tends (but not always) to be good for the state, for society, and for democracy.

Extrapolating and summarizing from the list of twenty reasons to be cautious about the concept analyzed above, three problems seem to be especially important. The first is the incredible variety of civil society forms, their diverse underlying philosophical, social, and cultural assumptions, the frequently mixed and "crazy-quilt" patchworks that exist, the distinct definitions, meanings, and priorities accorded civil society. The second, related, is the problem of ethnocentrism: our (particularly American) inability to comprehend and accept forms (Confucian, Islamist, clientelistic, statist, corporatist) of civil society and state-society relations, let alone democracy, other than our own. The third problem is politicization of the concept by everyone and for private political or economic purposes: local elites in Third World countries, foundations, the AFL-CIO, the Chamber of Commerce, AID, NED, U.S. embassies abroad, successive U.S. governments. Once that happens, and the issue gets enmeshed in our and other domestic politics and our politicized foreign policy, it is probably hopelessly lost, and we should, therefore, expect the gaffes, shortsightedness, and frequent misfires that have, in fact, occurred in many countries.

The ethnocentrism, biases, failures of understanding and empathy, private agendas, and all the other problems identified here may be a cause for despair among those, of whom I count myself one, who favor the growth of civil society. Three points need to be made. First, the civil society agenda, like the democracy one, is now so deeply entrenched in the international lending agencies, the foundations, and U.S. and other aid and foreign policy programs that it is certain to continue despite our reservations about it. Second, *on balance*, the concept of civil society and what it stands for—democracy, pluralism, participation, a group life apart from the state—are still worth working for, despite the frequent miscues and insensitivities. Third, therefore, let us continue with the program of assisting civil society, meanwhile trying to fix the problems indicated but not jettisoning the entire program. For even in its stumbling, bumbling, ethnocentric way, U.S. aid over time has produced some change, development, and the socioeconomic basis for greater democratization and civil society.

Civil society cannot "save the world," as some of its advocates have suggested. One is tempted to say, cynically, that civil society may have already peaked, that it is already too late, that we should forget about the idea and just wait for the next cure-all panacea to come down the pike. But that is too negative and, in fact, ignores the political process and positive factors that I have argued need to be taken into account. That, in turn, implies acceptance or at least understanding on the part of civil society advocates and practitioners of the compromises, mixed forms, and the frequent use and misuse of civil society in the political process. Hence, let us support and aid civil society—it is still a good idea—but do so with our eyes wide open, realistically, and recognizing both the opportunities and the limits that championing civil society in other people's countries offers.

NOTES

1. John Ehrenberg, *Civil Society* (New York: New York University Press, 1999).

2. The title of a recent conference on civil society.

3. Robert Putnam, *Bowling Alone: The Collapse and Revival of American Community* (New York: Simon & Schuster, 2000).

4. Thomas Carothers, *Aiding Democracy Abroad: The Learning Curve* (Washington, DC: The Carnegie Endowment for International Peace, 1999).

5. Howard J. Wiarda, *Corporatism and Comparative Politics: The Other Great "Ism"* (New York: M. E. Sharpe, 1996).

6. Howard J. Wiarda, *Civil Society* (Boulder, CO: Westview Press, 2003).

7. Anheir, *The Third World's Third Sector in Comparative Perspective* (Baltimore: Johns Hopkins University, The Johns Hopkins Comparative Nonprofit Sector Project, 1997).

8. A balanced assessment is Carothers, *Aiding Democracy*; also Marina Ottaway et al. (eds.), *Funding Virtue: Civil Society Aid and Democracy Promotion* (Washington, DC: Carnegie Endowment, 2000).

9. Putnam, *Bowling Alone*.

10. Samuel P. Huntington, *Political Order in Changing Societies* (New Haven: Yale University Press, 1968); Linn Hammergren, *Development and the Politics of Administrative Reform: Lessons from Latin America* (Boulder: Westview Press, 1983).

11. A. H. Somjee, *Parallels and Actuals of Political Development* (London: Macmillan, 1986); Howard J. Wiarda, *Ethnocentrism and Foreign Policy: Can We Understand the Third World?* (Washington, DC: American Enterprise Institute for Public Policy Research, 1985).

12. Carothers, *Aiding Democracy*; Salamon and Anheir, *The Third World's Third Sector*; Ronald Inglehart, *Culture Change in Advanced Industrial Society* (Princeton: Princeton University Press, 1990).

13. Neil Harvey (ed.), *Mexico: Dilemmas of Transition* (New York: St. Martin's, 1993); and Wayne Cornelius et al. (eds.), *Transforming State-Society Relations in Mexico* (San Diego University: Center for U.S.-Mexican Studies, Univ. of California, San Diego, 1994).

14. Christopher Sabatini, "Whom Do International Donors Support in the Name of Civil Society?" Paper prepared for delivery at the 2000 meeting of the Latin American Studies Association, Miami, March 16–18.

15. Howard J. Wiarda, *The Democratic Revolution in Latin America: History, Politics, and U.S. Policy* (New York: The Twentieth Century Fund, Holmes and Meier, 1990).

10

✿

The Developing Nations:
What Works in Development
—and What Doesn't

In the late 1950s and early 1960s the developing nations made their big splash onto the world stage. Latin America had become independent from Spain and Portugal in the 1820s, a handful of countries had gained independence after World War I, and India and Pakistan as well as parts of North Africa and the Middle East had become independent following World War II. But by 1960 a host of countries in Africa, Asia, the South Pacific, the Middle East, and the Caribbean had become newly independent. As an indicator of these changes the United Nations swelled to a membership of over 150 nations, and power began gradually to pass from the major countries represented in the UN's Security Council (the United States, Russia, China, France, Great Britain) to the more democratic (one nation, one vote) General Assembly. The sudden proliferation of so many new nations marked a turning point in world history; the emergence of scores of new political entities also broadened enormously the universe of comparative politics.

In Bandung, Indonesia, in 1956, Prime Minister Sukarno, Gamel Abdul Nasser of Egypt, and many other leaders from these new and largely non-Western nations got together to plan a common strategy. This was the beginning of the nonaligned movement, or what we commonly call the "Third World." The leadership of this movement and the countries represented actually had few things in common (China and Yugoslavia were also members), but most of them did share common histories of poverty, backwardness, and colonialism; a desire for socialism or maybe central planning; and a hope that, by remaining neutral and playing the then two great superpowers, the United States and the Soviet Union, off against each other, they could preserve their independence and reap assistance from the major powers for themselves. Thus was born not only the post–World War II tripartite organization of the world's nations into First World (developed capitalist states), Second World (developed communist states), and Third World (developing states), but also a fundamental feature of the Cold War, with both the United States and the Soviet Union competing for influence in numerous, often marginal Third World nations.

Now this structure of the post–World War II world has collapsed or is changing very rapidly. The former Soviet Union, Eastern Europe, China, and other previously communist nations are undergoing fundamental transformations. In addition, the Third World has learned, or is beginning to learn, that in the modern global economy socialism and central state planning do not work very well; some kind of free market is necessary. But more than these epochal changes, it may be that, in the absence of a viable Second World or communist threat, the very concept of a Third World independent from and playing the other two "worlds" off against each other has lost all meaning. What can it possibly mean to be "nonaligned" these days? With the Soviet Union having collapsed, who is there left to play the United States off against? In this chapter, therefore, we examine not only what has changed in the Third World's strategy of development but also where the Third World now fits in the organization of world power.

THE THEORY OF DEVELOPMENT

In the 1950s, when the early academic literature on development was written, Western economists had almost no experience in the developing nations and almost no literature on which to build. Whatever had been written about these Third World areas that were now, suddenly, independent nations was mainly by cultural anthropologists and a handful of journalists. Political scientists had not spent much time in these formerly colonial territories, nor did economists have a sure handle on how to stimulate development there. In the absence of either experience or prior literature, economists fell back on the models of development that they did know: the United States and Western Europe.

Most of the economists who wrote about development in those early days—John Kenneth Galbraith, Raúl Prebisch, Paul Rosenstein-Rodan, Albert Hirschman, Robert Heilbroner, Everett Hagen, W. W. Rostow, Lincoln Gordon—were Keynesians, brought up on the politics and economics of Franklin Delano Roosevelt's New Deal, who believed in strong state intervention in the economy.[1] Their beliefs were backed by the leading European economists and sociologists such as Gunnar Myrdal.[2] Some of these economists were socialists, but most were social democrats who were often more strongly committed to central planning than to free-market mechanisms.

During the 1950s, when Dwight Eisenhower was president and a conservative economic policy still reigned, most of these Keynesian economists were located in universities where they wrote the first articles and books on what was called "development economics." In fact, since a lot of the early literature was written at Harvard and MIT, this emerging body of literature came to be known as the "Charles River School," after the river that flows by both campuses and out into Boston Harbor. But when John F. Kennedy was elected president in 1960, many of these academic economists from the Cambridge, Massachusetts, area went with him to Washington where they filled influential government posts in the new administration and helped design such programs aimed at the Third World as the Alliance for Progress, the Peace Corps, and the Agency for International Development. All these programs were based on the assumptions of a leading role for the state in promoting development, central planning, a "balance" between private and public ownership, and a guiding, directing function for a plethora of new state regulatory agencies. The private sector, entrepreneurship, and markets received almost no attention either in the literature on development or in the main programs of the Kennedy administration.[3]

These emphases of the development economists corresponded closely with the preferences of leaders in the developing nations. For one thing, many of the early leaders of the new nations were themselves socialists (Sukarno, Nasser, Nkrumah, Kenyatta) or social democrats, having been trained in many cases at the London School of Economics (LSE) or perhaps the Sorbonne in Paris. At the ideological level, therefore, they mostly agreed with or went beyond their American advisers.[4]

But these political leaders in the emerging nations often had a second, political agenda that the well-meaning Americans who advised them seldom understood: that more power, resources, and economic control concentrated in the hands of the central state vastly increased these leaders' political power. It gave them greater patronage, sinecure positions, levers of authority, and hard cash that could be used for graft, the rewarding of friends, or the paying off of enemies. Often unbeknownst to the sometimes naive American academics who helped design and rationalized these Third World development programs, the money was used not always for development but too often for these essentially graft, patronage, and political functions.

Expanding state size was the main cause of the massive political corruption that came, unfortunately, to be endemic in many Third World countries. That was not, of course, the purpose that the foreign economists had in mind when they designed these programs, but it was one of

the unintended consequences. Moreover, the longer these early independence leaders stayed in power, the higher the level of graft and corruption
required to keep them there. It is an unfortunate fact of life, regardless of
ideological or political preferences, that the amount of corruption was directly proportional to the size of the state sector. As the size of the state increased, so did the amount of graft. Eventually, the corruption reached
such a level that it largely squeezed out what was left of the private sector, bankrupted many Third World economies, discredited the state and
its leaders, and led to the situations of mass starvation, incredible inefficiency, national disintegration, and widespread violence that are prevalent in some of these countries today.

The theory of development advanced by these early scholars joined by
most Third World leaders was state-led economic growth. It paid very little attention to markets, entrepreneurship, or private business. Rather, it
was the state that was to lead economic development, channel the resources, make decisions on investment and consumption, set prices and
wages, and centrally plan the economy. In most Western nations, including the United States, we now recognize that such strict central economic
control and so many programs run by the central government do not
work very well and are neither efficient nor productive; imagine, then,
how inefficient and downright disastrous such programs would be in
countries lacking the institutions to carry them out effectively.

In addition, in part because the theory was fashioned mainly by economists, it had an economic determinist foundation of undergirding assumptions that proved to be quite wrong. The theory assumed that economics was the driving force in development. It also assumed that social
change—a rising middle class, responsible trade unions, trickle-down benefits to the poor, greater societal pluralism, moderation and resistance to
extremist appeals, a better-informed and participatory citizenry—would
all result from economic development. Importantly for our purposes, it
further assumed that democratization and stable governments would, inevitably and universally—regardless of cultural and historical differences—follow from economic development. All we needed to do, therefore, was prime the pumps, provide foreign aid, and stimulate investment;
democracy would seemingly be the automatic result of the economic engine of change. But of course the actual practice of development proved to
be far different, more complex, and disappointing than the theory.

THE PRACTICE OF DEVELOPMENT

Recall that in the 1950s when the early literature on development was
published, we had very little actual experience with the developing na-

tions. There was no literature on the subject, so scholars largely fell back on the experiences they knew: the United States and Western Europe. This helps explain why, in the absence of experience or much empirical data, the models of development presented tended to be highly abstract, very theoretical, and without solid grounding in actual Third World realities.

But now, some forty years later, we have abundant experience with development. Our models need no longer be so abstract and theoretical—we can now ground them in reality and experience instead of abstractions. We now generally know what works and what doesn't work in development.

Where, then, did early development theory go wrong? The question is particularly poignant because to most of us, as Americans, it seems so reasonable. All we need do is provide the economic wherewithal and some advice, and democracy and pluralism will presumably flower. The question may be especially difficult for Americans because, after all, so much of the model was based on our own experience. That complicates matters because when we say the theory of development went wrong, we are also saying that maybe the American or, more broadly, Western experience of development doesn't work in, or has little or no relevance to, the Third World. That is a heretical proposition that flies in the face of the widespread U.S. belief not only that our institutions are the best there are but that we have a duty and an obligation to export them to less-favored lands.

In fact, this belief contains elements of truth: Some of our institutions and practices *are* useful, workable, and transferable in somewhat modified form to the developing nations, and others are not. We need, therefore, to sort out what is valuable, universal, and exportable in the American experience and what is not. Clearly, many aspects of the U.S.-inspired development theory are not workable abroad—although some aspects of it are.

Here are some of the key dilemmas in the U.S.-based development theory. First, we believed that by pouring in assistance the money would trickle down to the poor and the middle class, but in many Third World countries the funds were monopolized by the elites in control of the government and never reached the poor. Second, development theory assumed that a larger middle class would be a bastion of democracy and stability, but in many developing countries the emerging middle classes mimicked upper-class ways, disdained those who worked with their hands, and turned to the military to protect their interests from the lower classes. Rather than democracy, authoritarianism was the result. Third, we assumed that nonpolitical labor unions could be created that would be assimilated into the existing system, but in fact in many developing nations unions turned out to be highly political and often revolutionary.

The list of wrong, misleading, or only partially correct assumptions in development theory goes on. Fourth, developmentalism assumed that the leaders in these countries were public-spirited and desirous of benefitting their people, but in too many cases the leadership proved greedy, selfish, and rapacious; instead of serving the public interest, its main goal was to serve its own private interests—or those of its family, cronies, clan, community, or tribe. Fifth, development theory assumed that a professional, apolitical military could be created, but instead, the middle-class officer corps shared the ambitions and fears of the middle class more generally and often intervened to snuff out democratic movements and to frustrate the desires of peasants and workers. Sixth, development theory assumed a commitment to national development on the part of Third World bureaucracies and to carrying out effective public policies, but instead, what was presented as public policy too often actually served to line the pockets of the bureaucrats and their friends.

The most egregious mistake of development theory, however, was that it completely ignored political and cultural variables. It assumed that economic development would automatically generate social change (pluralism, a larger middle class, and so on), which would automatically produce political democratization. Furthermore, these processes were thought to be universal; once the great engine of industrialization got started, nothing could stop it and no local culture could resist it. But democratization does not just happen as a result of some inevitable process: It requires hard work, skilled political leaders, party organizers, well-run public programs, well-organized political groups, and so on. There is nothing *inevitable* about democracy; rather, democracy has to be *built*; it is an independent variable and not just dependent upon economic factors. Obviously, economic development helps to stimulate social change and can serve to make democracy more secure—although the recent great wave of transitions from authoritarianism back to democracy came at a time of economic recession, not prosperity, in most of the Third World. In short, democracy has to be seen as something worth working and fighting for and not just as the inevitable by-product of economic growth.

Related was the issue of culture, which development theory largely ignored. It assumed that economic development would produce a leveling of culture, a homogenization, in which cultural differences would become less apparent and less important. Hence the theory paid very little attention to historical, regional, religious, or cultural differences. It assumed that what worked in the United States would also work in Latin America, that what worked in Latin America would also work in Africa, and so on. But culture, like politics, is an independent variable, not a dependent one. It is preposterous to think that religious beliefs, legal systems, history, value patterns, and traditional ways of doing things do not have an impact on development, or that they are erased and disappear as development proceeds. Japan is the clearest example: a country that has achieved phenomenal economic growth but that has also preserved its own culture. Its culture stresses harmony and consensus in social relations rather than the conflict of American-style pluralism; culture also helps explain the chumminess of Japanese business-government relations and the continuity and stability of its political system. The Japan case and numerous others illustrate that culture and development exist in a dynamic relationship: culture shapes the path and peculiarities of development, while development in turn also has a long-range effect on culture. In either case, culture, like politics, cannot be ignored as it was in early development theory.

We could easily extend this list to include virtually every assumption of development theory.[5] Many proved wrong or, at best, only partially correct. What went wrong? How could our theories lead us so far astray?

There are several key (and lots of small) reasons, most of which are interrelated and which flow from the previous points. First, prior to 1960, virtually none of the early theorists of development had ever actually spent much time in a developing nation; they often held an antiseptic, even romantic view of development, untainted by the hard political realities of actually living in the Third World. Second, the models they used, as we have seen, derived from the American and European experiences and had very limited relevance for Third World nations with different histories and cultures. And that leads to the third main explanation: They ignored crucial political, cultural, and regional variables, and instead assumed that once the great motor force of economic development began, the outcomes socially and politically in all countries would be the same. But, of course, development does not occur that way, and it is wrong and misleading to think so. In fact, culture has been a filter of development, a way of keeping some Western ideas out and allowing others in, a factor in forcing development either to adapt to local conditions or to produce failures and unintended consequences. The ignoring of these factors by development theory doomed both the overall model and many specific programs to failure.[6]

Some countries, however, did begin to develop. They developed far faster economically and socially than they did politically. Beginning in the 1960s quite a number of Third World countries began to grow economically. Their per capita incomes increased by 2, 3, 4 percent or even higher per year, industrialization went forward, and affluence began to increase. In addition, social changes took place, the middle class increased in size, trade unions were organized, literacy and urbanization increased, peasants began to mobilize, and so on. But these changes, while often impressive, did not lead to any inevitable, let alone universal, situations of pluralism, secularism, or the fading of traditional culture and behavior as the theory suggested. Nor, as we have seen, did they lead necessarily to democracy.

While the economic direction in most developing countries in the 1960s and 1970s was slowly upward, toward increased economic development, some other countries, mostly in East Asia but elsewhere as well, experienced truly phenomenal growth—rates of 5, 6, or 7 percent per year. At the same time, other countries remained mired in poverty, without improvement. All three of these patterns—the spectacular growers, the slow growers, and the true disaster areas—command our attention in the next section. But note again that in none of the three patterns was economic development correlated automatically or necessarily with the growth of democracy.

CASES AND PATTERNS OF DEVELOPMENT

We often use the terms *Third World* or *developing nations* to designate a certain group of countries that have been poor and that have recently begun the development process. But these terms gloss over the enormous variations that exist within the Third World. The differences among these countries are in fact growing wider—so wide that a single designation is no longer applicable to them. Later in the chapter, on this and other grounds, we suggest that the term *Third World* has outlived its usefulness.

East Asia: The NICs

Newly industrialized countries (NICs) is a term invented by the World Bank. It is used to designate those countries, mostly concentrated in East Asia but not exclusively so, that have undergone exceedingly rapid economic growth in the last forty years. In fact, their growth has been nothing short of phenomenal. Industrialization, GNP, and per capita income have often shot up exceedingly rapidly. These countries are the true wonders of the developing world.

The most successful NICs have been South Korea, the Republic of China (Taiwan), Hong Kong, and Singapore. The first two countries, although small in size and resources, became economic giants, matching, and in some areas surpassing, the miraculous growth rates of Japan. The latter two countries are manufacturing and trading/commercial centers.

Their formula has been export-led growth. They have skillfully exploited external markets, principally in the United States, and they have been smart and flexible enough to shift products and exports as the markets change. They now export clothing, plastics, wood products, steel, manufactured goods, and high-technology items, as well as many other products. These countries have an educated, hard-working labor force, and they are disciplined and well organized. They utilize open markets but they also employ state assistance. They value education and skills highly. Their social systems are orderly yet accommodative; their political systems, while not always fully democratic, have similarly accommodated themselves to change and to the new requirements of greater democratization and human rights observance. Political order and stability have given them the internal peace necessary to develop their economies. They have enacted vast social programs to assist their citizens in living longer, more creative, and more productive lives. Some of these East Asian economies have also experienced recession but, since they have the basics in place (stability, education, a work ethic, discipline, organization, greater political freedom), they are again on the road to recovery with increasing growth rates in the last several years.

So what is the key factor in explaining the growth of the East Asian "tigers"? Is it the structural institutions (business-government cooperation) that these nations have put in place to encourage development, or is it the work ethic of their common Confucian culture? The answer is, some of both. No doubt the institutions put in place to encourage growth, such as government assistance to beginning industries, planning, careful market research, cartels, and strong state ministries and bureaucracies, had a strong impact on growth. But remember this story also: Once, while riding on a plane between Singapore and the Philippines, the author sat next to a gentleman of Chinese background, married to a *Filipina*, who also had business connections in the Philippines. We conversed for a time about his life and business, and then I asked him to explain to me why Taiwan, Hong Kong, and Singapore had done so well while the Philippines had not. My companion thought, looked around to make sure no one was listening (the passengers were mostly Filipinos), and then whispered: "They're not Chinese!" This response was not only a reflection of his own prejudices but probably a widespread Asian belief in the importance of Confucian cultural factors (hard work, belief in education, strong family values, initiative) as well.

However, it is not just in Asia where we find examples of successful NICs, successful development. In Latin America, Brazil, Chile, and Mexico have also achieved some phenomenal growth rates. These are all quite large countries, with sizable internal markets, substantial natural resources, and, increasingly, the political stability and democratic institutions on which economic growth can be built. All have taken significant steps recently to move away from the state-directed, import-substitution, mercantilist policies of the past, toward more open-market economies. All have evolved toward pluralism and greater human rights observance, and all have expanded social programs to provide for the poorest of their citizens.

Nor is it only the "tigers" of East Asia that have done well. Other countries of that area, historically mired in poverty, are now also beginning to develop. Myanmar, Thailand, Malaysia, the Philippines, and Indonesia have all begun to pick themselves up. All of these in the past have tied themselves to the great motor force of Asian development: Japan; now China has emerged as a major Asian, and global, economic power as well. All have used the formula that is becoming increasingly associated with economic growth: more open markets, export-oriented growth, political stability, encouragement of entrepreneurial spirit, allowance for social change and provision for social programs, and increasing openness to democracy.[7] Let us see how these features are working in other areas of the globe.

Oil-Exporting States

The oil-exporting states of the Middle East, which suddenly became wealthy because of their vast petroleum, occupy a special place in our catalog: they don't fit. On the one hand, such states as Saudi Arabia, Kuwait, Bharain, Dubai, and Abu Dhabi are enormously wealthy in per capita terms—right up there with the wealthiest nations in the world. On the other hand, their social development (education, social programs, pluralism, egalitarianism) and, even more so, their political development (numbers of civic groups and interest associations, institutionalization, and, above all, democratization) lag way behind other developed nations. They also lag behind many other developing nations, who are much poorer economically than the oil-exporting nations but are sometimes more advanced socially and politically.

These oil-exporting nations are basically sheikdoms or sultanships that have undergone some limited modernization but whose social and political systems are still mainly traditional, often anachronistic. They are exceptional cases. As alternative future scenarios, one could expect that continued economic prosperity would give rise over time to greater demands for social and political development, or else that the regimes in these countries would be obliged to use more absolute or totalitarian controls to stay in power while their populations become increasingly restless. As we have seen in numerous other cases, such authoritarian regimes cannot hold in check forever the social and political forces that modernization sets loose.

The oil-exporting countries thus constitute exceptions—so far—to the rules of development we have observed.

Latin America

Latin America has long been a kind of laboratory, or experiment station, for U.S. efforts to encourage reform and development in the Third World.

ﺳﻌﻴﻮﻥ

When we speak of "developing nations," it is usually Latin America (and a few others—Egypt, India, Indonesia) that we have in mind.

Latin America has long been committed to a statist model of development. Depending on the country, the state in Latin America may generate anywhere from 30 to 70 percent of GNP. That means that Latin America has considerably less state ownership than the present or former communist countries, but considerably more than the United States or most capitalist countries. Indeed, it is useful to think of the differences between communism and capitalism as forming a continuum, not a simple two-part categorization (see figure 10.1).

What we are suggesting is that, in addition to the capitalist and communist economies with which we are more familiar, there is a third category that we can call statist or mercantilist. Statist economies are intermediary between capitalism and communism. Typically in statist economies, the state will own and generate at least a third, maybe a half, perhaps even three-quarters as in Mexico, of the GNP. The state will usually own or monopolize the oil, petrochemical, steel, communications, transportation, and insurance industries as well as all utilities, banking, liquor, and gambling; it will also hold considerable interest in other economic sectors. In addition to its actual ownership, the state will usually be heavily involved in central planning; will often itself (rather than the market) set price, wage, and production levels; and will tightly regulate that part of the economy that is still privately owned.

Several lessons follow from this description of statist economies—which are not very much different from the lessons learned about communist

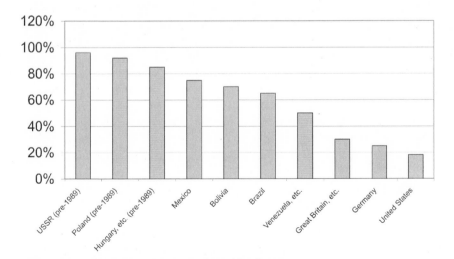

Figure 10.1. Percentage of GNP Generated by the State

countries. First, they are very inefficient because, in the absence of market incentives, there is very little reason to be streamlined or efficient. Second, they tend to be quite corrupt because corruption is often the only way to make the system work. Third, they tend to be top-down bureaucracies bloated with excess red tape, because efficiency is not rewarded and there is no reason to process work speedily. Fourth, they tend to become gigantic sinecure, patronage, or spoils agencies because, in the absence of efficiency as a criteria of appointment, that is how friends, cronies, allies, and family members are rewarded. Fifth, they breed a dependence on government (as distinct from entrepreneurship) because the state is virtually the only source of employment and because it is *the* source of contracts, licenses, and permits.

The list could go on, but enough has been said to indicate that these systems have not historically been very efficient economically in stimulating growth and that the statist regimes of Latin America and elsewhere, like their communist counterparts, have been very poor performers as compared with the East Asian NICs. Mexico and Venezuela have done well in the past because they almost literally float on oil (and thus have features comparable to the Middle Eastern oil-exporting nations), and Brazil is so big and resource-rich that it continues to grow even in the face of a statist regime ("Brazil develops at night," it is said, "while the government sleeps"). But when such factors as richness of resources are held constant, most statist regimes have performed very poorly. Many of these countries, especially Chile, Argentina, and now Brazil and Mexico, have recognized the debilitating effects of statism and have begun to move away from it.

In addition, a close connection may be made between countries that have statist economies and authoritarianism politically. When so much power and control are exercised by the state economically in terms of employment, licenses, contracts, monopoly, patronage, regulation, and so on, it is a very short step to political control. The connections are twofold: direct, in the form of control over individual employment possibilities, because the state is by far the country's largest employer and one does not criticize, let alone rebel against, the government that is paying one's wages; and indirect, in the form of all those licensing and regulatory procedures that can be used to hamstring political as well as economic activities. In short, developing nations that are heavily statist economically tend also to be authoritarian politically.

When Latin America began its impressive transitions to democracy in the late 1970s and early 1980s, it initially did so without changing its economic substructure. It made a political transition to democracy but not an economic one. As the inefficiency and bankruptcy of the statist model became increasingly apparent, as the successes of the East Asian NICs highlighted Latin America's deficiencies, and as the United States and the international lending agencies began to exert pressure, the Latin American countries began to change. They realized they would have to liberalize and free up their economies. In a time of declining foreign assistance, they could no longer rely on outside aid, nor could they blame all their internal problems on outside forces—as in dependency theory. After all, the successful East Asian NICs had been just as dependent on outside markets and capital as had Latin America, but East Asia had turned these conditions to advantage while Latin America remained mired in poverty. Beginning in the late 1980s, however, all the Latin American countries were sending trade missions to Asia to learn how the Asians had achieved such phenomenal development. Latin America was forced to become serious about development. It began to introduce privatization and free markets in the economic sphere just as it had earlier reintroduced political freedom and democratization.

A variety of reforms ensued in all the Latin American countries—though some were more successful than others. The Latin American countries moved to streamline their bloated bureaucracies, to open their markets to competition, to remove the various layers of red tape that hamper business dealings, to emphasize exports, to privatize state-owned enterprises, to reduce the size of their public sector, and in general to free up their economies. The pace of change was often exasperatingly slow because it is hard to find buyers for inefficient public industries or to actually fire people from public sector jobs. Sometimes they would fire thousands of public workers while the International Monetary Fund (IMF), whose loans were contingent upon serious structural reform, was watching, and then hire thousands back when they thought the IMF wasn't looking.

Nevertheless, the reforms in some nations have been impressive. Inefficiency has been reduced, the economies of the area have been partially privatized, more open market systems are being established, new investment is coming in, and economic growth has been stimulated. The most successful economy has been Chile, although Brazil, Colombia, Mexico, and Venezuela are also showing improvement. These are all, again, the larger and resource-rich countries. Some of the smaller nations are also doing reasonably well and beginning to pull slowly out of the depression conditions of the 1980s and 1990s—what is referred to in Latin America as the "lost decade." But quite a number of others, who have few resources and have not reformed their economies, are still locked in their historic poverty and in fact are slipping backward.

Latin America, along with East Asia, thus provides us with the clearest-cut case of the need for structural as well as cultural, social, and political reform in order to achieve development. The correlation is not exact or one-to-one, but it is not far from that mark. Those countries that have democratized and moved toward open, free markets are doing very well. Those countries that have not freed up their economies are not doing well, nor are they likely to until the necessary reforms are made.

India

India is the world's most populous democracy and, next to China, the second most populous country in the world. It has become *the* regional power in South Asia, including the possession of nuclear weapons. What happens in India, therefore, has immense consequences for the rest of the developing world.

India is a case par excellence of a country governed in the past by a small elite educated at the London School of Economics (LSE) and determined to follow a socialist/state planning model of development. India not only fashioned many of its political institutions after its former colonial master, Great Britain, it took its economic model from the LSE as well. For a long time the Indian elite rested comfortably in the belief that it had all the right answers, which included a (sometimes vaguely) socialist economy and centralized state planning.

But in recent years the political elite has been shaken in its beliefs. The Congress party, which had governed India for most of its independence period since 1947, has seen its near-monopoly on political office broken at the polls; in addition, the central planning system has not been working very well. Central planning can work in a small, homogeneous country like Denmark, but in large, chaotic, ethnically diverse India a single set of guidelines emanating from New Delhi cannot possibly take into account all the local contingencies.

Hence, at the political level India has moved toward greater pluralism, and economically it is also changing. While still clinging in some quarters to socialism as a goal, the Indian elite has also recognized the need to make the public bureaucracy more efficient, to streamline and rationalize the economy, to open the country to outside investments and freer trade, to allow private markets to operate, and to liberalize the system. It is allowing greater economic freedom, encouraging entrepreneurship, and permitting the business skills of its people to flourish. At the same time, as in Latin America, there is a certain reluctance by the state to let go, to relax government controls, because of the fear that change may get out of hand. Thus, again, as in Latin America, the changes so far have been often piecemeal, limited, cautious. But if India truly wishes to be more prosperous, then it will likely have to go farther toward reform and economic liberalization. The main question is, as in Latin America, whether the elites are willing to possibly upset their own applecarts by making the changes necessary.

China   ~~won't wor~~

China is the world's most populous country, with 1.3 billion people. It is also one of the world's last remaining Marxist-Leninist states—along with North Korea, Vietnam, and Cuba. At the same time, China is trying desperately to develop economically. So the key question is: can China succeed in developing economically without fundamentally changing its communist and often-repressive political system as well?

The Chinese formula so far has been to maintain a Marxist-Leninist system of *political* controls, while allowing in some areas a considerable degree of economic freedom. Thus, eastern coastal cities like Shanghai as well as areas in the south near the commercial city of Hong Kong enjoy considerable degrees of economic freedom and autonomy, while in much of the central, northern, and western areas of China communist controls are still in place. But can you have economic freedom in some of these areas without that inevitably translating into a demand for political freedom that would undermine the very basis of communist rule?

It is not an easy question to answer. The Marxist-Leninist rulers of China believe they can allow enough economic freedom to raise the country's prosperity, but without that leading to political upheaval. To that end, they have also allowed somewhat greater political, religious, and cultural freedom in the increasingly trendy capital city of Beijing as a way of providing young people and a rising middle class with a political escape valve, while also keeping tight controls over other areas of the country. Meanwhile, Western countries are betting on just the opposite scenario: that greater trade and contacts with China and rising prosperity will eventually result in greater political freedoms and human rights.

While China is a huge country in terms of size, resources, and especially population, it is still exceedingly poor with a per capita income of only $600 to $700 per year, a very small middle class, and therefore a small market for imported products. While China is beginning to modernize, it is still about 80 percent rural; and if it industrializes and goes through roughly the same changes that other, earlier industrializers did, the majority of that rural population (nearly a *billion* people) will be moving to the cities in the next generation or two. No country *ever* has experienced that kind of urbanization, with its likely attendant problems of housing, education, health care, water supplies, electricity, sanitation, crime, delinquency, social breakdown, etc.

The Chinese leadership is gambling that it can maintain stability and control in the face of these mammoth changes. But what if it cannot or does not? What if neither of the two options mentioned earlier, a continuation of Marxism-Leninism or a gradual evolution to democracy, works out? To these two earlier scenarios for China, we need therefore to add a

third one: the possibility of fragmentation, social unraveling, ungovernability, and breakdown.

The Middle East

The Middle East has long been divided between rich and poor Islamic
states, as well as between Arab states and Israel. The wealthier oil-pro-
ducing states (Saudi Arabia, Kuwait, the Persian Gulf emirates) have already been discussed; here we focus on the poorer states: Iraq, Iran, Syria,
Jordan, Egypt, Tunisia, Libya, and Algeria. It may be noted that there is
enormous diversity among these countries and that they do not always
get along very well; recall that one of the key reasons for Iraq's invasion
of Kuwait in 1990 was Iraqi resentment of the far-richer Kuwaitis.

There is great variety among these states but some common features as
well. Since the ouster of their traditional monarchies (Jordan's King Hus-
sein is the sole monarch left), most of them have been committed to an
Arab, or Baathist, form of socialism. Several of them (Iraq, Syria, Libya)
did not do altogether badly under this kind of regime because they had
considerable oil reserves that enabled them to generate some economic
benefits no matter how inefficient they are. Egypt is able to subsidize its
inefficient economy through immense U.S. and Saudi assistance programs; similarly, Jordan is propped up by the United States, the wealthier
Arab states, and Israel. Algeria and Tunisia receive benefits chiefly from
the fact that they lie close to prosperous Western Europe. None of these
regimes is very efficient, nor could any of them be even remotely described as democracies (although a limited democratic opening may have
occurred in Tunisia).

The pattern here is clear. In the political realm all these regimes remain
top-down and authoritarian, although several of them have experienced
a degree of political opening. Economically, some have done reasonably
well lately not because they are efficient or self-sufficient but because of
oil, foreign subsidies, or proximity to wealth that rubs off on them. At the
same time, these remain poor countries and with immense social gaps between rich and poor. Hence, these countries are not very good illustrations of what works in development and what doesn't. Oil alone or foreign aid alone do not make for a successful economy or society. Their
"Arab socialism" has not been very successful and has served as a legit-
imizer for some rather authoritarian, even miserable, regimes. None of
them have successfully made a transition to democracy or even shown
much sign of wanting to do so; nor have any of them begun seriously to
streamline, privatize, and open up their economies. These are examples
not of how to achieve democratic development but of how *not* to do it.

Depressed Areas

There are about forty countries in the world that have not done and are not doing very well either economically or politically. Most of these countries are located in sub-Saharan Africa, but some are located in Asia (Bangladesh, for example) and others can be found in Latin and South America (Haiti, Nicaragua, Bolivia, Guyana). These are among the world's poorest countries. Even worse, they show few signs of being able to improve their situations. That is why we label them "depressed areas."

The problem with most of these countries is that they lack basic economic resources. They have no oil, no valuable minerals, and seldom even decent agricultural land. Nor do they have the organization and institutional infrastructure, either economic or political, to carry out a sustained development effort. Virtually none of them have undertaken a transition to democracy, nor do they have the social and economic base to sustain democracy successfully should it be tried. The difficulty for these countries is that their poverty and underdevelopment are so great that probably no systemic change—presumably toward democracy and more open markets—can help them, and certainly not in the short run. They will remain poor and backward whether they have socialism or capitalism, democracy or authoritarianism.

Having said that, we must also note that there *are* some positive steps these poor countries could take. The benefits would probably be marginal for a time, but at least there would be benefits—and they might conceivably lead to better things. First, almost everyone agrees by now that the socialism many countries followed in the early decades of independence has not been productive; eliminating that system and the institutions that go with it would probably be a useful first step. Second, reducing the size of the public sector would help immensely, since we now recognize the close relationship between the size of the public sector and the level of corruption. A smaller state sector simply gives the regime and its bureaucrats fewer opportunities to steal; if private entrepreneurship could simultaneously be encouraged, that would also be helpful. Third, many of these unfortunate countries are governed by exceedingly brutal, corrupt, and rapacious dictators; getting rid of them could not help but improve the situation—unless the successor was equally bad, in which case nothing would have been lost.

Some success stories do exist, however, in this otherwise bleak picture from which lessons can be drawn. The Ivory Coast for a time, while not democratic by our standards, allowed some considerable degree of freedom; and in the economic sphere its longtime (now former) president, Félix Houphouët-Boigny, provided both stability and an openness to free market activity that was unique on the African continent. The Ivory Coast remained a poor country, but it was certainly better off than its neighbors; and the fact that the regime allowed, in the absence of a developed capitalist infrastructure, informal and low-level (street vendor) markets to operate gave it an economic vitality that most of the newly independent countries lacked.[8] Other depressed countries in Africa, Asia, the Middle East, and Latin America may also be slowly edging their way toward somewhat greater prosperity.

Eastern Europe

All of the Eastern European countries under Soviet control and a Marxist-Leninist economy were depressed, but some were worse off than others. Those that had the most Stalinist totalitarian regimes and the most tightly controlled economies—Bulgaria, Romania, and Albania—remained the most economically depressed and the most backward. East Germany was also Stalinist, but it had considerable resources—and now, unity with the prosperous West in a united Germany. Others—Poland and the Czech Republic—allowed a somewhat greater degree of economic freedom and activity, and they were not as bad off; these countries currently also have good prospects for democracy and economic growth. The one country—Hungary—that allowed the greatest degree of economic freedom and capitalism even while functioning within a communist regime was also the best off economically in terms of living standard and was best able to take advantage of the new freedoms and economic opportunities once the Marxist-Leninist regime collapsed in 1989. In contrast, the former Yugoslavia has split apart along ethnic, nationality, and religious lines: some areas (Slovenia, Croatia) are doing better politically and economically, while others (Serbia, Bosnia-Herzegovina, Kosovo, Moldova) have been torn by conflict and their futures are uncertain.

Thus, the pattern that we have been observing—that freer and democratic political systems and less statist, more open-market economies are the best indicators of developmental success—holds in these former communist countries of Eastern Europe as well as in the developing nations.

A word about geographic labels and nomenclature is in order here. What we have called "Eastern Europe" no longer wishes to be called that. Instead, since the fall of the Iron Curtain and the collapse of the Soviet Union, the countries of Eastern Europe prefer the designation "Central Europe." Or perhaps just "Europe." In their view, "Eastern Europe" has moved farther east to encompass the Ukraine, Belarus, and the Baltic States (Estonia, Latvia, Lithuania). So comparative politics will need to adjust its regional nomenclature to take these changes into account.

New Trading Blocs

Although the theme of new global trading blocs is a bit outside traditional comparative politics, it does have a bearing on the subject particularly as it relates to regional groupings, the developed and developing nations, and the political-economic models these countries are using.

Much of the world has now organized itself into trading blocs. The first, most important, and most long-standing is the European Economic Community (EEC), now the European Union (EU). It includes most of the countries of Western Europe; many of the countries of Eastern (now Central) Europe have also been included within it. Quite a number of developing nations also have special arrangements to buy and sell within the EU without cumbersome tariff restrictions. The EU has reduced tariffs among member countries and these others, has developed a common currency, has already developed numerous common regulations and quality controls among the member countries, and is to an extent erasing Europe's old national boundaries and even the concept of national sovereignty itself. For example, citizens of the member countries can now travel quite freely throughout the area without passports; at the same time, police in hot pursuit in one country can chase suspects across the border in another. The EU has developed central institutions in Brussels, Belgium, and Strasbourg, France, as well as other countries; it has written a new, pending constitution; it is the most developed of the several common markets; and it seems likely to proceed even further toward common economic and political policies (foreign and defense) as the twenty-first century proceeds.

A second and less well-known trading bloc has formed in the Asia/Pacific Rim region. There the driving force has been mainly Japan but China and India are also jockeying for leadership roles. The so-called "Asian Tigers"—South Korea, Taiwan, Hong Kong (now part of China), and Singapore—have shown miracle growth rates, and the developing economies of Indonesia, Malaysia, Thailand, and the Philippines have been stimulated by internal reforms as well as the power of their neighbors' economies. The Asian bloc is newer and less institutionalized than the European one; in addition and often in competition with each other, the Asian nations are all trying to increase their exports as well as defending bloc interests.

The third major trading bloc, the North American Free Trade Association (NAFTA), includes the United States, Canada, and Mexico. The United States has moved to include other Latin American nations in this bloc, but those plans suffered a setback when Congress denied fast-track negotiating authority to the president. Meanwhile, impatient at the U.S. delays and eager to pursue their own agendas, some of the major South

American countries (Argentina, Brazil, and others) formed their own free trade association, MERCOSUR (literally, Southern Market), which lowered tariffs, significantly expanded trade among the member countries, *and* began negotiating separately with the EU and Asia. But the power of the U.S. economy is such that, with or without an expanded NAFTA, it will remain the dominant economic power in the Western Hemisphere.

But note also the striking patterns. First, all three of these superblocs are primarily market-oriented; there is no longer a socialist bloc. Second, a scramble is underway among almost all developing nations to achieve cover under one or another of the three umbrellas; those who are not a part of one or more of the blocs are likely to be left out in the economic wilderness, unprotected, vulnerable, and without markets for their goods. Third and particularly among the larger, more powerful economies (the United States, Japan, Germany, China, and others), an effort is being made both to integrate neighboring economies into a free trade bloc *and* to remain free to trade with other nations and blocs outside of one's own area. Thus, regional trade agreements are being formed at the same time that global trade is also increasing; the most dynamic economies try to increase their markets in *all* these areas.

WHAT WORKS IN DEVELOPMENT

Economic development is generally taken to mean economic growth. Growth is sought in order to achieve better living standards and higher well-being for the people of the country. Economic growth and higher living standards also increase the prestige and power standing of the country involved. Economic growth is usually measured in terms of increases in the gross national product (GNP). However, since it cannot be called real growth if population increases mean larger numbers of people continuing to live in grinding poverty, growth is usually measured in GNP per capita. That is, not only must the GNP go up, but average income per person must also increase. Hence an essential element of development is to increase investment, and thereby productivity, at a rate greater than that of the population growth. In this effort both agricultural development and industrialization will typically be involved.

Less-developed countries (LDCs) are not the only areas where the study of economic growth is relevant. The study of economic development enables us to understand both where the already developed nations have come from and what is likely to be their future trajectory. It also enables us to examine how such recently developed countries as Brazil or South Korea achieved their impressive growth records. Furthermore, these principles of economic growth are relevant to the problems of structural reforms and development in the formerly communist countries of the Soviet Union and Eastern Europe. The ex-communist countries may serve as illustrations of the limits to the growth that can be achieved by capital investment in the absence of real structural reform.

Since World War II, the onset of the Cold War, and especially the surge of new, developing nations onto the world scene, economists and others have been debating what strategies or models can best achieve development. What policies should be employed to stimulate development, and what should be the role of the state or government in the process? A leading early theory, that of W. W. Rostow, which, because of Rostow's positions in the State Department and the White House, also was incorporated into U.S. foreign aid policy, saw development in terms of linear stages that would be approximately the same in all nations. This theory focused on the fundamental need for investment, regardless of cultural traditions or political institutions, to generate increased productivity and output.

A second theory, identified most closely with economist W. Arthur Lewis, focused on the need for structural change in the Third World. Lewis's discussion of economic growth was more subtle than the "stages" thesis; it involved an analysis of the transition from an agricultural to an industrial economy and the ways in which the country's main institutions of both government and economics needed to be restructured to facilitate those transformations. However, this theory was seldom embedded in actual policy, as Rostow's was.

Dependency was a third theory. As analyzed by its leading early spokesman Raúl Prebisch, who headed the United Nations' Economic Commission for Latin America, it argued that Latin America (and other developing areas) was underdeveloped because it was too heavily dependent on outside markets and called for a protectionist, import substitution policy. This strategy demanded central planning and state-led development rather than reliance on open markets.

The current consensus in development theory may be termed neoclassical. It emerges from the experience of the last forty years as recounted in the previous discussion, and not from theory. It suggests that development is markedly faster and more sustainable if fundamental reliance is placed on markets for the allocation of goods and services, and not on an all-powerful government.[9] Some central planning, coordination, and resource allocation by the state may still be necessary, but not at the expense of primary reliance on open markets. Socialism has been shown to be woefully inefficient and not conducive to development, and so have the excessively statist economies of Latin America. Hence governments should focus on areas that are not well handled by the market, such as infrastructure (roads, communications), education, macroeconomic policy, social welfare, the environment and other externalities, and a legal system or policy framework that permits markets to operate and ensures optimum incentives to economic activity.

This approach considers openness to international markets (both imports and exports) as essential in order to discipline domestic prices, end the antiexport bias of the older import substitution model, and provide markets for new areas of production. Hard work, organization, and discipline are also necessary. Political stability, effective leadership, and democratic government over a considerable period of time enormously facilitate capital investment and hence growth. Political stability is best achieved, we now know, not by either Marxism-Leninism (witness Eastern Europe) or authoritarianism, but by democracy, which entails respect for elections, human rights, pluralism, and freedom. Stability is also best achieved through the provision of adequate levels of social services, education, and social justice for the nation's citizens. Without social justice and a stable political order achieved through democracy, all the best-laid plans for economic growth—as both the communist and authoritarian regimes found out—can go astray. Of course, there will still be questions about what precise percentage of scarce resources should go into investment and what into social programs; those questions can only be resolved in a democratic political process, as they should be. Also useful in terms of stimulating economic growth are programs to control excessive population growth.

There we have it: an agenda for development. After forty years of experience the consensus on what works in development is widespread:

- Hard work, discipline, organization
- Free, open markets
- Democracy and human rights
- Stability and internal security
- Widespread literacy and good public education at all levels
- Social programs and modernization
- Efficient and honest public administration
- Intelligent, rational, but limited state planning systems
- An effective legal system
- Family planning

These are the *sine qua non* for development. With these features development in the emerging countries is feasible and highly likely; without them, or most of them, development is highly unlikely.

IMPLICATIONS FOR U.S. POLICY

In the past, U.S. assistance programs directed toward the developing nations have not always been based on this formula. Instead, foreign aid, influenced by Rostow, has been based on the "stages" theory. If only we can invest enough capital, Rostow argued, economic development will occur, and social modernization and political development will automatically follow. But in the past they did not follow; Rostow got the cart before the horse. It is not enough merely to encourage investment and economic growth; rather, stable, effective, democratic political institutions and programs that promote education, equity, and social justice are also necessary. The agenda must then be well balanced to include political and social reforms as well as economic ones. There is nothing automatic or inevitable (as Rostow assumed) about investment automatically or inevitably producing economic development, because if the government and bureaucracy are corrupt, greedy, and mainly interested in lining their own pockets (as in the Philippines under Marcos or Indonesia under Suharto), growth will benefit the few rather than the many and will not help the country in long-range terms.

The issue becomes even more complicated. A strong argument can be made that in the early stages of development, a country needs a strong, stable (not necessarily democratic) government to stimulate growth, overcome the weight of traditional practices, and get the process of self-sustained growth started. That was the strategy of the successful Asian "tigers" (Hong Kong, Singapore, South Korea, Taiwan) in their early stages of development. But even if the government at this stage is nondemocratic, it must be honest, efficient, and dedicated to national growth, not just private enrichment. Moreover, as economic development goes forward, it gives rise to new social groups (trade unions, businessmen, middle class) that must be politically accommodated and incorporated into the system if growth is to continue. In other words, even a development strategy that starts under nondemocratic leadership soon requires a more open and democratic system to manage the new pressures and pluralism to which development itself gives rise. Furthermore, in the present context, the pressures of global lending agencies, the media, the international community, and neighboring countries all but *force* a developing nation to take a democratic route.

None of this was acknowledged in the U.S. foreign aid program where, under Rostow's influence, the emphasis was on economic assistance and large construction projects, and not on democracy or social justice. Political, social, and cultural variables in achieving development were largely ignored. Moreover, the Rostow model and U.S. aid tended also to emphasize central planning and the role of the state in development, not the role of open markets and private entrepreneurship. U.S. development assistance in the early days thus ignored the need to direct its funds toward effective democratic governments and often favored authoritarian and dictatorial regimes whose records in stimulating national development were often weak. Many of these early foreign aid programs ended in failure.

The U.S. foreign assistance program in developing nations has gone through several incarnations since the 1960s. First came the emphasis on large infrastructure projects (dams, power companies, highways) and agrarian reform. But the infrastructure projects mainly benefitted the elite groups in the society, and agrarian reform, under governments controlled by these same elites, was never carried out seriously. Next came the emphasis in the 1970s on "basic human needs"—feeding the poorest of the poor—but that program, however laudable in design, was woefully inadequate to meet the need and ignored long-term development projects. Republican administrations emphasized private business while the Democrats championed "sustainable development."[10]

None of these programs provided the balanced, comprehensive program that the developing nations truly needed. Look back at the preceding list: from this list and the accompanying analysis, it is clear that successful development requires political, economic, social, and cultural-psychological transformations all at once. Attacking one problem in isolation from the others will not work. Economic development cannot be achieved unless you have a political system committed to it; you also need the right social programs and a value system or political culture supportive of modernization. But most aid programs have concentrated on economic factors to the exclusion of political and cultural factors, which helps explain why so many of them have been failures. A successful development program has to be comprehensive in scope and take *all* relevant factors into account.

THE TRANSFORMATION OF THE WORLD

Is the model that seems most successful in the developing countries also appropriate in the formerly communist world? Can open markets and political democracy be made to work in previously Marxist-Leninist regimes? The answer is: no one knows for sure. We hope and tend to assume so, and much of our aid to Russia and Eastern Europe is based on the assumption of a successful transition to democracy and free markets. Certainly the formerly communist states themselves also tend to think so and are putting lots of their eggs in the free-market basket. But the outcome remains uncertain, and large obstacles stand in the way. Marx and Lenin tried to show us how capitalism would give way to socialism, but when we set sail on the reverse course—from socialism to capitalism—we are sailing into uncharted waters. So the issue of whether a transition from communism to capitalism is possible or feasible remains a big unknown.

In comparative politics, a number of scholars have tried to use the models of transitions to democracy in Southern Europe (Greece, Portugal, Spain) and apply them to postcommunist Eastern Europe. But Southern Europe already had some democratic traditions and institutions on which to build, the economies of the area were considerably more developed than Eastern Europe, vast social and cultural changes had already occurred in Southern Europe *before* the onset of democratization, and—most importantly—the Southern European economies already had market systems in place to help facilitate both political and economic transitions. Eastern Europe not only lacked the institutions of either political democracy or open markets, it also had to undertake all of these changes—political, economic, social, cultural—at once and without a base on which to build. Many scholars now believe that the Southern European model is *not* appropriate for Eastern Europe, which must begin their transitions from scratch, and that it will be necessary to develop entirely new models to explain these postcommunist transitions. But that is a daunting task since, until recently, there had never been a case—and therefore no road maps— of a former communist country returning to democracy and free markets.

Nevertheless, it is significant that these large *system* transformations are changing the face of the globe. In the 1970s and 1980s many previously authoritarian and right-wing regimes undertook the transition to democracy. Then, beginning in 1989, Eastern Europe and the former Soviet Union began their transitions *both* to democracy and to more open market systems. Not only did these involve some stupendous changes in the countries affected, but it also meant, for comparative politics, new and particularly significant transformations to study and, related, the need for new models and new approaches to help us understand these remarkable events. In systems terms, it also meant the discrediting and disappearance of many authoritarian as well as Marxist-Leninist regimes. The result in 2004 was that only democracy in the political sphere and some form of open markets in the economic sphere enjoyed widespread legitimacy, although countries would and could differ considerably over the precise forms that these could take. But the great systems debate of the past appeared to be over: Democracy and free markets had won and there were no other serious challengers.

These changes also implied the need for new classifications and new nomenclature in comparative politics. The First World of industrialized, democratic nations remained standing but, of course, it consisted of a great variety of countries (Japan, Germany, the United States) with quite different economic and political systems. Meanwhile, the Second World of developed communist states had disappeared, replaced by a variety of transitional regimes seeking mainly to emulate the First World. And the Third World was divided between those countries making it into the level of modern nations and those lagging behind, not only still mired in extreme poverty and underdevelopment but also unable any longer to try to play off the First World against the Second World.

It is, therefore, clear that the terms used for the past fifty years (the era of the Cold War) to categorize the world's political systems no longer have much basis in reality. The Cold War is over and the world (or much of it) has changed. Comparative politics badly needs a new set of definitions and categories to describe and help us analyze these newer economic and political realities.

NOTES

1. A useful collection on the major figures in development is Gerald M. Meier and Dudley Seers (eds.), *Pioneers in Development* (Oxford: Oxford University Press, 1985).

2. Gunnar Myrdal, *Asian Drama: An Inquiry into the Poverty of Nations* (New York: Random House, 1972).

3. An exception is Peter Nehemkis, *Latin America* (New York: Knopf, 1964).

4. Paul Sigmund (ed.), *The Ideology of the Developing Nations* (New York: Praeger, 1972).

5. Devastating critiques may be found in two volumes edited by Claudio Veliz, *Obstacles to Changes in Latin America* (London: Oxford University Press, 1965) and *The Politics of Conformity in Latin America* (London: Oxford University Press, 1967).

6. A. H. Somjee, *Parallels and Actuals of Political Development* (London: Macmillan, 1986); and Howard J. Wiarda, *Ethnocentrism in Foreign Policy: Can We Understand the Third World?* (Washington, DC: American Enterprise Institute for Public Policy Research, 1985).

7. Thomas W. Robinson (ed.), *Democracy and Development in East Asia* (Washington, DC: American Enterprise Institute for Public Policy Research, 1991).

8. Hernando de Soto, *The Other Path: The Invisible Revolution in the Third World* (New York: Harper & Row, 1989).

9. See, for example, Peter L. Berger, *The Capitalist Revolution: Fifty Propositions about Prosperity, Equality, and Liberty* (New York: Basic Books, 1986); Michael Novak, *The Spirit of Democratic Capitalism* (New York: Simon & Schuster, 1982); and Howard J. Wiarda (ed.), *The Relations between Democracy, Development, and Security: Implications for Policy* (New York: Global Economic Action Institute, 1988).

10. For AID's own view, see its publications: *Economic Growth and the Third World: A Report on the AID Private Enterprise Initiative* (Washington, DC: U.S. AID, 1987); *AID Policy Paper: Private Enterprise Development* (Washington, DC: U.S. AID, 1985); and *Development and the National Interest: U.S. Economic Assistance into the 21st Century* (Washington, DC: U.S. AID, 1989).

11

⁂

Frontiers of Research in Comparative Politics

Comparative politics is a dynamic field. The entire globe is our re-search terrain and things are constantly changing, in flux. There are always new issues, new approaches, new political movements, and even new countries to explore and explain. To most of us in the field, these changes and the dynamism engendered are what make the subject matter of comparative politics so interesting.

In this chapter we examine some of these new issues. The topics ex-plored include women in politics, drug policy, immigration, regionalism and decentralization, gay rights, and pollution and the environment. Our purpose is not to exhaustively examine these subjects (which cannot be done in one short chapter) but to introduce them and to offer some pre-liminary comments concerning the dimensions of these issues and the ap-proach of diverse countries or regions to them, to show how comparative politics can increase our understanding and analysis of them. Hopefully, the discussion will stimulate other scholars and students to explore the is-sues more fully and in a variety of national contexts.

WOMEN IN POLITICS

The comparative study of women in politics is a subject of growing inter-est in the field.[1] On the one hand, women are playing an increasingly im-portant political role in many countries; on the other, the place, position, and political influence of women varies greatly from country to country and region to region. That is precisely the kind of issue that comparative politics seeks to explore, involving change and new dynamics (women in politics) but also variation among countries and regions.

To begin, let us make some distinctions. First, the movement to involve more women in politics has been stronger in the developed countries than in the developing nations. Second, it has been stronger in the Western countries: North America (the United States, Canada), Western Europe, and the countries that are offshoots of Western civilization (Australia, New Zealand). In contrast, Japan, South Korea, Taiwan, Hong Kong, and Singapore—the developed and emerging market economies of Asia—have so far lagged behind in terms of women in politics, although that is now changing. Third, women in the developing areas have similarly lagged behind women in the developed nations, although that is also changing. And there are major differences between the roles and position of women in Africa, Latin America, and the Middle East (Islamic society).

If we examine the number of women at cabinet levels (figure 11.1) in the developed, Western countries, some interesting patterns emerge. Note that the top three countries and four of the top five countries are in Scandinavia. Sweden is the top-ranking country in terms of number of women cabinet members, but it has recently been matched by Spain, which was not even in the top ten in our 2001 listing.

In general, the wealthier the country, the higher the percentage of women cabinet members; the poorer the country, the fewer women in higher government posts. Note that only Hungary from poorer Eastern Europe makes the list and, very recently, only Spain from Southern Europe. Catholic countries seem to rank behind Protestant countries in numbers of women cabinet members; Northern or Northwest European countries rank ahead of other European regions.

The numbers of women at cabinet or ministerial levels are, in most countries, a product of the numbers of women who gain prior experience at local and then national parliamentary levels (figure 11.2). So when we look at the number of women in parliament, it is not surprising that the same countries lead the way. Sweden has the most women parliamentarians (45 percent) followed by the Netherlands and Norway at 37 percent, then Germany at 33 percent, and so on. Note again that it is the wealthier, Northern, Protestant countries that have the most women parliamentarians. However, such wealthy countries as France, Italy, and Japan are way down the list.

The leading countries have a large number of women cabinet members because they have a large pool of women parliamentarians from which to choose. It is striking that those countries with few women cabinet members also have, for the most part, few women parliamentarians and, thus, have a narrower pool of candidates for higher office. In other words,

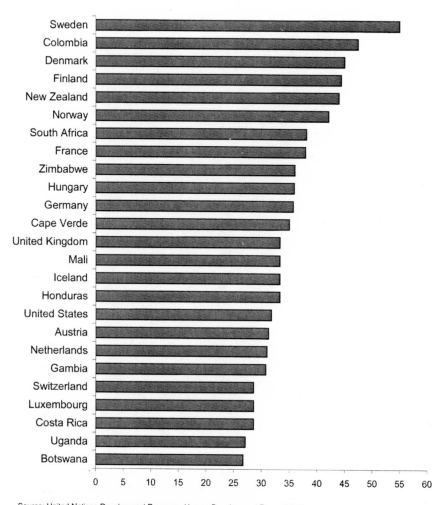

Source: United Nations Development Program, *Human Development Report 2004.*
*Some of these countries have high numbers due to mandated quotas.
**In 2004 Spain leapfrogged to a position tied with Sweden at the top.

Figure 11.1. Percentage of Women in National Ministerial Positions in 2001: Top Twenty-five Countries

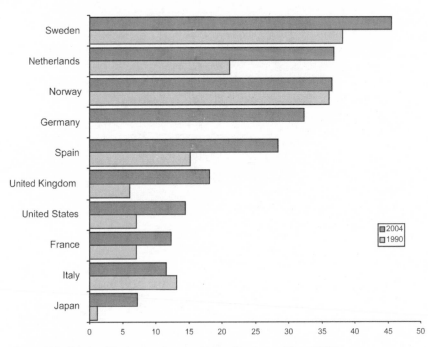

Source: United Nations Development Program, *Human Development Report 2004.*
*The *Human Development Report 2004* listed Germany's Women in Parliament 1990 data as unavailable, most likely due to the reunification in process at that time.

Figure 11.2.   Women in Parliament (% of Total)

training and experience at the local and parliamentary levels is crucial if women wish to be selected for higher-level cabinet positions.

However, even in the progressive Scandinavian countries, women tend to get the "softer" cabinet positions: health, education, culture, social welfare. The "harder" portfolios (defense, finance, foreign affairs, justice) tend still to be reserved for men—although that is also changing. Only in Finland have women, at one time or another, held every type of cabinet position. Women prime ministers are still fairly rare; only Norway and Great Britain.

Now let us turn to the developing nations. Figure 11.3 provides figures on the numbers of women cabinet members in the leading countries of Latin America, Asia, Africa, and the Middle East. A word of caution: Some of these countries have mandated quotas on numbers of women in parliament and other high positions, thus skewing the rank orderings.

In Latin America, based on what was said earlier, one would expect the more-developed countries like Argentina and Uruguay to be high on the list, but they are not there; only Chile among the wealthier countries ranks

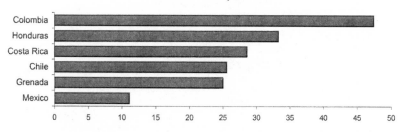

Top Five Latin American and Caribbean Countries, Plus Mexico for Comparison

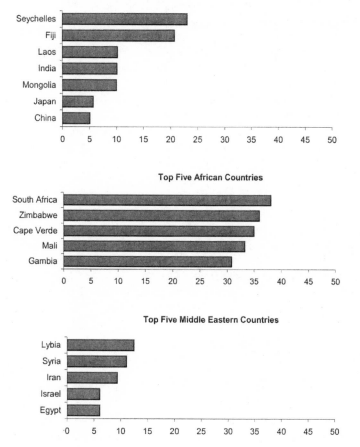

Source: United Nations Development Program, *Human Development Report 2004.*

Figure 11.3. **Percentage of Women in National Ministerial Positions in 2001: Top Developing Countries**

high. In Asia the Seychelles and Fiji islands, both former British colonies, have the highest percentage of women; other countries, including India, Japan, and China, lag far behind.

Several of the leading African countries have used quotas to enhance their rank, although some of the countries are clearly committed to the advancement of women. Note that the Middle Eastern and Islamic countries rank not only low but also behind other developing areas in numbers of women in ministerial positions.

At least three main hypotheses emerge from these data. One is that the percentage of women in high government positions is related to socio-economic development: the wealthier the country, the greater the number of women in office. A second hypothesis is that religion and culture are important variables: Protestant countries score higher than Catholic countries; Christian countries score higher than Muslim ones. A third hypothesis has to do with colonialism: Women do better in former British colonies in the Third World, including Granada, Seychelles, Fiji, South Africa, Zimbabwe, and Gambia, than in the former colonies of other countries. It is likely that the British legal system and providing educational opportunities for women even under colonialism had something to do with these high rankings.

In all the developing areas there remain major cultural, religious, social, and economic barriers to women's advancement. However, in both Asia and Latin America well-educated women are increasingly occupying professional positions (including in politics), while less-well-educated women are increasingly finding work outside the home in manufacturing and service industries. Nevertheless, in both these areas a glass ceiling still blocks women from most high-level governmental positions. But in Africa and the Middle East, strong cultural, religious, and social barriers as well as underdevelopment, lack of education, and lack of jobs still frequently block most women from participation in the gainfully employed workforce, which in turn also contributes to a lack of political influence.

All of these are, of course, preliminary findings and speculation; the subject of women in politics viewed from a comparative perspective clearly calls out for more detailed and thorough analysis.

COMPARATIVE DRUG POLICY

Drugs, almost everyone agrees, are a scourge and a menace.[2] Not just in the United States but in Western Europe as well, and increasingly in other countries, drugs are poisoning our youth, adding to social and health problems, and leading to increased crime and violence. At the same time the profits from drug growing, transport, and dealing are enormous.

Farmers in the producing countries can get as much as twenty times more from growing drugs as from growing more traditional crops; the production and shipment of drugs have turned some of the narco-traffickers into multimillionaires who may in their own countries also operate like patronage politicians bestowing benefits on their neighbors in return for loyalty and service. At the same time, military officers and bureaucrats in the sending countries often supplement their meager salaries by assisting or winking their eyes at the traffickers, and governments in those countries often benefit as well, as drugs become their major export crop and increase GNP, yet corrupt their courts, legislatures, and police.

Drugs are a complex problem and there are no easy solutions. The United States tried initially to stem the use of drugs on the consumer side but found its efforts to administer drug tests randomly to key sectors of the population (teachers, airline pilots, truckers, and train engineers) stymied by constitutional guarantees and the opposition of these groups' unions. Frustrated in its efforts on the domestic side, the United States turned to the international or production side and instigated the "war on drugs" in an effort to interdict and cut off the flow into the United States. But that proved no more successful than the earlier effort. President George H. W. Bush sought to implement a balanced approach that combined education, interdiction, public affairs advertising, rehabilitation, and a focus on money laundering. That approach made a modest dent in the drug program for a time, but by the mid-1990s drug use was again up along with the crime and violence associated with it.

Western Europe is in general more tolerant than is the United States on drug use; at the same time, that policy is made easier by the fact Europe does not have the same levels of crime and violence associated with drugs as does the United States. The most tolerant of the European countries is the Netherlands, followed by Switzerland (which provides free needles to drug users to prevent the spread of disease), and the Scandinavian countries. In Holland, cannabis (marijuana), though officially illegal, may be openly bought and sold in small quantities, usually on the street or in "coffee shops." The logic of the Dutch experiment is that, if drugs are cheap and openly sold, the criminal and violent elements associated with drugs are removed; that by tolerating the retail trade in cannabis, young people are kept away from dealers who might lure them into more dangerous drug use; and furthermore that this way the government can raise revenues by taxing the open drug transactions, without looking too closely at the source of supply. In Holland, even the use of hard drugs is usually not prosecuted.

Neither France, Germany, Britain, nor other European countries have yet been willing to go so far toward legalizing or tolerating drugs as the Dutch. Their policy has been generally to tolerate individual, low-level drug use as long as it does not cause a disturbance or get out of hand, but to crack down hard on the criminal or violent aspects of drugs. The U.S. government has been strongly critical of the Dutch approach. And, while some advocates in the United States have been urging a similar decriminalization of drugs, public opinion surveys tell us that less than 10 percent of the population is willing to follow that route. With such a low percentage of the public supporting decriminalization, American politicians have been unwilling to consider this option.

Americans tend to see the drug issue in moral and religious terms (drug use is wrong and sinful and, therefore, must remain illegal), and not in the purely pragmatic terms of price and criminal statistics, which is how most Europeans view it. In addition, the United States is a quite different society and culture as compared with Western Europe, having significantly higher levels of violence and criminality more generally which are then exacerbated by the drug problem. So the solutions will likely have to be different as well. A third variant among industrial countries is Japan where, because of close-knit families and Confucian-style social obligations, drug use, though rising, is considerably lower than it is in either the United States or Western Europe.

Drug policy is a very complex issue having to do with the relations between producing and consuming countries, the economics of the drug trade, levels of social and economic development, and a host of other factors. Also, distinct countries and regions have very different attitudes toward drugs and drug use, have different societies and cultures in which the drug issue is played out, and have different government attitudes and policies concerning drugs. So here again we have both a fascinating, challenging, and controversial issue and the very "stuff" of comparative politics: drug policy (which we will call the dependent variable) and then a *host* of factors—social, cultural, economic, political, religious, international—that must be included in any explanation of the policy and that varies enormously from country to country. It is another area of the field that cries out for further, more detailed analysis.

IMMIGRATION

Globalization, we saw in an earlier chapter, affects all countries. When we think of globalization, we usually think of increased trade in goods, services, and materials, as well as culture and ideas. But globalization has also been a factor in the increased drug trade considered above, in immigration (traffic of people and labor rather than goods), and in the environment and pollution considered below. All these new trends and new issues are either products of globalization or were accelerated by it.

Immigration is another one of those hot, complex, front-burner issues, like drugs.[3] Immigration affects many countries, not just the United States. The general pattern is: people go from poorer, low-wage, fewer-benefits countries toward wealthier, higher-wage, greater-benefits countries. Moreover, we need to think that immigration affects not just the receiving countries, in the form of more people as well as, usually, pressures on housing, schools, utilities, social services, health care systems, and law enforcement, but also the sending countries often in the form of loss of its most skilled, educated, and ambitious persons.

The United States currently tends to receive immigrants mainly from Mexico, Central America, and the Caribbean but now from other countries as well. Britain receives immigrants mainly from its former colonies in the Caribbean, Africa, and South Asia (India, Pakistan). Continental Europe receives immigrants from three main sources: across the Mediterranean from North Africa and sub-Saharan Africa, from Turkey and the Middle East, and now increasingly, since the Iron Curtain has been torn down, from Eastern Europe and Russia. Japan is much more restrictive in its immigration policy and has brought in few immigrant laborers. But remember the rule of migration from poorer to richer countries. That means that oil-rich Saudi Arabia and the Gulf emirates bring in laborers from other, poorer Arab countries; that Nicaraguans emigrate to wealthier Costa Rica; Bolivians and Paraguayans, to richer Argentina and Chile; Malays, to Singapore; Chinese, to Hong Kong; and so on. Such patterns of immigration are nearly universal.

There has, of course, always been immigration but in recent decades the pace has greatly accelerated. The main factors are faster and easier transportation, modern communications which tell the story of greater affluence in the developed countries and provide a magnet for people to emigrate, and reduced immigration/passport restrictions because of the lowering of barriers among common market countries. Increased immigration may also stem from one country's political or diplomatic strategies abroad or from conscious decisions to import labor, either in general or to do low-level work that citizens of the receiving country no longer are willing to do.

In the 1960s and early 1970s, for instance, a number of the European countries were booming ahead so rapidly that they developed severe labor shortages, especially in low-paid jobs. So they began to import Spanish and Portuguese workers to do physical labor—persons from countries that were still in the economic doldrums. But then the Spanish and Portuguese economies began to expand, reducing the incentive for their workers to emigrate. Still needing labor, however, the wealthier European nations—primarily West Germany but others as well—began to bring in workers from farther afield: Turkey, the Middle East, North Africa. The flow of immigrant labor eventually numbered in the *millions*, so that nowadays, if you buy a Mercedes, BMW, or Volvo, the chances are quite good it will have been made mainly by immigrant labor.

At first, immigration was thought to be temporary. The term used was "guest workers"—comparable to the earlier *"bracero"* program in the United States. That is, workers (male) who would leave their families behind, work and earn money in the receiving country on a temporary (seasonal) or short-term (two or three years) basis, and then return to their own countries. But over time these workers began to stay longer, to bring their wives and children along, to *have* children in the host countries (which thus often qualified them for citizenship), to reside permanently in the host country. By this time their children have also grown up in the host country, attended its schools, speak German or Swedish and maybe not the language of their parents, and often marry into host-country families. This means they have become permanent residents and often citizens; they will not go back to their original countries; and often a host of racial, religious, and cultural conflicts arise—with which persons in the United States are not unfamiliar. As long as the host country economy is booming ahead, these problems are often minimized; but when the economy turns stagnant, the charge is often raised that the immigrants (now often full citizens) are taking host-country jobs, don't fit, are "difficult," etc. And that is when right-wing, xenophobic, neo-Nazi parties and political movements spring up aimed at punishing the immigrant minorities, forcing them out, or, at a minimum, pushing for tougher immigration laws.

Another source of large-scale immigration has been political or diplomatic decisions made by the host country. The main criterion has been human rights violation or persecution in some other country; the most sympathetic countries responding to these abuses have again been the Scandinavian countries and Holland. Sweden, for example, which has long opened its arms wide to political refugees, has about 20,000 Chileans—refugees from the dictatorship of Augusto Pinochet in the 1970s who have stayed in Sweden long after Pinochet has gone. It has about 50,000 Iranians, refugees both from the Shah's authoritarian regime and from the ayatollah's, as well as numerous exile communities from other dictatorial regimes.

The Swedish policy, as in the United States, was one of assimilation, the "melting pot," although Swedish immigration policy was far more generous. It gave the immigrants an apartment, education, training, money for up to a year, and eventually a job. It sought to create "Swedes" out of all these usually dark-haired, dark-eyed peoples. But increasingly, as in the United States, the Swedes and other receiving countries found many of the immigrants didn't want or failed to assimilate; retained their own language, customs, and ethnic ways; and failed to conform to the Swedish/Scandinavian ethic of orderliness, cleanliness, and hard work. Increased culture clashes resulted and a widespread wringing of the hands over what to do about the "immigrant problem."

A variation on this problem of political immigrants is presented in Britain and Holland. Many people of the British Commonwealth either have British passports or lay claim to having British citizenship. Before modern transportation and communication, this was not a major issue, but in recent decades the flow of people into a more prosperous Britain has become a larger tide. And like their counterparts in Germany and Scandinavia, the immigrants have now often been in Britain for two or more generations, were born in Britain, went to school in Britain, and are full British citizens—but are often the victims of racial prejudice because of their darker skins. Similarly in Holland: Because of its former colonial empire, Holland has thousands of Indonesians, Moluccans, Surinamese, Arubans, and others living within its borders who are fully Dutch citizens but no longer sure they want to forsake their old ways and become "little Dutchmen." Once again, cultural, racial, and eventually political discord is the result. To varying degrees, the same kind of clashes over identity, citizenship, and assimilation are occurring in other countries.

It is, of course, easier to assimilate small numbers of immigrants than large ones. Among the developed countries the United States has both the largest numbers of and the most diverse ethnic immigrant communities: perhaps 15 to 20 percent of the population. But in France, Germany, and Britain the number of immigrants now numbers in the millions; perhaps 5 to 10 percent of the population. Handling or assimilating 5 to 10 percent is far easier than dealing with 15 to 20 percent; nevertheless, in *all* the receiving countries the level of racial, ethnic, and political tension over immigration issues is rising. Multiculturalism may be the goal; but in countries like France or Holland, multiculturalism is present mainly when their racially diverse soccer teams take the field.

Immigration is thus another hot, current, comparative politics issue. And like drugs, pollution, and the environment, it is both a domestic and an international policy issue, a combination of *international* and *domestic* which is thus called "inter-mestic." Once again the now-familiar comparative politics questions are present: if immigration policy is the dependent variable, then what are the independent or explanatory factors behind that policy, and how do they vary from country to country? Is it economic factors (the need for immigrant workers), political or diplomatic initiatives (opening the doors to political refugees), a sense of social or cultural superiority, or downright racial prejudice? Could it be (as in some countries) a result of war and the displacement of peoples, of famine and starvation causing people to flee, or the desire for a better life for one's self and one's family? Or varying combinations of several or all of these? We do not provide the final answer here, only hints and suggestions; the comparative politics methodology, however, points toward more detailed and systematic ways to explore answers to this question.

REGIONALISM/DECENTRALIZATION

Regionalism and decentralization have become the rallying cries for many peoples in many nations.[4] Here is the paradox: At one level, globalization is going forward and countries are integrating into ever larger trading blocs, but at another they are being divided into smaller units by ethnic, nationality, political, religious, cultural, economic, and geographic differences.

The causes of this trend toward regionalism and decentralization are several. One cause is the upsurge in ethnic nationalism, not just in historically unsettled countries like Spain or the former Yugoslavia but also in previously unified countries like France (autonomy movements in Normandy, Brittany), Britain (Scotland, Wales, Northern Ireland), and Canada (Quebec). Another cause is that of good government and the sense that putting government and policy making closer to the people at local or regional levels serves that purpose. A third cause is the end of the Cold War: so long as the Cold War was being waged, the big superpowers effectively policed, discouraged, or snuffed out divisive ethnic or nationality movements within their spheres of influence; but now that the Cold War is over, they cannot do that effectively, and, hence, ethnic and nationality movements that were suppressed so long are again surfacing. A fourth cause is a sense of economic injustice on the part of certain regions: both the North of Italy and the Basque and Catalan regions in Spain contribute more in taxes than other areas to the national treasury or than they get back from the central government in public services, and they would like a redress of this imbalance.

The form that regionalism may take also varies greatly. Germany has the only federal system in Western Europe where, like the United States, power is constitutionally divided between the federal government and the states (*laender*). In Britain and France—historically more centralized countries—the issue is how much autonomy to grant to distinct regions that want to preserve their own language and culture. In Spain the issue is a thousand-year conflict that has ebbed and flowed over the centuries between a central state in Madrid seeking to enhance its power, and historically separatist regions that are seeking to reestablish their traditional rights to self-government. In Russia and Eastern Europe the trends seem to be toward disruptive and often chaotic ethnic nationalism, while in Scandinavia the primary motive of decentralization may well be old-fashioned, "boring" (compared with these others) *good government*.

The politics of regionalism and decentralization are fascinating. Here we present only two brief illustrations. In Italy we have a nation divided into a very wealthy, dynamic North and a poor, underdeveloped, almost Third World South. The North is well integrated into Europe, a center of fashion, art, prosperity, and creativity; while the South is isolated, more "Mediterranean," wracked by poverty, and dominated by patronage and traditionalism. For decades, if not centuries, the wealthy North has been heavily subsidizing the poor South, seemingly without having made more than a minor dent in the area's poverty and traditionalism, and now many Northerners have grown weary of the effort. The issue ebbs and flows but there are many in the North (and even a separate political party) who would cut the South off, let it go its separate ways, and declare an independent nation in the North. That has not happened yet and may even be inconceivable, but because a split is even being discussed, students of comparative politics must consider it seriously.

Another interesting case is Portugal, where regionalism is being pushed mainly by the government as well as the Communist Party. Portugal is a comparatively small country where regional government may not be needed and may only add a new layer of bureaucracy to an already overly bureaucratic government. That is precisely what the government wants: a new layer of public administration that it can fill with its own supporters and use for patronage obligations. The Communist Party has a different set of motives: while it is declining in voter support at the national level, it nevertheless still dominates local government, particularly in Portugal's South. The party knows that, under new EU rules, European community assistance money can be channeled directly to these new regional governments rather than funneled through the national ministries in Lisbon which are controlled by another party and not about to share much of its budget with Communists. So the Communist Party is betting that, with the creation of regional governments, it can control the South region, receive funding directly from the EU, and thus accomplish programs at the local and regional levels that, with its declining share of the vote, it cannot hope to do at the national level.

These are fascinating issues. Some political scientists feel that a focus on state, regional, or local government must be terribly boring. But when issues of regionalism and decentralization get tied into issues of ethnic nationalism, regional autonomy, the actual or potential breakup of larger states (Yugoslavia, Czechoslovakia, the Soviet Union, Canada), or the fascinating political maneuvering as here described for Italy and Portugal, that becomes very exciting material for further research.

LEGAL RIGHTS FOR GAYS

The issue of homosexual rights remains controversial and unsettled in most developed countries, although the trend is toward greater tolerance.[5] In this respect, Europe is close to the United States, though there are interesting differences and variations.

In most of Europe unwed couples who are living together, whether gay or heterosexual, have no or little protection under the law to ensure pensions, inheritances, or health care for their partner if they should become sick or die. Whether it is taxes, retirement income, welfare, inheritance, life insurance, or housing, unwed partners are mainly treated in law as people without family. But now France has enacted a law called a "contract of social union" that gives cohabitating couples of whatever sexual orientation the same social, fiscal, and inheritance rights as those enjoyed by wedded partners. Other countries have already or are in the process of enacting similar provisions.

These changes in law reflect, as in the United States, the changes that have taken place in social, cultural, and religious attitudes toward marriage, informal unions, and gays in recent years, especially among young people. In France, for example, in a population of nearly sixty million, over two million couples now live together out of wedlock, twice the number fifteen years earlier. The figures show that 38 percent of French children are born outside of marriage, which gives France one of the highest illegitimacy rates in the world, ahead of Britain at 36 percent and just behind the Swedish and Danish figures. As regards homosexuals, the French have long been homophobic, but opinion polls now show two-thirds of the public willing to grant equal rights to gays as married couples, which helps explain the new social-union legislation. The same poll shows that more than 50 percent of the Finnish could "accept" a homosexual son or daughter.

The new laws and attitudes put France roughly in the middle of the European countries on the issue of gay rights. At present, there is still a wide range of attitudes as well as legal standing for gays in European and other developed countries. Table 11.1 shows the age of consent for both heterosexual and homosexual persons and whether there is legal recognition for homosexual couples. At this time, legal rights for homosexual couples are recognized by all the Scandinavian countries. Spain, Holland, Belgium, and, recently, France have enacted or are in the process of drafting legislation that, with some national variations, grant similar rights. Elsewhere in Europe, homosexual couples have no legal standing.

Table 11.1 indicates that the age of consent also varies. Among European countries, the most common age of consent for both heterosexual and homosexual sex is sixteen. But in Sweden, Denmark, and France it is

Table 11.1. Legal Rights for Homosexual Couples in Europe and Age of Consent

	Legal Recognition		Age of Consent Heterosexual	Age of Consent Homosexual
Belgium	y		16	16
Denmark	y		15	15
Finland	y		16	16
France	y		15	15
Germany	y	2000	14/16	14
Hungary	y	1995	14	14
Netherlands	y		12/16	12
Norway	y		16	16
Portugal	y	2001	16	16
Sweden	y		15	15
United Kingdom	y	2003	16	16
Austria	n		14	18
Greece	n		15/17	17
Ireland	n		17	17
Italy	n		14	14
Poland	n		15	15
Russia	n		14/16	14
Spain	n		13	13
Turkey	n		15/16	18

Sources: Council of Europe; The Advocate; and Gay and Lesbian Rights Lobby.

fifteen. Significantly, some countries—Austria and Turkey among them—have higher age requirements (eighteen) of consent for homosexual sex than for heterosexual sex. In Spain the age of consent for both homosexuals and heterosexuals is thirteen.

It is clear that in Western Europe as well as the United States (less so in other areas), traditional moral, religious, and personal attitudes toward sex, marriage, and homosexuality are changing. And these changed attitudes are now being reflected in changed laws as well as practices. Our purpose here is not to make moral judgments about these changes but only to suggest that this is another intriguing, current, front-burner issue worthy of further study and about which comparative politics and the comparative perspective have interesting data to present.

ENVIRONMENTAL ISSUES AND POLLUTION

The environment has also become a major, hot issue in recent years—and not just in the United States.[6] Once again, our purpose in these few pages is not to try to solve the issue but to suggest areas of inquiry and research and to show how comparative politics can shed light on the subject.

Environmental issues are a lot like other issues—hunger, overpopulation, immigration, drugs—that have emerged in recent years and that are a product both of globalization and of new, rising consciousness. First, these issues are at one and the same time both global and national issues. All of us understand that acid rain, pollution, global warming, and the environment generally are not just local or national issues but, since they cross frontiers and national borders and affect us all, international and global issues. Nor can they be solved by one nation acting unilaterally; international cooperation is necessary. At the same time, since international organizations are weak, often ineffective, and lack enforcement mechanisms, national societies and national legislatures are usually the first arenas of political activity where effective action is taken on the issue. And the problem for those who see the issue in purely global terms is that these nations often have quite different interests and perspectives on the issue. That, to students of comparative politics, makes the issue more interesting and should not necessarily be cause for lamentation.

The sharpest split has been between developed and developing nations. The developed or industrialized nations are often the largest polluters, and the results of their earlier polluting industries, automobiles, and habits are all around. They are usually the first to ring the alarm on any further environmental degradation. The developing countries in contrast are just that: poor and underdeveloped. They often want the industries, even the polluting ones and the jobs and economic growth that go with them, that the developed nations are inclined to reject. They resent the industrialized nations, which have already made it to developed status and are rich and prosperous, telling them that they should not develop their resources (such as in the Brazilian Amazon), or they should not build factories and smokestacks for the sake of what are often vague, future, environmental goals. They see "sustainable development" as an euphemism for outsiders to regulate their development and keep them poor. They also insist that, since the industrialized nations are responsible for the vast majority of the world's pollution, they and not the developing countries should pay for cleaning it up. The dilemma, of course, is that, while everyone (or nearly so) is against damaging the environment, that stance may come at the cost of keeping the developing countries poor. And that is neither a realistic nor a politically or morally sustainable position.

Problems also exist between and among the developed countries. Canada blames the United States for the acid rain that begins as airborne pollutants from American factories in the Midwest but mainly falls as rain on Canadian provinces. Japan tends to blame both China and South Korea for the pollution that the prevailing westerly winds blow over the Japanese islands. The United States blames Mexico for the pollution in the border area between the two countries and the sewage that drifts across the Gulf of Mexico or flows from Tijuana into San Diego Bay. Western Europe with its clean streets and (mainly) fresh air looks aghast at American wastefulness, grime, pollution, and the "throwaway" society that contributes to these conditions.

Environmental issues can be approached on three main levels: national, regional, and international. At the national level, there is much that individual societies can do to reduce harmful emissions, clean up the air and water, and improve the environment. Most of the Western European countries and Japan are far ahead of the United States in these respects; a good comparative politics project would be to investigate how, why, and in what specifics. A second approach is regional, and at this level—beyond national politics but below the global dimension—a great deal can be accomplished. For example, under the North American Free Trade Agreement (NAFTA) the United States and Mexico are cooperating on a wide range of activities to improve environmental standards and quality in the border region. Across the Mediterranean Sea, the nations of North Africa and those of Southern Europe are cooperating on fishing agreements, the discharge of pollutants, sewage treatment plants, and industrial waste in an effort to save the Mediterranean.[7] Similarly in the north of Europe, the Scandinavian nations of Denmark, Finland, Norway, and Sweden have entered into agreements with the newly independent Baltic nations of Estonia, Latvia, and Lithuania, plus Poland and Germany, to try to improve the condition of the Baltic Sea. One could think of some fascinating comparative politics research projects involving not just the attitudes and policies of the different countries involved but also a comparison between groups of nations and their cooperation levels in the Mediterranean and Baltic projects.

At the global level, given the absence of either strong institutions or consensus, it is likely that less can be accomplished. Nevertheless, there is much that can be done in terms of education about environmental issues and the raising of consciousness. Global conferences about the environment can also be useful, both in terms of generating publicity for the goals desired and in enacting resolutions that national governments are then called to act upon. But so far—and that is what makes the issue so interesting to students of comparative politics—most of the action on environmental issues has come at the national and, secondarily, the regional levels.

The environmental issue, like many of those raised here, is interesting not only for its own sake but also for the comparative politics issues it raises. For like these others, the environment brings up questions of political culture and national values, of economic needs and demands, of dependency and the relations between developed and developing nations, of conflict and cooperation at the regional and international levels, of laws and comparative institutions as well as social forces.

It should not be thought that the issues raised in this chapter—women in politics, drugs, immigration, gay rights, the environment—exhaust the list of new and interesting issues. There are many others—terrorism, land reform, water rights, tourism, trade, population, hunger, energy, and many more—that are also worth studying from a comparative perspective. All of these are fascinating, current, front-burner issues that are not only worth knowing more about but that are also filtered through national values, interest groups, political party maneuvering, elections, and institutions. And these, of course, all vary from country to country and region to region. But that is what comparative politics is all about: trying to better understand the similarities as well as differences between countries, regions, and the public policies that they pursue. Comparative politics and the comparative method offer us the tools both to understand these issues better and, if we are actively engaged, to advance the policy issues which we care deeply about.

NOTES

1. Among the better comparative studies of women in politics are: Jane S. Jaquette, *Women and Democracy* (Baltimore: Johns Hopkins University Press, 1998); Jaquette, *Women in Developing Countries* (New York: Haworth, 1983); Ann M. Pescatello, *Power and Pawn: Women in Latin America* (Westport, CT: Greenwood, 1976); and Susan Bourque, *Learning about Women* (Ann Arbor: University of Michigan Press, 1989).

2. For some background on drugs and drug policy, see Renssalaer Lee, *The White Labyrinth* (New Brunswick, NJ: Transaction, 1989); and Scott B. MacDonald, *Mountain High, White Avalanche* (New York: Praeger, 1989).

3. Immigration is discussed in Jack Millman, *The Other Americans* (New York: Viking, 1997); Roberto Suro, *How Latino Immigration Is Transforming America* (New York: Knopf, 1998); Daniel James, *Illegal Immigration: An Unfolding Crisis* (Washington, DC: Mexico-United States Institute, 1991); and Barry R. Chiswick (ed.), *The Gateway: U.S. Immigration Issues and Policies* (Washington, DC: American Enterprise Institute for Public Policy Research, 1992).

4. Regionalization/decentralization are discussed in Richard Sagar, *Local Control and Accountability* (Thousand Oaks, CA: Corwin, 1996); Joel F. Handler, *Down from Democracy* (Princeton: Princeton University Press, 1996); *Regionalism and Global Economic Integration* (New York: Routledge, 1998); Raquel Fernandez, *Return to Regionalism* (Washington, DC: World Bank, 1997).

5. The data and analysis in this section derive from *The Economist* (July 5, 1997), 52.

6. On environmental issues, see Sheldon Kamieniecki (ed.), *Environmental Politics in the International Arena* (Albany: State University of New York Press, 1993).

7. Peter M. Haass, *Saving the Mediterranean* (New York: Columbia University Press, 1990).

PART IV

COMPARATIVE POLITICS: TOWARD NEW FRONTIERS

12

❧

The End of the Great Systems Debate? Implications for Comparative Politics

M ost of the present leadership in the comparative politics field came of age, intellectually and as scholars, during the 1960s, 1970s, and 1980s. It was an exciting time. A host of new nations had emerged onto the world stage; there were exciting new approaches and methodologies for studying these changes; U.S. foreign policy through such agencies as the Peace Corps and the U.S. Agency for International Development (USAID) was paying serious attention to the Third World for the first time; and the developing nations of Africa, Asia, Latin America, and the Middle East offered fascinating new "living laboratories" for the study of social and political change. Not only was the subject matter new and challenging, but the comparative politics field advanced some of the most innovative and exciting theory and conceptual approaches in all of political science as well: studies of political culture, political socialization, developmentalism, dependency and interdependency, corporatism, bureaucratic-authoritarianism, organic-statism, transitions to democracy, and so on. The combination of new and exciting research terrains and provocative, innovative theory served to attract the best young graduate students to the field.[1]

Comparative politics and its conceptual theories were so exciting during this period because the questions they addressed involved large, complex, *systems* issues. These included the questions of capitalism versus communism, democracy versus totalitarianism or authoritarianism, free markets versus planned economies, political evolution versus revolution. When those early waves of young scholars fanned out to the developing areas in the 1960s, 1970s, and 1980s—and this is what made it so exciting—*all* the options seemed open: democracy, authoritarianism, Marxism,

253

revolution, corporatism, totalitarianism, fragmentation and disintegration, and civil war. Quite frankly, none of us knew what the outcome of
these conflicting viewpoints, forces, and systems might be; in a context of
new, still inchoate, often violent politics, almost any outcome seemed possible.[2] And to many young students, it was this very uncertainty, the
many competing options open, that seemed to make comparative politics
so exciting as a field of study.[3]

But by now many of those earlier issues have been decided. The great
systems debates of earlier decades have been (mostly?) resolved. Democracy has largely triumphed in the political sphere; certainly democracy is
the only system of government that enjoys widespread global legitimacy.
No regime wants to be called authoritarian or "Marxist-Leninist" anymore; both of these *system* alternatives have been discredited. In addition,
with the collapse of the Soviet Union, the Cold War conflict between capitalism and communism has largely run its course, and there is only one
real superpower left. The success, particularly of the East Asian
economies and the failures of Cuba, Nicaragua, and Eastern Europe,
demonstrated the advantages of private market initiatives over a totally
controlled system. Obviously, there is and will continue to be debate between advocates of freer markets and state downsizing, and those who
would preserve statism and a larger welfare state, but increasingly these
involve the politics of compromise and moderation (socialist governments in the UK and Germany following free-market strategies, right-of-
center governments in Portugal and Italy expanding welfarism, virtually
everyone else also seeking to combine free-market policies with strong social programs) rather than the politics of "either/or."

The great systems debates of earlier decades is now largely over, at least
in the more advanced industrial countries and in much of the Third World
as well. There has been a certain decline of ideology;[4] as Francis
Fukuyama famously put it, history has "ended."[5] By that he meant not literally that history is over, only that, in the great competition of ideas of
the last two hundred years plus, democracy has won out. Democracy now
has triumphed in the political sphere almost universally; at the same time,
an open market system or some mix of free markets and state regulation
(the mix may vary from country to country) has won out economically.
Relatively few countries still lie outside of this consensus.

The end of the great systems debates, however, does not mean that
comparative politics is any less interesting as a field of study. Some questions have been largely answered but new ones are constantly coming to
the fore. Will China also democratize? Is Russia now slipping back into its
older bad (authoritarian) ways? Will democracy in Latin America be consolidated? Will Africa develop over time and stabilize? How wide will the
gap between the European and American political systems (and foreign

policies) become? Will the Islamic countries also undergo democratization? How will the advanced industrial countries handle new social issues (e.g., immigration, an aging population, bankrupted welfare systems)? These are only some of the exciting issues that come to mind. Comparative politics has a lot to say about these and many other hot topics.

COMPARATIVE POLITICS: THE QUEEN OF THE DISCIPLINE

In 1955 Roy Macridis launched a diatribe against traditional comparative politics.[6] He accused the field of being formal-legalistic (studying formal institutions over nonformal political processes), descriptive rather than analytic, case study–oriented rather than genuinely comparative, and Eurocentric with its emphasis on Great Britain, France, Germany, and the Soviet Union. Macridis's critique had a strong effect on the younger scholars beginning to write in the field in those days. In addition, the revolution then occurring in political science more generally—behavioralism, the study of decision making, the emphases on informal actors such as political parties and interest groups, research on public opinion and political processes—also had a profound impact on comparative politics.[7]

Along with the Macridis critique, in the late 1950s and early 1960s came the sudden emergence onto the world scene of a large number of new nations. The decolonization of that period doubled the number of independent countries in the world and opened up new research opportunities in a variety of heretofore unexplored countries in Africa, Asia, and the Middle East. With the pioneering work of Gabriel Almond, David Apter, Lucian Pye, Sidney Verba, Myron Weiner, and the Social Science Research Council/Committee on Comparative Politics, the study of "non-Western"[8] or "developing" areas[9] came to the fore. The growth of new and exciting theory accompanying these developments made comparative politics the most innovative and provocative field within political science. For these reasons, comparative politics also attracted the best and brightest of political science graduate students who planned to write doctoral dissertations on the developing areas.

"Developmentalism" was the dominant conceptual paradigm at this time, incorporating both the effort to find and study development *and* the effort, through such agencies as USAID, the Alliance for Progress, the Peace Corps, and others, to bring development to less-favored ("developing" or "emerging") countries. It was obvious that not only were the developing nations very exciting to study but also that U.S. foreign policy was also increasingly interested in them and was seeking to find a noncommunist theory of development to counter the appeals of Marxism-Leninism. At the time (pre-Vietnam), most scholars interested in development saw no contradiction between their academic interest in development and the serving of U.S. foreign policy goals, presumably incorporating the same objectives.[10]

Meanwhile, by the mid-to-late 1960s, many of the younger scholars trained in development returned from the field with their dissertations under their arms, having found precious little "development"—functioning political parties or party systems, independent trade unions, functioning legislatures, and so on. The sentiment eventually grew that it was not just "their countries" that were "dysfunctional" for lacking these assumed accoutrements of development, but that the theory of development was itself flawed and based on misplaced assumptions.[11] The critiques of the developmentalist approach and logic grew louder; at the same time the 1965 U.S. intervention in the Dominican Republic, the escalation in Vietnam, the assassinations of Robert F. Kennedy and Martin Luther King, Jr., and then the presidency of Richard Nixon and the Watergate scandal led many scholars to become thoroughly disillusioned with both the theory of development and the practice of U.S. politics and policy on which so much of the developmentalist model had been based. The critiques of developmentalism were eventually so powerful and widespread that the theory went into eclipse and was largely ignored in comparative politics in the 1980s and 1990s.

Two main alternatives to developmentalism arose in the early 1970s and, over time, gained widespread attention: dependency theory and corporatism. Both these alternative approaches were strongly critical of developmentalism; both arose as conscious alternatives to it. Dependency theory,[12] mainly Marxian in origin, criticized the dominant developmentalism for ignoring domestic class factors as well as international market and power factors in development, and was particularly critical of U.S. foreign policy and multinational corporations. It suggested, contrary to the earlier development theory, that the development of the already industrialized nations and that of the developing ones would not go together hand-in-hand; instead, dependency theory argued that the development of the West had come on the shoulders and at the expense of the non-West. The corporatist approach criticized developmentalism for its Euro-American ethnocentrism and indicated that there were alternative organic, corporatist, often statist ways to organize government and state-society relations besides the dominant liberal-pluralism that undergirded developmentalism.[13] Although the dependency and corporatist "schools" often feuded within and between themselves, together they largely squeezed and criticized the developmentalist approach out of the picture.

During the later 1970s and on into the 1980s, still reflecting the backlash against developmentalism, a number of other theories and approaches emerged.[14] These included bureaucratic-authoritarianism,[15] organic-statism,[16] political economy, and indigenous concepts of change.[17] Eventually, rational choice theory and the new institutionalism joined the list of comparative politics approaches. Later, in the 1980s, new subject matters, if not new approaches, came similarly to the fore: transitions to democracy, the politics of structural adjustment, neoliberalism, and privatization. Some of the early scholars of development resented these new approaches as undermining and breaking the unity of the field (as well as their own monopoly of it), but others saw them as adding healthy diversity, providing an alternative variety of approaches and enlightening subject areas not covered by the earlier developmentalist perspective.[18]

The debate and excitement within the field from the 1960s through the 1980s reflected the large issues with which comparative politics had to wrestle. It bears repeating that these were *grand systems* issues. The ongoing debate between advocates of the developmentalist, dependency, corporatist, and other schools mentioned was not just an academic debate over proverbial small stakes; rather, it was a vigorous discussion about the future direction of developing and transitional nations themselves. Would they be capitalist or socialist? Would they have liberal-democratic, corporatist-authoritarian, or communist-totalitarian political systems? Would their path of development be by revolution, civil war, or gradual evolutionary change? Would they be viable as societies and nation-states or would they break down into chaos, ungovernability, and civil war; and what was the best political and economic system for achieving viability and avoiding breakdown?

Complicating all these already large and complex questions was the sometimes overt and sometimes covert foreign-policy issue: With which side in the Cold War would the developing nations be aligned and which model of all those discussed above would best assure the Cold War goals set by the superpowers? These were big issues; the stakes involved were enormous. The importance of the debate as well as the intellectual excitement created by the complex and often conflicting theories involved made comparative politics during this period the most exciting field in the political science discipline and development studies the most innovative field in the social sciences.

THE ECLIPSE OF SYSTEMS ISSUES

As the 1980s dawned, the world remained a tumultuous and uncertain place. The first of the "third-wave" transitions to democracy had begun but their outcome still remained fragile and uncertain.[19] The Cold War remained hot in such far-flung regions of conflict as Southern Africa, Afghanistan, Central America, the Horn of Africa, and the Middle East;

and at the time the question of which of the superpowers would emerge victorious was by no means certain. Marxism in its various forms, corporatism, authoritarianism, revolution, *and* democracy all seemed to be possible outcomes in many so-called developing nations. The Asian Tigers (Hong Kong, Singapore, South Korea, and Taiwan) had begun to show impressive economic growth but the term *newly industrialized countries* (NICs) had not yet been coined and no one quite expected the Asian NICs to blossom into global models.

But during the course of the 1980s and on into the 1990s, many of these earlier conflicts were resolved. More than that, after some thirty years of experimentation and experience (as distinct from the earlier theory), it became quite possible to say (see chapter 10) what works in development and what doesn't.[20] In addition, the older ideological, partisan, and class passions began to fade in some countries or were ameliorated somewhat. Many countries whose economic, social, and political systems had seemingly been "up for grabs" settled down to become more normal countries; democracy in one form or another was largely institutionalized. While it is not quite certain that history has "ended" in some definitive way, it is clear that the older ideological conflicts have declined and that, along with the end of the Cold War, the great systems debates of earlier decades are largely over. Democracy, consumerism, and neoliberalism or a mixed form of capitalism and social welfare appear to have emerged triumphant.

All of these real-world changes also carry immense implications for the field of comparative politics. Our purpose here is not to offer a complete or definitive analysis of all these transformations (impossible in a few pages), but to provide a region-by-region survey of some of the major changes in each area, to suggest how these have affected the great systems debates of earlier years, and then to explore the broad implications of these changes for comparative politics. A more detailed, systematic, and thorough explanation must be reserved for a later time. At this stage our hope is to offer a provocation, a set of research suggestions, and a number of hypotheses in narrative form, not a full and final treatment.[21]

The first countries to experience the "third-wave" transitions to democracy in the mid-1970s were the Southern European countries of Greece, Portugal, and Spain. All three had long been perceived as being on the periphery of Europe, dependent on the center in economic and political terms, and backward and underdeveloped socially, economically, and politically. At the time of their transitions in 1974–1975, *all* options seemed to be open: continued authoritarianism and corporatism, democracy, Marxian revolution, breakdown and fragmentation, even the possibility of civil war. These were exciting, large-scale systems issues; one suspects it was the systems-wide magnitude of the issues involved that attracted so many scholars to Southern Europe in the 1970s.

But since that time, Greece, Portugal, and Spain have settled down, become "normal" countries. Democracy has triumphed; elections are held regularly; a more-or-less stable party system has emerged; and in all three countries there have been at least two elections in which power has passed peacefully to the opposition—usually thought of as a key indicator of the consolidation of democracy.

All three countries are now members of the EU and NATO. Per capita income has risen to roughly 70–80 percent of the European average and a stable middle class has emerged. Ideological passions have cooled; depoliticization has taken place and consumerism has triumphed. Socialist governments carry out neoliberal economic policies while right-of-center governments expand social welfare. Democracy's triumph has been so definitive and enjoys such high legitimacy that a left-wing revolution or a right-wing coup are unthinkable. All the great systems issues have been resolved; politics revolves around "more or less" (a little less social welfare, a little more privatization, or vice versa) rather than the make-or-break issues of the past. As elsewhere in Europe, there is widespread consensus on democracy, employment, stability, welfare, markets, continued growth, consumerism, and something akin to a guaranteed income. Arguments still occur around the margins of these issues but not on the basics.[22]

Some parallel developments have occurred in Asia. First, the authoritarian political systems of earlier decades in South Korea, Taiwan, and Singapore have become more open, democratic, and pluralist. Second and relatedly, the authoritarian, state corporatism of the past has become more participatory and socially just ("societal corporatism"). Third, the economies of the area boomed: the four Asian Tigers (Hong Kong, Singapore, South Korea, and Taiwan) became NICs and began to challenge the already industrialized nations on several economic fronts. Fourth, this economic boom spread to other, previously less-developed countries (Indonesia, Malaysia, the Philippines, Thailand); while, fifth, even such communist countries as China and Vietnam have seen the benefits of opening their markets even as they still utilize the political controls of a command regime. Sixth, India has now been a political democracy for fifty years; recently, and looking at the example of its Asian neighbors, it has taken steps to reform and free up its economy as well. Thus, in both the political and the economic realms, the future path in Asia, despite recent and probably temporary downturns, seems clear: greater pluralism and democracy coupled with a combined statist-bureaucratic and more open-market system.[23]

A personal anecdote may help illustrate the point. In 1987 the author and Soviet Union specialist Jerry Hough were part of an academic delegation visiting Singapore. In a variation on the "mouse that roared" theme (small countries that make big headlines), Hough made front-page news in all the Singapore newspapers by claiming—with only a little hyperbole—that it was "little" Singapore that had won the Cold War! He argued that it was the dynamism and success of the Singapore economy (and that of the other Asian Tigers) that had shown to the Soviets, other developing countries, and the world that market capitalism was far more productive and superior to Marxist-Leninist economies. One can see why this assessment was so well received by the Singapore press: city-state-sized Singapore had become a model for the *world*.

Latin America's political systems are more fragile than those of Southern Europe and its economies less developed, but many of the same trends present in Spain, Portugal, Greece, and even Asia are also present in Latin America. Indeed, the two Iberian countries, especially Spain, like to present themselves as models for Latin America. Here are a few, perhaps surprising, statistics for comparison: in 1960 Latin America was 70 percent rural (and agrarian reform was a major issue); now it is 70 percent urban. In 1960 Latin America was 70 percent illiterate; now it is 70 percent literate. In 1960 Latin America's per capita income was in the $300–$400 range; now it is quadruple that, and most countries have reached middle-income levels. Latin America is currently one of the most dynamic areas economically in the world. In 1977 (at the height of the wave of bureaucratic-authoritarianism) fourteen of the twenty Latin American countries were under military rule and in three other countries the military was so close to the surface of power as to make the line between civil and military all but invisible. In 1997, in contrast, nineteen of the twenty countries (all except Cuba) could be said to be democratic or en route to democracy.[24]

Polls show that 60, 70, or 80 percent (depending on the country) of the population support liberal, democratic, representative rule. Almost no one wants Marxism-Leninism or a return to authoritarianism and corporatism anymore, although "strong, effective government" is still often preferred. While the legitimacy of democracy is thus high, the precise meaning of democracy ("controlled," "tutelary," "delegative," "Rousseauian"—democracy with adjectives) is not so clear-cut. Moreover, the public support for what we think of as democracy's essential pluralist underpinnings—political parties, trade unions, etc.—is often low, in the range of 10, 15, or 20 percent. Electoral democracy has clearly triumphed in Latin America but liberal democracy has not yet been firmly entrenched.[25] Nor are Latin Americans fully convinced of the efficacy of a neoliberal economic order, although they lack a viable alternative model.

As was the case with Southern Europe, a large number of young scholars were attracted to Latin America in the past because of the excitement and romance of the major changes taking place there and because it offered a marvelous laboratory of social and political transformation. Latin America was a systems area *par excellence*. Democracy, revolutions, coups, guerrilla struggles—all the options seemed possible. But with democracy now triumphant, most guerrilla movements suing for peace or reconstituting themselves as political parties and joining the electoral political process, and coups d'état a thing of the past in most countries, the great systems conflicts of previous decades have died down. Latin America, too, like Southern Europe and Asia, is now more prosperous, more middle class, less ideological, more consumerist, more affluent, thus providing a stronger socioeconomic base for democracy.

While Latin America is presently strongly democratic, its democracy is not so firmly established or institutionalized as that of Southern Europe. The precise meaning of democracy (patronage in Brazil, welfarism in Uruguay, often organic and corporatist elsewhere) is still not entirely clear, and the institutions of democracy are often weak. The large, well-endowed South American countries have in general stronger economies and better institutionalized political systems than the weaker countries of Central America; hence, there is still the possibility of a coup d'état in some of the latter countries, although probably not a whole wave of authoritarian takeovers as occurred in the 1960s and 1970s. In addition, the Latin American political process is still more anomic, chaotic, and conflict-prone than in the more-developed countries, with street demonstrations, strikes, riots, structured violence, property takeovers, and so on that have the potential to produce more open-ended politics. Equity and social justice issues are still critical; class and racial divisions remain sharp; and the neoliberal agenda has not yet produced the economic gains expected.[26] However, with both Marxism-Leninism and traditional statism/mercantilism discredited, there is presently no real alternative to the neoliberal model. Political debate has largely concentrated on the pace and extent of these changes, not on the need for reform itself. Once again it is the politics of "more or less" rather than that of either-or that is emerging triumphant—less dramatic than Latin American politics in the past but probably more hopeful, too.

Russia and Eastern Europe are presently going through many of the same systems changes as did Southern Europe, Asia, and Latin America in previous decades. Indeed, one is struck by the remarkable parallels between these four areas. To use a now almost forgotten phrase from W. W. Rostow,[27] it may be that not only was Marxism-Leninism a "disease of the transition" (to modernity) but also that authoritarian-corporatism was similarly a "disease" of the same transition. That is to say that both Marxism-Leninism on the left and authoritarian-corporatism on the right were products of a certain vulnerable stage of the transition from tradition to modernity, a stage and time period where system breakdown and extremism of both left and right were possible. We have long known that communism and fascism were not only often bitter enemies but also exhibited numerous parallels,[28] and now we know another reason why: they were products of the same time period and of many of the same wrenching, divisive, potentially morbific social and political forces. But now, after a long interregnum (forty years of authoritarian corporatism in Spain and Portugal, seventy years of Marxism-Leninism in the USSR), those conditions have dramatically changed and so have the two kinds of countries discussed.[29]

Let us make some preliminary distinctions, which are well worth further comparative politics research.[30] First, because of geography, proximity, history, culture, and sociology—to say nothing of the fact that its Marxism-Leninism was imposed by invading and occupying Soviet armies—Eastern Europe is, in general, currently closer to the Western model politically (democracy) and economically (mixed market economies) than is Russia. Second, within Eastern Europe there are also major differences: Poland, Hungary, the Czech Republic, Slovakia, the Baltic states, and Slovenia are closer to the West politically and economically (democracy and a free market/mixed economy) than are Romania, Bulgaria, Croatia, Bosnia, and Serbia. Almost all these countries have joined NATO and the EU or are en route to membership. Except perhaps for Albania, Kosovo, and Bosnia, the great systems debate in Eastern Europe of recent years over which direction to pursue seems to be mainly over as well; democracy and a mixed economy are becoming triumphant here as in other areas surveyed—even though numerous structural reforms are still required in these countries.

Russia and some members of the Commonwealth of Independent States constitute a more difficult case.[31] On the one hand, Russia in the past fifteen years has made remarkable strides toward democracy and a more open market system. On the other, Russia's democracy remains weakly institutionalized; its democratic leadership is uncertain; authoritarianism is still strong; and the economy is often run in a corrupt and patronage-based way. At the same time, nationalistic Slavophile forces are assertive and there exists at least the *possibility* of a communist return to power or, alternatively, a military coup. These system possibilities help make Russia a fascinating country to study and have lured a new generation of scholars to the area. But while these alternative systems models are still possibilities, a more likely outcome is a continuation of the status quo: an uncertain and sometimes wobbly democracy combined with a form of entrepreneurial capitalism. In this sense, Russia is reminiscent of Greece, Portugal, and Spain in the late 1970s: on the way to democracy and freer markets but with the changes not yet institutionalized or consolidated.

With regard to the Commonwealth of Independent States, some further distinctions need to be made. Because of geography, culture, level of development, and proximity to Europe, it seems likely that the Baltic states,

Georgia, the Ukraine, and perhaps Belarus—to say nothing of Russia it-self—will follow, in one form or another, the European polity (democracy) and economy (open markets, mixed economy) model. However, such ar-eas as Chechnya, Azerbaijan, Kazakhstan, Uzbekistan, Tajikistan, Kyr-gyzstan, and Turkmenistan may come closer to the earlier East Asian model of a form of authoritarianism politically and a more statist model economically. In these areas of the former Soviet Union, the systems de-bate of the past would seem to be still lively.[32]

The two other areas of the world where the question of system is, for the most part, still intensely debated and often fought over, are sub-Saha-ran Africa and the Islamic world. While some countries of sub-Saharan Africa are stabilizing and demonstrating economic and political progress, other countries remain unstable, torn apart by conflict, revolution, civil war, or coup d'état.[33] While Marxism has in many countries been discred-ited, authoritarianism—often disguised by the rhetoric and appearance of democratic elections—is still prevalent. In addition, the idea of an indige-nous, homegrown model of development—whatever that might mean and with all its problems of implementation[34]—is still attractive in the context of sub-Sahara Africa. Although progress toward democracy and free markets often seems glacial, change is occurring in the form of greater decentralization and privatization that may lead to systems change and improvements in the future. The recent changes in Africa as well as the systems options still open have attracted both renewed policy attention and scholarly interest to the area.

The Islamic world has similarly been slow in moving toward either po-litical or economic reform. Or, if it has moved toward democracy and elec-tions (Algeria), it has sometimes had to cancel the democratic opening be-cause of the threat or actuality of victory by Islamic fundamentalists. The result is that, of all the world's geographic or culture areas, the Islamic world has continued to lag depressingly behind in both the economic and political spheres.[35] Economically, many of the Islamic countries are still dominated by elites, oligarchies, and royal families who monopolize most of the wealth for themselves; elsewhere a bureaucratic-statist and often highly politicized or militarized model remains in place that has inhibited economic growth. Politically, much of the Islamic world is still dominated by authoritarianism and a top-down model of political control; only in a handful of countries (Jordan, Iran, Turkey, Kuwait) have even the earliest and quite limited forms of political opening taken place. In addition, there are strong, ongoing efforts to fashion a distinctly Islamic model of devel-opment as an alternative to the Western one—one that, as in Africa, is be-set by difficulties.[36] It is perhaps no coincidence that the Islamic world constitutes one of the main cases in Samuel P. Huntington's writing on "the clash of civilizations."[37]

Hence, in virtually all global areas (sub-Saharan Africa and the Islamic world are the major exceptions), we have seen in recent years a significant gravitation toward more open political and economic systems. The main alternatives of Marxism-Leninism and corporatism-authoritarianism have been uprooted and largely discredited; only democracy and free markets (usually combined with welfarism and some form of statism) now enjoy widespread legitimacy. It may be democracy or free markets with adjectives (controlled democracy, tutelary democracy, delegative democracy, limited democracy), but it is democracy nonetheless; even the adjectives seem to reinforce that it is only *democracy* that has legitimacy. The precise meanings of democracy and free markets may vary somewhat but increasingly, in grand systems terms, the politics of compromise and pragmatism has replaced the politics of ideological either/or. All of this suggests, with immense implications for comparative politics, that the great systems debates of the past are largely over. And the field is now turning its attention to other, newer issues and controversies.

FUTURE RESEARCH TERRAINS

To say that the large systems issues of the past have mainly been resolved at this stage in favor of democracy and open markets is not, of course, to argue that comparative politics as a field is now any less interesting. The move away from the grand systems debates of previous decades forces us to reorient the field but not to abandon it. In fact, there is a host of interesting issues for students in the field to examine; herewith a partial list.

First, let us recognize that the debate over grand political and economic systems is not yet ended. In China, the Commonwealth of Independent States, much of the Islamic world, and sub-Saharan Africa, the systems debate is by no means over. Even in Russia, parts of Asia, and some countries of Eastern Europe and Latin America, the question of system may not yet be as resolved as implied here. And these issues involve some big, important countries and regions.

Second, even if the question of grand system has been resolved in many countries, it remains important to understand how and why that occurred. The literature on "transitions to democracy" seems to me incomplete and unsatisfactory in various ways, and it leaves unanswered a variety of questions. Is it social, political, economic, cultural, or geostrategic (the winding down of the Cold War) factors—or some combination of them—that best explains these changes? How do the transitions from communist regimes differ from the transitions from authoritarian-corporate regimes? How do the transitions from well-entrenched and institutionalized authoritarian regimes (Portugal, Spain, Mexico, Taiwan, South

Africa) differ from those in less-well-institutionalized military dictator-ships? How much continuity as well as change is there in these transi-tions? How precisely do we account for the variations among countries en route to democracy, and so on?

Third, even if the triumph of democracy and open markets has largely ended the grand systems debate over these issues, students of compar-ative politics should continue to be fascinated by the distinct forms, the-oretical bases, and institutional arrangements of democracy and neolib-eral economics in distinct countries and regions. How does Asian or Latin American democracy differ from European or North American de-mocracy? How does Asian neo-corporatism differ from European neo-corporatism? What are the processes involved in Latin America transi-tioning from an older state corporatism to a newer societal corporatism or even to (usually limited) pluralism? How do civil society, pluralism, and state-society relations differ in these distinct regions? These issues would seem to present as much substance for comparative analysis as the great systems debates of the past.

Fourth, while "on the ground" in terms of actual countries and conti-nents, there seems to have been considerable evolution toward a common agenda of democracy and freer markets, comparative politics theory has not yet quite reflected these changes. The different schools of thought in-clude developmentalists, dependency theorists, theorists of corporatism, advocates of political culture explanations, structuralists, institutionalists, and so on. Reflecting the real changes in the world, we now need our the-oretical models to catch up, to focus on such topics as the relations be-tween development, dependency, and interdependency, or the relations between dependency and corporatism.[38] We need to build bridges be-tween these several islands of theory to reflect the changing situation of the world and the interrelations and interdependence of the various coun-tries in it.

A fifth area calling for further research lies in the politics of managing social and economic policy in this new era of rather constrained choices, and of the accompanying coalition formation and management. For ex-ample, Spain, Germany, and the UK all have socialist governments, but all three are practicing the financial restraint that would seem to be associ-ated with neoliberalism and a more conservative political-economy agenda. At the same time, Portugal and Italy have right-of-center govern-ments that have done little to privatize, roll back state size, or curtail so-cial welfare. In other words, the post–Cold War consensus on neoliberal-ism is forcing *all* governments, left and right, to coalesce around a fairly agreed-upon policy of opening markets and downsizing the state, but only modestly, and also reducing welfare but also only modestly. All gov-ernments of both left and right are following this essentially centrist agenda, pursuing the politics of "more or less," and thus altering both their electoral strategies and their search for coalition allies.

Sixth, these changes also help explain the new emphasis on institutions (neoinstitutionalism) in comparative politics. The implications of the argument presented here are that ideologies, party labels, and particularly extremist parties of left and right in this new era of relative consensus on political economy are becoming less important, giving way to increasingly important emphasis on corporatist forms of management and administration. With parties, ideologies, and perhaps even elections in decline, there is renewed emphasis on institutions of government, particularly the efficiency, proper organization, cost-effectiveness, and deliverability of services of these institutions. Hence, within comparative politics there is a new interest in and emphasis on institutions and institutionalization that may, after a forty-year interregnum, lead us back to the quite sophisticated work on institutions of Carl Friedrich, Herman Finer, or Karl Loewenstein in earlier decades, or Peter Merkl or Jorgan Rasmussen still today.[39] New approaches to studying institutions are, of course, needed but the usefulness of the institutional focus itself is clear.

However, if the state is changing and/or contracting, seventh, we will need to modify our views of state-society relations as well. The structure, main institutions, and practice of corporatism and neo-corporatism will also need to be reviewed and our interpretations reformulated. Similarly, the politics of interest group activity, particularly the incorporation of interest groups into state decision making, will require new approaches and new ways of thinking.[40] In addition, the relations between the central state, regional entities, and local government will need to be reevaluated, particularly since decentralization is now widely seen as a more effective way to deliver public services—back to institutional issues again.

Eighth, comparative politics is also likely to focus in the future on lower-level, more technical, narrower, and specialized topics. These will include studies of voting behavior, public opinion, electoral strategies, coalition management, public policy issues, and foreign and international policy. All of these are fascinating topics of research.

WRAPPING UP

Comparative politics is a quite different field from what it was twenty, thirty, and forty years ago. Then, big changes were in the air; the field changed to reflect the great systems debate then stirring, particularly in the Third World. All options seemed open: capitalism, socialism, mercantilism, democracy, authoritarianism, corporatism, totalitarianism, revolution, coup d'état, civil war, disintegration. These were exciting times, for the world and for comparative politics. New, innovative, and exciting models of change and development emerged to provide conceptual frameworks for comprehending the vast changes taking place.

Now much of this has changed. The Cold War is over as well as many of the superpower and proxy rivalries that went with it. In addition, we now know pretty much what works in development, as compared with the largely theoretical discussion of alternatives of thirty to forty years ago. Furthermore, much of the Third World is more affluent, urban, literate, bourgeois, consumerist, and middle class than before; it has less use for the impassioned ideological quarrels of the past. These changes in the social and economic realms have provided a more solid base for democracy than before; that and the end of the Cold War have given democracy greater legitimacy. In turn, a consensus has also emerged on the main directions and requirements of economic policy, although with ongoing differences over the details. The great systems debates of the past decades are dying down; the better administration and management of policy are now a main focus. All this is, or ought to be, having an impact on the field of comparative politics as well.

There is still much for students of comparative politics to do. The topics outlined here (and doubtless others as well) remain interesting and important. Nor should we forget that in many countries—China, many of the Islamic countries, sub-Saharan Africa—the great systems debate is not yet over. Or that it could be reversed in some areas—Russia, the Commonwealth of Independent States, Latin America—that are currently undergoing democratic slippage. On both the older issues and the newer ones, there is still much for comparative politics to do—and a *whole world* of political systems to explore and analyze.

NOTES

1. For the background, see Myron Weiner and Samuel P. Huntington (eds.), *Understanding Political Development* (Boston: Little, Brown, 1987); and Howard J. Wiarda, *Introduction to Comparative Politics* (Belmont, CA: Wadsworth, 1993).

2. For a conceptual perspective, see Merle King, "Toward a Theory of Power and Political Instability in Latin America," *Western Political Quarterly* 9 (1956), pp. 21–35.

3. See, for example, Willard A. Beling and George O. Totten (eds.), *Developing Nations: Quest for a Model* (New York: Van Nostrand, 1970).

4. Daniel Bell, *The End of Ideology* (Cambridge, MA: Harvard University Press, 1988).

5. Francis Fukuyama, *The End of History and the Last Man* (New York: The Free Press, 1992).

6. Roy Macridis, *The Study of Comparative Government* (New York: Random House, 1955).

7. See Heinz Eulau, *The Behavioral Persuasion in Politics* (New York: Random House, 1963); and David Easton, *A Framework for Political Analysis* (Englewood Cliffs, NJ: Prentice Hall, 1965).

8. Lucian Pye, "The Non-Western Political Process," *Journal of Politics* 20 (1958), pp. 468–86.

9. The pioneering work was Gabriel A. Almond and James S. Coleman (eds.), *The Politics of the Developing Areas* (Princeton, NJ: Princeton University Press, 1960).

10. Irene I. Gendzier, *Managing Political Change: Social Scientists and the Third World* (Boulder, CO: Westview Press, 1985); and Arturo Escobar, *Encountering Development: The Making and Unmaking of the Third World* (Princeton, NJ: Princeton University Press, 1995).

11. See the Introduction by the editor in Howard J. Wiarda (ed.), *New Directions in Comparative Politics* (Boulder, CO: Westview Press, 1992).

12. See especially Fernando Henrique Cardoso and Enzo Faletto, *Dependency and Development in Latin America* (Berkeley: University of California Press, 1979). But see also Theodore Moran, *Multinational Corporations and the Politics of Dependence* (Cambridge, MA: Center for International Affairs, Harvard University, 1975).

13. Frederick B. Pike and Thomas Stritch (eds.), *The New Corporatism* (Notre Dame, IN: Notre Dame University Press, 1974); and Howard J. Wiarda, *Corporatism and Comparative Politics: The Other Great "Ism"* (New York: M.E. Sharpe, 1997).

14. These approaches are summarized and a critique provided in Wiarda, *New Directions in Comparative Politics.*

15. Guillermo O'Donnell, *Modernization and Bureaucratic-Authoritarianism* (Berkeley: Institute of International Studies, University of California, 1973).

16. Alfred Stepan, *State and Society: Peru in Comparative Perspective* (Princeton, NJ: Princeton University Press, 1979).

17. A. J. Somjee, *Parallels and Actuals of Political Development* (London: Macmillan, 1986); and Howard J. Wiarda, *Ethnocentrism in Foreign Policy: Can We Understand the Third World?* (Washington, DC: American Enterprise Institute for Public Policy Research, 1985).

18. Wiarda, "Introduction," in *New Directions in Comparative Politics.*

19. The reference is to Samuel P. Huntington, *The Third Wave: Democratization in the Late Twentieth Century* (Norman: University of Oklahoma Press, 1991).

20. Howard J. Wiarda et al., *The Relations between Democracy, Development, and Security: Implications for Policy* (New York: Global Economic Action Institute, 1988).

21. The analysis in the following section is based on a review of the literature as well as an extraordinarily busy eighteen months of travel in 1996–1998 by the author that took him to Europe on four occasions and to Russia, Eastern Europe, Asia, and Latin America on three occasions, providing a firsthand and invaluable comparative perspective.

22. For data and background, see Howard J. Wiarda, *Politics in Iberia: The Political Systems of Spain and Portugal* (New York: HarperCollins, 1993); and Howard J. Wiarda, *Iberia and Latin America: New Democracies, New Policies, New Models* (Lanham, MD: Rowman & Littlefield, 1996).

23. Thomas W. Robinson (ed.), *Democracy and Development in East Asia* (Washington, DC: American Enterprise Institute for Public Policy Research, 1991).

24. Howard J. Wiarda, *Latin American Politics: A New World of Possibilities* (Belmont, CA: Wadsworth, 1994).

25. This useful distinction has been made by Larry Diamond, "Is the Third Wave Over?" *Journal of Democracy* 7 (1996), pp. 7–19.

26. The limits, qualifications, and problems of democratization in Latin America are discussed in Howard J. Wiarda, *Democracy and Its Discontents: Development, Interdependence, and U.S. Policy in Latin America* (Lanham, MD: Rowman & Littlefield, 1995).

27. W. W. Rostow, *The Stages of Economic Growth* (Cambridge, UK: Cambridge University Press, 1960).

28. Carl Friedrich and Zbigniew Brzezinski, *Totalitarian Dictatorship and Autocracy* (New York: Praeger, 1962).

29. See Howard J. Wiarda, "Political Culture and the Attraction of Marxism-Leninism: National Inferiority Complexes as an Explanatory Factor," *World Affairs* 151 (1989), pp. 143–50.

30. The analysis follows that of Dale K. Herspring, "Eastern Europe: Successful Transitions or Descent into Chaos?" in Howard J. Wiarda (ed.), *U.S. Foreign and Strategic Policy in the Post Cold War Era* (Westport, CT: Greenwood, 1996), pp. 85–105.

31. See Steve D. Boilard, *Russia at the Twenty-first Century* (Fort Worth, TX: Harcourt Brace, 1998).

32. Carol Barner-Barry and Cynthia A. Hody, *The Politics of Change: The Transformation of the Former Soviet Union* (New York: St. Martin's, 1995).

33. Marina Ottaway, "African Democratization: An Update," *CSIS Africa Notes* 171 (1995).

34. Lana Wylie, "Sub-Saharan Africa: Western Influence and Indigenous Realities," in Howard J. Wiarda (ed.), *Non-Western Theories of Development: Regional Norms versus Global Trends* (Fort Worth, TX: Harcourt Brace, 1998).

35. An excellent survey is by John Lancaster, the *Washington Post*, Part 1 (3 August 1997) focusing on the stalled economies and Part 2 (4 August 1997) dealing with autocratic politics.

36. Anwar H. Syed, "The Islamic World: Western Influences and Islamic Fundamentalism," in Wiarda, *Non-Western Theories of Development*.

37. Samuel P. Huntington, *The Clash of Civilizations and the Remaking of World Order* (New York: Simon & Schuster, 1997).

38. John D. Martz and David J. Myers, "Understanding Latin American Politics: Analytic Models and Intellectual Traditions," *Polity* 16 (1983), pp. 214–41; Howard J. Wiarda, "Toward Consensus in Interpreting Latin American Politics: Developmentalism, Dependency, and 'The Latin American Tradition,'" *Studies in Comparative International Development* (1999).

39. The references are to Carl Friedrich, *Constitutional Government and Democracy* (Boston: Ginn, 1950); Herman Finer, *The Theory and Practice of Modern Government* (New York: Holt, 1949); Karl Loewenstein, *Political Power and the Governmental Process* (Chicago: University of Chicago Press, 1937); Jorgen S. Rasmussen and Joel C. Moses, *Major European Governments* (Belmont, CA: Wadsworth, 1995); and Peter H. Merkl, *Modern Comparative Politics* (Hinsdale, IL: Dryden Press, 1977).

40. See Wiarda, *Corporatism and Comparative Politics*.

13

Conclusion

INTRODUCTION

Comparative politics has long been one of the leading fields in political science, if not *the* leading field. It has a long history, a rich body of theory, and a distinguished tradition of research. Many of its scholars are leaders in the profession. It offers wonderful opportunities for travel, analysis, and exploration. Remember that it is the *world* that is our laboratory of inquiry, all 240-some political entities within it. One cannot think of a more exciting field of research, at all levels: local, national, regional, global.

Comparative politics has, like all fields, had its ups and downs; these changes are usually related to larger mega trends and forces at the global level that add spice and new research terrains to our agenda. For example, for a long time comparative politics concentrated on studying the advanced European political systems; but in the 1960s, when a large number of former colonial possessions became independent, the field shifted to a focus on development and the developing areas. When the Cold War was on, there was much for students of comparative politics to do; but when the Cold War ended, there was less interest in international affairs generally, including on the part of the public and government officials alike. But now after 9/11 and with the war on terrorism and the rise of Islamic fundamentalism, there has been a renewed spike in interest in comparative politics. With the world becoming more globalized and international, in addition, it seems likely that comparative politics will remain a leading field, attracting some of the best students and scholars.

One of the main themes of this book is the great systems debate that has waxed and waned over the decades and even centuries. That debate was three-sided, pitting the defenders of liberal, representative democracy against the advocates of left-wing totalitarianism and communism, on the one hand, and against the proponents of right-wing authoritarianism and fascism, on the other. In this epic battle, it appears that democracy and free, open markets have now finally won out, have become "the only game in town," or nearly so.

That is probably true in the advanced industrial countries of Western Europe, North America, Japan, and the British Commonwealth nations of Canada, Australia, and New Zealand. But it is far less conclusive in the Third World where, although democracy appears ascendant, authoritarian and/or Marxist solutions are still often seen as attractive. Recall the case of India, a country of a billion people whose democracy is still precarious, or of China—1.3 billion people—which is becoming more open-market oriented but is still governed by a Marxist-Leninist political system and in which accelerated social change and urbanization could still produce conflict and fragmentation. Or Latin America, now mainly democratic but still expressing preference for "strong government." Or Africa or the Islamic Middle East where democracy has made only weak and limited inroads, and where Islamic fundamentalism may come to challenge what appeared to be democracy's global triumph and the supposed "end of history."

COMPARATIVE POLITICS APPROACHES

In this book we have concentrated not so much on individual countries and regions but on the *approaches* or "handles" that comparative politics uses to get at and understand these areas. Recall that initially the approach used was formal-legal and focused on institutions, and that was probably not entirely inappropriate given that comparative politics in these early years was largely focused on Europe where the formal-legal rules and institutions largely operated as they were designed to operate. But when in the 1960s we turned our attention to the developing areas, it became obvious that a new approach was necessary, one that focused (a change already occurring in political science) on more informal groups, more fluid and changing politics, and informal processes rather than formal institutions.

As a new approach, however, developmentalism also proved less than satisfactory. It opened new vistas on the emerging nations, but it was also ethnocentric, based on the prior Western developmental experience rather than the actual experiences of the developing areas, did not adequately take into account non-Western cultures and the differences between them, largely ignored international factors in development, and exhibited a considerable number of other logical and methodological flaws. By the 1970s the developmentalist approach had largely fallen into disfavor.

Developmentalism was initially supplanted by two new approaches, dependency theory and corporatism. Dependency theory *did* pay attention to international forces; in its Marxist versions it argued that the advanced countries' development came at the expense of the Third World—although we saw that one need not be a Marxist to understand various dependency relations in the world. The corporatist approach was important for two main reasons: (1) it focused on the relations between the state and societal or economic interest groups that liberal theory largely ignored, and (2) it tried to understand foreign countries on their own, often corporatist (controlled, limited, regulated interest-group activity) terms rather than through the lenses of American liberal-pluralist preferences.

During the course of the 1970s and 1980s, a number of other approaches also came to the fore in comparative politics. Some of these presented themselves as alternative theories; others, as complements to already-existing approaches. These new approaches included political economy, state-society relations, indigenous theories, the new institutionalism, and rational choice theory. Meanwhile, the defenders of developmentalism continued to champion their approach; and in the 1990s, as democracy and liberalism seemed for a time everywhere triumphant, the developmentalist approach enjoyed something of a comeback. By the end of this period, students of comparative politics had a wide gamut of approaches from which to choose.

Some advocates of these individual "schools" or approaches continued to advance exclusivist claims for their point of view, arguing that *theirs* was the best or most encompassing approach. But most scholars of comparative politics took a more pragmatic and eclectic viewpoint. Their argument was: (1) let us end the internecine "warfare" among these various approaches and their proponents, (2) let us borrow selectively from and use each of these approaches where it is useful and sheds light on the subject matter, and, meanwhile, (3) let us go on to study the various issues, problems, and subject matters that we and comparative politics are interested in.

And that is what happened in comparative politics in the 1990s and continuing to today. The fervent debate among the rival approaches discussed here has died down. Instead, what most scholars do is utilize *whichever* of these approaches best helps her or him to understand the issues. So if dependency theory is useful, let us use that; if corporatism or state-society relations are helpful, let us use those. The approach one uses depends on the issue one chooses to study. Thus, if you're interested in the politics of labor relations and how both labor and employer groups relate to government policy making, then the corporatism literature will be useful to you. But if you're interested in the international flow of capital or how the U.S. government or big multinational corporations operate abroad, then some of the dependency theory literature will be useful to you. The point is, the choice of a research approach ought to be a pragmatic one and not the result of some ideological position.

This focus on pragmatism and eclecticism in the use of approaches helps explain the direction of comparative politics contemporaneously. By now most scholars in the field have come to accept the fact that *all* these approaches, or various combinations of them, have something to offer. We don't need to argue about that so much anymore. So let us go on, avoiding the ideological and methodological disputes of the past, and explore the issues and problems that we are interested in, using where appropriate the approaches set forth here.

That is why in Part III of this book we shifted direction somewhat to focus on hot issues and problem areas, and not so much on approaches. We examined such issues as transitions to democracy, the rise of civil society, what works (and what doesn't) in development, as well as some of the newer, frontier issues in comparative politics—women in politics, the legal and institutional position of gays viewed comparatively, immigration, and environmental issues. Each of these issues can be studied using, as appropriate, one or a combination of the approaches examined earlier.

Most scholars in comparative politics think that the diversity of approaches in the field as outlined here has been healthy and good. We now have a variety of approaches from which to choose. Depending on the issues or problems we wish to explore, we can now select from a wide array of different models and methodologies. We are also able to combine the best of several different approaches—for example, political economy and developmentalism or corporatism and state-society relations. Almost all of us believe that this pragmatic, eclectic way of approaching comparative politics is good for the field and good for us as individual students and scholars.

NEW HORIZONS AND FUTURE TASKS

Part of the message here is that we need to be both pragmatic and eclectic in our choice of the approaches that best serve our research and scholarly needs. None of these approaches is set in stone, nor should we reify them or elevate them to an elevated or all-encompassing importance that they may not deserve. Remember that the models and approaches we use are meant to assist us in enlightening, clarifying, and organizing our research. Where they are useful, use them; where they are not, find another approach.

The other message, therefore, is that we need to remain open to new approaches and new combinations of them. For none of these approaches has an exclusive claim on that elusive phenomenon called "truth." At best, a model or an approach as outlined here gives us an approximation of reality, almost always a simplified version of it, a means of ordering and thinking about our data and subject matter—and surely those are useful activities. But we need also to be continuously open to new approaches, new *facts* that force us to reconsider our old approaches, and new ways of combining existing approaches that yield new insights and new theory.

What, then, are the tasks ahead for comparative politics? Here we return to the discussion of different types of studies presented in chapter 2, but with the advantage now of knowing much more about the different approaches in the field.

Case Studies. The first and easiest kind of study to carry out is the case study. This involves the study of a single country or some institution or issue in it. But in doing such a single case study, as comparativists, we're still interested in advancing theory and more general knowledge. That is why, even in a case study, we employ one or another of the approaches set forth in this book. Suppose we are interested in the possibilities of democracy in Iraq or Afghanistan. We would then examine the literature on transitions to democracy to see what is necessary for democracy to succeed—that is your theory or approach. Next we would look at the country itself and the main indicators within it: the level of socioeconomic development, whether the political culture is conducive to or supportive of democracy, the level of civil society and if it is participatory and democratic, ethnic and religious divisions that might tear the country apart, the level of institutionalization, and whether the government is capable of carrying out effective public policy. Now, in our conclusion, tying together our theoretical approach (democratic transitions) and our factual knowledge of the country researched, we are in a good position to assess the prospect or likelihood of democracy in that country.

Comparisons of Two (or More) Countries. A little more complicated but still possible to do in a paper or thesis. Take two countries rather than just one. Pick an issue that you're interested in—let us say, this time, whether the state or government allows freedom of association for all groups or whether it restricts interest group activity. Now find an appropriate body of theory, or approach, that is relevant to this issue—probably the corporatist or state-society relations literature. Apply that approach to your two countries—let us say China and India. Your hypothesis might be that India allows greater freedom of association than does China and is, therefore, a more democratic country. Test your hypothesis by various criteria that measure freedom of association. Draw conclusions that support (or fail to support) your hypothesis. Voilà! Your prize-winning paper is complete.

Regional Studies. Suppose your area of interest is a regional one: Africa, Asia, Latin America, or the Middle East. If you're an area specialist, there's an implicit assumption operating that there are certain cultural, social, and political institutions or practices common to the countries of your area also serve to distinguish it from other areas. An area studies focus makes your comparison somewhat easier than a comparison *across* areas because that way you can assume the culture to be a constant and not have to account in your study for that variable, too, as you would have to do in a cross-cultural research project.

Suppose you want to study the impact of the Roman Catholic Church on politics in two Latin American countries. In doing this comparison, because Latin America has long been predominantly Roman Catholic, you assume that you have here a solid basis for comparison. The approach you would use would most likely come from the literature on political culture or, perhaps, the new institutionalism. Again the procedure would be to state your hypothesis, discuss the approach or approaches that best speak to that issue, test your hypothesis in terms of the role of the Church and religion in your two countries, and then arrive at your conclusion.

The same methodology could obviously be used to study the impact of Islam on two countries in the Middle East. Or of Confucianism in East Asia. These are all valid studies, valid comparisons. But because the cultures of these two areas are so different, you do not need to be a methodology specialist to see that trying to compare *across* regions—Confucianism in an Asian country with Catholicism in a Latin American one—would be immensely more complicated, almost like comparing apples and oranges. It can be done but doing so is very tricky because, in social science terms, many more variables are involved—i.e., Catholicism is a religion but Confucianism is more a body of ethical beliefs and, therefore, philosophically you may be comparing two "religions" that are not really comparable.

Studies across Regions. As indicated, such studies *can* be done but they often get into tricky philosophical and methodological issues. One way scholars of comparative politics have increasingly approached such cross-regional comparisons is to focus on problems common to two or more areas, such as consolidating democracy, ending poverty, eliminating the military from politics, or protecting the environment. These are common problems that many developing countries in different parts of the world face. Moreover, they are problems that can be studied (and hopefully resolved) without getting tied up in impossible-to-resolve disputes over cultural differences and their importance as explanatory factors.

More and more students of comparative politics are focusing on these kinds of problem-solving issues. And once again your way of proceeding is the familiar one: State your hypothesis (let us say, this one deals with the importance of having strong political parties in the consolidation of democracy), discuss the issue within the context of your approach or a body of literature (in this case, probably the new institutionalism, transitions to democracy, and civil society literature), test your hypothesis by closely examining the strength of parties and the party system in your countries of research interest, and finally state your conclusions and show how they confirm or require modification of the general theoretical literature on transition to democracy.

Global Studies. Global comparisons are difficult because of the apples, oranges, and kumquats problem. By making a global comparison (let us say correlating democracy with levels of social and economic development), you are assuming that you are comparing the same thing in all countries, regardless of regional or cultural differences. But that may be a big assumption. For example, we know that such terms as "participation," "civil society," even "democracy" itself mean different things or carry different implications in different languages and cultures. For example, in America civil society means grassroots and democratic participation, but in Asia the translation of civil society usually implies state, official, or top-down authority—not the same thing at all. So by purporting to measure democracy or civil society on a global or universal basis, are we really measuring the same or similar phenomena? Do the United States, Europe, Asia, the Middle East, Africa, and Latin America all really mean and understand the same things by these terms? Probably not entirely. Hence, many of us in comparative politics find such global comparisons to be useful and suggestive of trends and patterns, but not necessarily conclusive.

So what then are the tasks of comparative politics? Obviously, our goal is greater understanding of the world's 240-some political systems. To accomplish that goal we need to study them analytically and systematically. And that requires the use of the analytic approaches set forth in this book.

We need, therefore, to continue the case study work set forth here; there is *always* more room for good case studies. But we'll also want to do more of our two-or-more country comparisons and more in-depth regional studies. They may be trickier and more difficult, but we'll similarly want to do more studies across regions, studies of the same global problems and issues in regions and cultures that are very different, and perhaps a global or universal study that suggests new paths of research.

Above and beyond these kinds of studies, we also need work, both empirical and philosophical, that improves comparative politics theory. We need to continuously refine and improve the various approaches set forth here. A particularly useful task in my mind is to build bridges among the various, distinct "islands" of theory that we already have—between political economy and developmentalism, between political culture and transitions to democracy, between corporatism or state-society relations and the civil society literature; doubtless, there are many such useful ways of combining theoretical approaches. And who knows, maybe out of such thinking and research work, *you* can come up with your own approach and theory. Or maybe you can arrive at your own grand synthesis of all these diverse theories and approaches as presented here. What an exciting development that would be!

Comparative politics is thus a very exciting field. It is exciting for all of the diverse countries and regions that you can study, visit, and, if you're lucky, live in for an extended period of time. But since the entire world is our field of study, it is also exciting for the great global issues and problems with which the world now has to grapple. We hope that our enthusiasm and sense of excitement about the field are contagious.

Suggested Readings

Allen, Christopher S., Mark Kesselman and Joel Krieger, et al. *European Politics in Transition.* 5th ed. Boston: Houghton Mifflin, 2006.

Almond, Gabriel A., and James S. Coleman, eds. *The Politics of the Developing Areas.* Princeton, N.J.: Princeton University Press, 1960.

Almond, Gabriel A., G. Bingham Powell, and Robert J. Mundt. *Comparative Politics: A Theoretical Framework.* New York: Harper Collins, 1996.

Ayittey, George. *Indigenous African Institutions.* New York: Transnational Publishers, 1991.

Barner-Barry, Carol, and Cynthia A. Hody. *The Politics of Change: The Transformation of the Former Soviet Union.* New York: St. Martin's, 1995.

Bell, Daniel. *The End of Ideology.* Cambridge, MA: Harvard University Press, 1988.

Bendix, Reinhard. "Tradition and Modernity Reconsidered." *Comparative Studies in Society and History* 9 (April 1967): 292–346.

Benedict, Ruth. *Patterns of Culture.* New York: Mentor Books, 1957.

Black, E. *The Dynamics of Modernization.* New York: Harper and Row, 1968.

Carothers, Thomas. *Aiding Democracy Abroad.* Washington, D.C.: Carnegie Endowment for International Peace, 1999.

Cardoso, Fernando Enrique, and Enzo Faletto. *Dependency and Development in Latin America.* Berkeley: University of California Press, 1978.

Dahl, Robert. *On Democracy.* New Haven: Yale University Press, 1998.

Deutsch, Karl. "Social Mobilization and Political Development." *American Political Science Review* 55 (Sept. 1961): 493–514.

Diamond, Larry, ed. *Political Culture and Democracy in Developing Countries.* Boulder: Lynne Rienner, 1994.

Dogan, Mattei, and Dominique Pelassy. *How to Compare Nations.* Chatham, N.J.: Chatham House, 1984.

Finer, Herman. *The Theory and Practice of Modern Government.* New York: Holt, 1949.

Friedrich, Carl. *Constitutional Government and Democracy.* Boston: Ginn, 1950.

Friedrich, Carl, and Zbigniew Brzezinski. *Totalitarian Dictatorship and Autocracy.* New York: Praeger, 1962.

Fukuyama, Francis. *The End of History and the Last Man.* New York: Maxwell Macmillan International, 1992.

Haass, Peter M. *Saving the Mediterranean.* New York: Columbia University Press, 1990.

Heidenheimer Arnold, et al. *Comparative Public Policy: Policies of Social Choice in Europe and America.* New York: St. Martin's Press, 1975.

Heisler, Martin, ed. *Politics in Europe.* New York: McKay, 1974.

Huntington, Samuel P. *The Clash of Civilizations and the Remaking of World Order.* New York: Simon & Schuster, 1996.

———. *The Third Wave: Democratization in the Late Twentieth Century.* Norman: University of Oklahoma Press, 1991.

Inglehart, Ronald. *Culture Change in Advanced Industrial Society.* Princeton: Princeton University Press, 1990.

Jaquette, Jane S. *Women and Democracy.* Baltimore: Johns Hopkins University Press, 1998.

Kamieniecki, Sheldon, ed. *Environmental Politics in the International Arena.* Albany: State University of New York Press, 1993.

Lipset, Seymour M. *Continental Divide: The Values and Institutions of the United States and Canada.* New York: Routledge, 1990.

Loewenstein, Karl. *Political Power and the Governmental Process.* Chicago: University of Chicago Press, 1935.

Macridis, Roy. "Some Social Requisites of Democracy: Economic Development and Political Legitimacy." *American Political Science Review* 53 (March 1959): 69–105.

Martz, John D., and David J. Myers, "Understanding Latin American Politics: Analytic Models and Intellectual Traditions." *Polity* 16 (1983): 214–41.

Mazrui, Ali. *The African: A Triple Heritage.* London: BBC Publications, 1986.

McCormick, John. *Comparative Politics in Transition.* Fort Worth, Tex.: Harcourt Brace, 2000.

Merryman, John Henry. *The Civil Law Tradition.* Stanford: Stanford University Press, 1969.

Migdal, Joel. *Strong Societies and Weak States.* Princeton, N.J.: Princeton University Press, 1986.

Moody, Peter. *Tradition and Modernization in China and Japan.* Belmont, Calif.: Wadsworth, 1995.

Moran, Theodore H. *Multinational Corporations and the Politics of Dependence.* Cambridge, Mass.: Harvard University, Center for International Affairs, 1975.

Ottaway Marina, et al., eds. *Funding Virtue: Civil Society Aid and Democracy Promotion.* Washington, D.C.: Carnegie Endowment, 2000.

Putnam, Robert. *Bowling Alone: The Collapse and Revival of American Community.* New York: Simon & Schuster, 2000.

————. *Making Democracy Work: Civic Traditions in Modern Italy.* Princeton: Princeton University Press, 1993.

Rostow, Walt W. *The Stages of Economic Growth: A Non-Communist Manifesto.* Cambridge, UK: Cambridge University Press, 1960.

Schmitter, Philippe, and Gerhard Lehmbruch, eds. *Trends toward Corporatist Intermediation.* Beverly Hills: Sage, 1979.

Skocpol, Theda, ed. *Bringing the State Back In.* Cambridge, UK: Cambridge University Press, 1985.

————. *States and Social Revolutions: A Comparative Study of France, Russia, and China.* New York: Cambridge University Press, 1979.

Somjee, A. H. *Development Theory: Critiques and Explorations.* London: Macmillan, 1991.

————. *Parallels and Actuals of Political Development.* London: Macmillan, 1986.

Stepan, Alfred. *State and Society: Peru in Comparative Perspective.* Princeton, N.J.: Princeton University Press, 1978.

Tiersky, Ronald, ed. *Europe Today. National Politics, European Integration, and European Security.* Lanham, Md.: Rowman & Littlefield, 1999.

Tilly, Charles, ed. *The Formation of the National States in Western Europe.* Princeton, N.J.: Princeton University Press, 1975.

de Tocqueville, Alexis. *Democracy in America.* New York: Knopf, 1960.

Tsebelis, George. *Nested Games: Rational Choice in Comparative Politics.* Berkeley: University of California Press, 1990.

Wiarda, Howard J. *Civil Society.* Boulder, Colo.: Westview Press, 2003.

————, ed. *Comparative Democracy and Democratization.* Fort Worth, Tex.: Harcourt College Publishers, 2002.

————. *Corporatism and Comparative Politics: The Other Great "Ism."* New York: M. E. Sharpe, 1996.

————, ed. *European Politics in the Age of Globalization.* Fort Worth: Harcourt Brace, 2000.

————. *An Introduction to Comparative Politics: Concepts and Processes.* 2nd ed. Fort Worth: Harcourt Brace, 2000.

————, ed. *New Directions in Comparative Politics.* 3rd ed. Boulder, Colo.: Westview Press, 2002.

————, ed. *Non-Western Theories of Development.* Fort Worth: Harcourt Brace, 1998.

Wiarda, Howard J., and Harvey F. Kline, eds. *Latin American Politics and Development.* 6th ed. Boulder, Colo.: Westview Press, 2006.

Index

About the Author

Howard J. Wiarda is the Dean Rusk Professor of International Relations and head of the Department of International Affairs at the University of Georgia. Much of his career was spent as professor of political science and comparative labor relations and the Leonard J. Horwitz Professor of Iberian and Latin American Studies at the University of Massachusetts, Amherst. He retains his positions as public-policy scholar of the Woodrow Wilson International Center for Scholars, and senior associate at the Center for Strategic and International Studies (CSIS) in Washington, D.C. Professor Wiarda began his career as a scholar of Latin American politics, and his writings on Latin America, Spain, Portugal, and the developing nations are well known in the field. While continuing these research and writing interests, over the last twenty years his scholarly interests have broadened to include Russia, Asia, Europe, sub-Saharan Africa, comparative democratization, civil society, and general comparative politics and American foreign policy.